The Ultimate Instant Pot

Cookbook 2024

2000+ Days of Fast and Easy Recipes for Effortless Cooking and Time-Saving Meals, Let you discover a new world of food. Beginner Friendly

Aaron J. Bishop

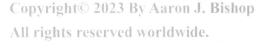
Warning-Disclaimer

The purpose of this book is to educate and entertain. The author or publisher does not guarantee that anyone following the techniques, suggestions, tips, ideas, or strategies will become successful. The author and publisher shall have neither liability or responsibility to anyone with respect to any loss or damage caused, or alleged to be caused, directly or indirectly by the information contained in this book.

Table of Contents

INTRODUCTION

Welcome to the world of Instant Pot cooking! This revolutionary kitchen appliance has taken the culinary world by storm, allowing you to cook delicious meals in a fraction of the time it would take with traditional cooking methods. And with this cookbook, you'll discover a whole new world of possibilities for your Instant Pot.

From classic comfort foods to more adventurous recipes, this cookbook has something for everyone. With easy-to-follow recipes and step-by-step instructions, even novice cooks can create delicious meals that will impress their friends and family.

But the Instant Pot is much more than just a faster way to cook. It's a versatile and powerful tool that can help you create a wide range of dishes.

And with features like pressure cooking, slow cooking, sautéing, and steaming, using the Instant Pot couldn't be easier. Simply add your ingredients, set the timer, and let the Instant Pot work its magic.

So why wait? Start exploring the endless possibilities of Instant Pot cooking today and take your culinary skills to the next level with the help of this cookbook. Whether you're a seasoned chef or a beginner in the kitchen, the Instant Pot Cookbook has everything you need to create healthy, delicious meals that your whole family will love.

Tips for Using

Using an Instant Pot is easy and straightforward. Here are the basic steps to get you started:

1. Familiarize yourself with the Instant Pot: Before using your Instant Pot, make sure to read the user manual and become familiar with its features and functions.

2. Prepare your ingredients: While the Instant Pot is preheating, prepare your ingredients by washing, cutting, and seasoning them as desired.

3. Add liquid: Most recipes will require some sort of liquid, such as water or broth, to create steam and build pressure inside the Instant Pot. Be sure to add the required amount of liquid according to the recipe instructions.

4. Set the cooking time and pressure: Once your ingredients and liquid are in the Instant Pot, set the cooking time and pressure according to the recipe instructions. The Instant Pot has several different settings, including pressure cooking, slow cooking, sautéing, and steaming.

5. Wait for the Instant Pot to come to pressure: Once you've set the cooking time and pressure, the Instant Pot will take some time to come to pressure.

6. Cook your food: Once the Instant Pot has come to pressure, it will start cooking your food according to the settings you selected. The cooking time will vary depending on the recipe and the type of food you're cooking.

7. Release the pressure: Once the cooking time is up, you'll need to release the pressure before opening the Instant Pot. There are two ways to do this: natural release and quick release. Natural release means letting the Instant Pot cool down on its own, while quick release means manually releasing the pressure using the valve on top of the Instant Pot.

8. Enjoy your delicious meal: Once the pressure has been released, open the Instant Pot and serve your delicious meal. You can enjoy perfectly cooked meals in a fraction of the time it would take with traditional cooking methods.

With these simple steps, you can easily use your Instant Pot to create healthy, delicious meals for you and your family.

Chapter ❶
Breakfasts

Almond Pancakes

Prep time: 10 minutes | Cook time: 15 minutes per batch | Serves 6

4 eggs, beaten	1 tablespoon avocado oil
2 cups almond flour	1 teaspoon baking powder
½ cup butter, melted	1 teaspoon vanilla extract
2 tablespoons granulated erythritol	Pinch of salt
	¾ cup water, divided

1. In a blender, combine all the ingredients, except for the ½ cup of the water. Pulse until fully combined and smooth. Let the batter rest for 5 minutes before cooking. 2. Fill each cup with 2 tablespoons of the batter, about two-thirds of the way full. Cover the cups with aluminum foil. 3. Pour the remaining ½ cup of the water and insert the trivet in the Instant Pot. Place the cups on the trivet. 4. Set the lid in place. Select the Manual mode and set the cooking time for 15 minutes on High Pressure. When the timer goes off, do a quick pressure release. Carefully open the lid. 5. Repeat with the remaining batter, until all the batter is used. Add more water to the pot before cooking each batch, if needed. 6. Serve warm.

Coddled Eggs and Smoked Salmon Toasts

Prep time: 5 minutes | Cook time: 10 minutes | Serves 4

2 teaspoons unsalted butter	and sliced
4 large eggs	2 radishes, thinly sliced
4 slices gluten-free or whole-grain rye bread	1 Persian cucumber, thinly sliced
½ cup plain 2 percent Greek yogurt	1 tablespoon chopped fresh chives
4 ounces cold-smoked salmon, or 1 medium avocado, pitted, peeled,	¼ teaspoon freshly ground black pepper

1. Pour 1 cup water into the Instant Pot and place a long-handled silicone steam rack into the pot. (If you don't have the long-handled rack, use the wire metal steam rack and a homemade sling) 2. Coat each of four 4-ounce ramekins with ½ teaspoon butter. Crack an egg into each ramekin. Place the ramekins on the steam rack in the pot. 3. Secure the lid and set the Pressure Release to Sealing. Select the Steam setting and set the cooking time for 3 minutes at low pressure. (The pot will take about 5 minutes to come up to pressure before the cooking program begins.) 4. While eggs are cooking, toast the bread in a toaster until golden brown. Spread the yogurt onto the toasted slices, put the toasts onto plates, and then top each toast with the smoked salmon, radishes, and cucumber. 5. When the cooking program ends, let the pressure release naturally for 5 minutes, then move the Pressure Release to Venting to release any remaining steam. Open the pot and, wearing heat-resistant mitts, grasp the handles of the steam rack and lift it out of the pot. 6. Run a knife around the inside edge of each ramekin to loosen the egg and unmold one egg onto each toast. Sprinkle the chives and pepper on top and serve right away. 7. Note 8. The yolks of these eggs are fully cooked through. If you prefer the yolks slightly less solid, perform a quick pressure release rather than letting the pressure release naturally for 5 minutes.

Tropical Steel Cut Oats

Prep time: 5 minutes | Cook time: 5 minutes | Serves 4

1 cup steel cut oats	¾ cup frozen mango chunks
1 cup unsweetened almond milk	1 (2-inch) vanilla bean, scraped (seeds and pod)
2 cups coconut water or water	Ground cinnamon
¾ cup frozen chopped peaches	¼ cup chopped unsalted macadamia nuts

1. In the electric pressure cooker, combine the oats, almond milk, coconut water, peaches, mango chunks, and vanilla bean seeds and pod. Stir well. 2. Close and lock the lid of the pressure cooker. Set the valve to sealing. 3. Cook on high pressure for 5 minutes. 4. When the cooking is complete, allow the pressure to release naturally for 10 minutes, then quick release any remaining pressure. Hit Cancel. 5. Once the pin drops, unlock and remove the lid. 6. Discard the vanilla bean pod and stir well. 7. Spoon the oats into 4 bowls. Top each serving with a sprinkle of cinnamon and 1 tablespoon of the macadamia nuts.

Blueberry Almond Cereal

Prep time: 5 minutes | Cook time: 2 minutes | Serves 4

⅓ cup crushed roasted almonds	white protein powder
¼ cup almond flour	2 tablespoons Swerve
¼ cup unsalted butter, softened	1 teaspoon blueberry extract
¼ cup vanilla-flavored egg	1 teaspoon ground cinnamon

1. Add all the ingredients to the Instant Pot and stir to combine. 2. Lock the lid, select the Manual mode and set the cooking time for 2 minutes on High Pressure. When the timer goes off, do a natural pressure release for 10 minutes, then release any remaining pressure. Open the lid. 3. Stir well and pour the mixture onto a sheet lined with parchment paper to cool. It will be crispy when completely cool. 4. Serve the cereal in bowls.

Cinnamon French Toast

Prep time: 10 minutes | Cook time: 20 minutes | Serves 8

3 eggs	Pinch salt
2 cups low-fat milk	16 ounces whole wheat
2 tablespoons maple syrup	bread, cubed and left out
15 drops liquid stevia	overnight to go stale
2 teaspoons vanilla extract	1½ cups water
2 teaspoons cinnamon	

1. In a medium bowl, whisk together the eggs, milk, maple syrup, Stevia, vanilla, cinnamon, and salt. Stir in the cubes of whole wheat bread. 2. You will need a 7-inch round baking pan for this. Spray the inside with nonstick spray, then pour the bread mixture into the pan. 3. Place the trivet in the bottom of the inner pot, then pour in the water. 4. Make foil sling and insert it onto the trivet. Carefully place the 7-inch pan on top of the foil sling/trivet. 5. Secure the lid to the locked position, then make sure the vent is turned to sealing. 6. Press the Manual button and use the "+/-" button to set the Instant Pot for 20 minutes. 7. When cook time is up, let the Instant Pot release naturally for 5 minutes, then quick release the rest

Bacon and Spinach Eggs

Prep time: 5 minutes | Cook time: 9 minutes | Serves 4

2 tablespoons unsalted butter, divided	Pinch of black pepper
½ cup diced bacon	½ cup water
⅓ cup finely diced shallots	¼ cup heavy whipping cream
⅓ cup chopped spinach, leaves only	8 large eggs
Pinch of sea salt	1 tablespoon chopped fresh chives, for garnish

1. Set the Instant Pot on the Sauté mode and melt 1 tablespoon of the butter. Add the bacon to the pot and sauté for about 4 minutes, or until crispy. Using a slotted spoon, transfer the bacon bits to a bowl and set aside. 2. Add the remaining 1 tablespoon of the butter and shallots to the pot and sauté for about 2 minutes, or until tender. Add the spinach leaves and sauté for 1 minute, or until wilted. Season with sea salt and black pepper and stir. Transfer the spinach to a separate bowl and set aside. 3. Drain the oil from the pot into a bowl. Pour in the water and put the trivet inside. 4. With a paper towel, coat four ramekins with the bacon grease. In each ramekin, place 1 tablespoon of the heavy whipping cream, reserved bacon bits and sautéed spinach. Crack two eggs without breaking the yolks in each ramekin. Cover the ramekins with aluminum foil. Place two ramekins on the trivet and stack the other two on top. 5. Lock the lid. Select the Manual mode and set the cooking time for 2 minutes at Low Pressure. When the timer goes off, use a natural pressure release for 5 minutes, then release any remaining pressure. Carefully open the lid. 6. Carefully take out the ramekins and serve garnished with the chives.

Breakfast Farro with Berries and Walnuts

Prep time: 8 minutes | Cook time: 10 minutes | Serves 6

1 cup farro, rinsed and drained	cinnamon
1 cup unsweetened almond milk	1 tablespoon pure maple syrup
¼ teaspoon kosher salt	1½ cups fresh blueberries, raspberries, or strawberries (or a combination)
½ teaspoon pure vanilla extract	6 tablespoons chopped walnuts
1 teaspoon ground	

1. In the electric pressure cooker, combine the farro, almond milk, 1 cup of water, salt, vanilla, cinnamon, and maple syrup. 2. Close and lock the lid. Set the valve to sealing. 3. Cook on high pressure for 10 minutes. 4. When the cooking is complete, allow the pressure to release naturally for 10 minutes, then quick release any remaining pressure. Hit Cancel. 5. Once the pin drops, unlock and remove the lid. 6. Stir the farro. Spoon into bowls and top each serving with ¼ cup of berries and 1 tablespoon of walnuts.

Pecan and Walnut Granola

Prep time: 10 minutes | Cook time: 2 minutes | Serves 12

2 cups chopped raw pecans	walnuts
1¾ cups vanilla-flavored egg white protein powder	½ cup slivered almonds
1¼ cups unsalted butter, softened	½ cup sesame seeds
1 cup sunflower seeds	½ cup Swerve
½ cup chopped raw	1 teaspoon ground cinnamon
	½ teaspoon sea salt

1. Add all the ingredients to the Instant Pot and stir to combine. 2. Lock the lid, select the Manual mode and set the cooking time for 2 minutes on High Pressure. When the timer goes off, do a natural pressure release for 10 minutes, then release any remaining pressure. Open the lid. 3. Stir well and pour the granola onto a sheet of parchment paper to cool. It will become crispy when completely cool. Serve the granola in bowls.

Cranberry Almond Grits

Prep time: 10 minutes | Cook time: 10 minutes | Serves 5

¾ cup stone-ground grits or polenta (not instant)	1 tablespoon unsalted butter or ghee (optional)
½ cup unsweetened dried cranberries	1 tablespoon half-and-half
Pinch kosher salt	¼ cup sliced almonds, toasted

1. In the electric pressure cooker, stir together the grits, cranberries, salt, and 3 cups of water. 2. Close and lock the lid. Set the valve to sealing. 3. Cook on high pressure for 10 minutes. 4. When the cooking is complete, hit Cancel and quick release the pressure. 5. Once the pin drops, unlock and remove the lid. 6. Add the butter (if using) and half-and-half. Stir until the mixture is creamy, adding more half-and-half if necessary. 7. Spoon into serving bowls and sprinkle with almonds.

Mini Spinach Quiche

Prep time: 5 minutes | Cook time: 15 minutes | Serves 1

2 eggs	¼ cup chopped fresh spinach
1 tablespoon heavy cream	½ teaspoon salt
1 tablespoon diced green pepper	¼ teaspoon pepper
1 tablespoon diced red onion	1 cup water

1. In medium bowl whisk together all ingredients except water. Pour into 4-inch ramekin. Generally, if the ramekin is oven-safe, it is also safe to use in pressure cooking. 2. Pour water into Instant Pot. Place steam rack into pot. Carefully place ramekin onto steam rack. Click lid closed. Press the Manual button and set time for 15 minutes. When timer beeps, quick-release the pressure. Serve warm.

Coddled Huevos Rancheros

Prep time: 5 minutes | Cook time: 10 minutes | Serves 2

2 teaspoons unsalted butter	½ cup chunky tomato salsa (such as Pace brand)
4 large eggs	2 cups shredded romaine lettuce
1 cup drained cooked black beans, or two-thirds 15 ounces can black beans, rinsed and drained	1 tablespoon chopped fresh cilantro
Two 7-inch corn or whole-wheat tortillas, warmed	2 tablespoons grated Cotija cheese

1. Pour 1 cup water into the Instant Pot and place a long-handled silicone steam rack into the pot. (If you don't have the long-handled rack, use the wire metal steam rack and a homemade sling) 2. Coat each of four 4-ounce ramekins with ½ teaspoon butter. Crack an egg into each ramekin. Place the ramekins on the steam rack in the pot. 3. Secure the lid and set the Pressure Release to Sealing. Select the Steam setting and set the cooking time for 3 minutes at low pressure. (The pot will take about 5 minutes to come up to pressure before the cooking program begins.) 4. While the eggs are cooking, in a small saucepan over low heat, warm the beans for about 5 minutes, stirring occasionally. Cover the saucepan and remove from the heat. (Alternatively, warm the beans in a covered bowl in a microwave for 1 minute. Leave the beans covered until ready to serve.) 5. When the cooking program ends, let the pressure release naturally for 5 minutes, then move the Pressure Release to Venting to release any remaining steam. Open the pot and, wearing heat-resistant mitts, grasp the handles of the steam rack and carefully lift it out of the pot. 6. Place a warmed tortilla on each plate and spoon ½ cup of the beans onto each tortilla. Run a knife around the inside edge of each ramekin to loosen the egg and unmold two eggs onto the beans on each tortilla. Spoon the salsa over the eggs and top with the lettuce, cilantro, and cheese. Serve right away.

Spinach and Chicken Casserole

Prep time: 5 minutes | Cook time: 15 minutes | Serves 5

1 tablespoon avocado oil	½ teaspoon kosher salt
1 tablespoon coconut oil	½ teaspoon freshly ground black pepper
1 tablespoon unflavored MCT oil	¼ cup sugar-free or low-sugar salsa
1 avocado, mashed	¼ cup heavy whipping cream
½ cup shredded full-fat Cheddar cheese	1 pound (454 g) ground chicken
½ cup chopped spinach	
½ teaspoon dried basil	

1. Pour 1 cup of filtered water inside the inner pot of the Instant Pot, then insert the trivet. 2. In a large bowl, combine and mix the avocado oil, coconut oil, MCT oil, avocado, cheese, spinach, basil, salt, black pepper, salsa, and whipping cream. 3. In a greased Instant Pot-safe dish, add the ground chicken in an even layer. Pour the casserole mixture over the chicken and cover with aluminum foil. Using a sling, place this dish on top of the trivet. 4. Close the lid, set the pressure release to Sealing, and select Manual. Set the Instant Pot to 15 minutes on High Pressure, and let cook. 5. Once cooked, carefully switch the pressure release to Venting. Open the Instant Pot, serve, and enjoy!

Pulled Pork Hash

Prep time: 10 minutes | Cook time: 15 minutes | Serves 4

4 eggs	1 teaspoon chopped fresh cilantro
10 ounces (283 g) pulled pork, shredded	1 tomato, chopped
1 teaspoon coconut oil	¼ cup water
1 teaspoon red pepper	

1. Melt the coconut oil in the instant pot on Sauté mode. 2. Then add pulled pork, red pepper, cilantro, water, and chopped tomato. 3. Cook the ingredients for 5 minutes. 4. Then stir it well with the help of the spatula and crack the eggs over it. 5. Close the lid. 6. Cook the meal on Manual mode (High Pressure) for 7 minutes. Then make a quick pressure release.
calories: 275 | fat: 18g | protein: 22g | carbs: 6g | net carbs: 5g | fiber: 1g

Streusel Pumpkin Cake

Prep time: 10 minutes | Cook time: 30 minutes | Serves 8

Streusel Topping:

¼ cup Swerve	or unsalted butter, softened
¼ cup almond flour	½ teaspoon ground cinnamon
2 tablespoons coconut oil	

Cake:

2 large eggs, beaten	2 teaspoons pumpkin pie spice
2 cups almond flour	
1 cup pumpkin purée	2 teaspoons vanilla extract
¾ cup Swerve	½ teaspoon fine sea salt

Glaze:

½ cup Swerve	almond milk
3 tablespoons unsweetened	

1. Set a trivet in the Instant Pot and pour in 1 cup water. Line a baking pan with parchment paper. 2. In a small bowl, whisk together all the ingredients for the streusel topping with a fork. 3. In a medium-sized bowl, stir together all the ingredients for the cake until thoroughly combined. 4. Scoop half of the batter into the prepared baking pan and sprinkle half of the streusel topping on top. Repeat with the remaining batter and topping. 5. Place the baking pan on the trivet in the Instant Pot. 6. Lock the lid, select the Manual mode and set the cooking time for 30 minutes on High Pressure. 7. Meanwhile, whisk together the Swerve and almond milk in a small bowl until it reaches a runny consistency. 8. When the timer goes off, do a natural pressure release for 10 minutes, then release any remaining pressure. Open the lid. 9. Remove the baking pan from the pot. Let cool in the pan for 10 minutes. Transfer the cake onto a plate and peel off the parchment paper. 10. Transfer the cake onto a serving platter. Spoon the glaze over the top of the cake. Serve immediately.

Bacon Spaghetti Squash Fritters

Prep time: 20 minutes | Cook time: 15 minutes | Serves 4

½ cooked spaghetti squash	¼ teaspoon pepper
2 tablespoons cream cheese	1 stalk green onion, sliced
½ cup shredded whole-milk Mozzarella cheese	4 slices cooked bacon, crumbled
1 egg	2 tablespoons coconut oil
½ teaspoon salt	

1. Remove seeds from cooked squash and use fork to scrape strands out of shell. Place strands into cheesecloth or kitchen towel and squeeze to remove as much excess moisture as possible. 2. Place cream cheese and Mozzarella in small bowl and microwave for 45 seconds to melt together. Mix with spoon and place in large bowl. Add all ingredients except coconut oil to bowl. Mixture will be wet like batter. 3. Press the Sauté button and then press the Adjust button to set heat to Less. Add coconut oil to Instant Pot. When fully preheated, add 2 to 3 tablespoons of batter to pot to make a fritter. Let fry until firm and completely cooked through.

Mexican Breakfast Beef Chili

Prep time: 5 minutes | Cook time: 45 minutes | Serves 4

2 tablespoons coconut oil	1 teaspoon hot sauce
1 pound (454 g) ground grass-fed beef	½ teaspoon chili powder
1 (14 ounces / 397 g) can sugar-free or low-sugar diced tomatoes	½ teaspoon crushed red pepper
	½ teaspoon ground cumin
½ cup shredded full-fat Cheddar cheese (optional)	½ teaspoon kosher salt
	½ teaspoon freshly ground black pepper

1. Set the Instant Pot to Sauté and melt the oil. 2. Pour in ½ cup of filtered water, then add the beef, tomatoes, cheese, hot sauce, chili powder, red pepper, cumin, salt, and black pepper to the Instant Pot, stirring thoroughly. 3. Close the lid, set the pressure release to Sealing, and hit Cancel to stop the current program. Select Manual, set the Instant Pot to 45 minutes on High Pressure and let cook. 4. Once cooked, let the pressure naturally disperse from the Instant Pot for about 10 minutes, then carefully switch the pressure release to Venting. 5. Open the Instant Pot, serve, and enjoy!

Pork and Quill Egg Cups

Prep time: 15 minutes | Cook time: 15 minutes | Serves 4

10 ounces (283 g) ground pork	1 teaspoon dried dill
1 jalapeño pepper, chopped	½ teaspoon salt
1 tablespoon butter, softened	1 cup water
	4 quill eggs

1. In a bowl, stir together all the ingredients, except for the quill eggs and water. Transfer the meat mixture to the silicone muffin molds and press the surface gently. 2. Pour the water and insert the trivet in the Instant Pot. Put the meat cups on the trivet. 3. Crack the eggs over the meat mixture. 4. Set the lid in place. Select the Manual mode and set the cooking time for 15 minutes on High Pressure. When the timer goes off, do a quick pressure release. Carefully open the lid. 5. Serve warm.

Kale Omelet

Prep time: 5 minutes | Cook time: 10 minutes | Serves 2

2 eggs	⅔ teaspoon white pepper
1 cup chopped kale	½ teaspoon butter
1 teaspoon heavy cream	

1. Grease the instant pot pan with butter. 2. Beat the eggs in the separated bowl and whisk them well. 3. After this, add heavy cream and white pepper. Stir it gently. 4. Place the chopped kale in the greased pan and add the whisked eggs. 5. Pour 1 cup of water in the instant pot. 6. Place the trivet in the instant pot and transfer the egg mixture pan on the trivet. 7. Close the instant pot and set the Manual (High Pressure) program and cook the frittata for 5 minutes. Do a natural pressure release for 5 minutes.

Vegetable and Cheese Bake

Prep time: 7 minutes | Cook time: 9 minutes | Serves 3

3 eggs, beaten	chopped
¼ cup coconut cream	3 ounces (85 g) provolone cheese, shredded
¼ teaspoon salt	1 teaspoon butter
3 ounces (85 g) Brussel sprouts, chopped	1 teaspoon smoked paprika
2 ounces (57 g) tomato,	

1. Grease the instant pot pan with the butter. 2. Put eggs in the bowl, add salt, and smoked paprika. Whisk the eggs well. 3. After this, add chopped Brussel sprouts and tomato. 4. Pour the mixture into the instant pot pan and sprinkle over with the shredded cheese. 5. Pour 1 cup of the water in the instant pot. Then place the pan with the egg mixture and close the lid. 6. Cook the meal on Manual (High Pressure) for 4 minutes. Then make naturally release for 5 minutes.

Cinnamon Roll Fat Bombs

Prep time: 5 minutes | Cook time: 5 minutes | Serves 5 to 6

2 tablespoons coconut oil	½ cup Swerve, or more to taste
2 cups raw coconut butter	½ teaspoon ground cinnamon, or more to taste
1 cup sugar-free chocolate chips	½ teaspoon vanilla extract
1 cup heavy whipping cream	

1. Set the Instant Pot to Sauté and melt the oil. 2. Add the butter, chocolate chips, whipping cream, Swerve, cinnamon, and vanilla to the Instant Pot and cook. Stir occasionally until the mixture reaches a smooth consistency. 3. Pour mixture into a silicone mini-muffin mold. 4. Freeze until firm. Serve, and enjoy!

Chicken and Egg Sandwich

Prep time: 5 minutes | Cook time: 15 minutes | Serves 1

1 (6 ounces / 170 g) boneless, skinless chicken breast	1 egg
	1 cup water
¼ teaspoon salt	¼ avocado
⅛ teaspoon pepper	2 tablespoons mayonnaise
¼ teaspoon garlic powder	¼ cup shredded white Cheddar
2 tablespoons coconut oil, divided	Salt and pepper, to taste

1. Cut chicken breast in half lengthwise. Use meat tenderizer to pound chicken breast until thin. Sprinkle with salt, pepper, and garlic powder, and set aside. 2. Add 1 tablespoon coconut oil to Instant Pot. Press Sauté button, then press Adjust button and set temperature to Less. Once oil is hot, fry the egg, remove, and set aside. Press Cancel button. Press Sauté button, then press Adjust button to set temperature to Normal. Add second tablespoon of coconut oil to Instant Pot and sear chicken on each side for 3 to 4 minutes until golden. 3. Press the Manual button and set time for 8 minutes. While chicken cooks, use fork to mash avocado and then mix in mayo. When timer beeps, quick-release the pressure. Put chicken on plate and pat dry with paper towel. Use chicken pieces to form a sandwich with egg, cheese, and avocado mayo. Season lightly with salt and pepper.

Avocado Green Power Bowl

Prep time: 10 minutes | Cook time: 10 minutes | Serves 1

1 cup water	½ cup kale, sliced into
2 eggs	strips
1 tablespoon coconut oil	½ clove garlic, minced
1 tablespoon butter	½ teaspoon salt
1 ounce (28 g) sliced	⅛ teaspoon pepper
almonds	½ avocado, sliced
1 cup fresh spinach, sliced	⅛ teaspoon red pepper
into strips	flakes

1. Pour water into Instant Pot and place steam rack on bottom. Place eggs on steam rack. Click lid closed. Press the Manual button and adjust time for 6 minutes. When timer beeps, quick-release the pressure. Set eggs aside. 2. Pour water out, clean pot, and replace. Press the Sauté button and add coconut oil, butter, and almonds. Sauté for 2 to 3 minutes until butter begins to turn golden and almonds soften. Add spinach, kale, garlic, salt, and pepper to Instant Pot. Sauté for 4 to 6 minutes until greens begin to wilt. Press the Cancel button. Place greens in bowl for serving. Peel eggs, cut in half, and add to bowl. Slice avocado and place in bowl. Sprinkle red pepper flakes over all. Serve warm.

Chicken, Mozzarella, and Tomato Pizza

Prep time: 5 minutes | Cook time: 20 minutes | Serves 4 to 5

Crust:

2 eggs	1 cup grated full-fat
2 tablespoons salted grass-fed butter, softened	Parmesan cheese
	⅓ cup blanched almond
1 pound (454 g) ground chicken	flour

Topping:

1 (14 ounces / 397 g) can fire roasted sugar-free or low-sugar tomatoes, drained	1 cup chopped spinach
	½ teaspoon dried basil
	½ teaspoon crushed red pepper
2 cups shredded full-fat Mozzarella cheese	½ teaspoon dried oregano
	½ teaspoon dried cilantro

1. Pour 1 cup of filtered water into the inner pot of the Instant Pot, then insert the trivet. In a large bowl, combine the eggs, butter, chicken, cheese, and flour. Mix thoroughly. Transfer this mixture into a greased, Instant Pot-friendly dish. Cover loosely with aluminum foil. Using a sling, place this dish on top of the trivet. 2. Close the lid, set the pressure release to Sealing, and select Manual. Set the Instant Pot to 10 minutes on High Pressure and let cook. 3. Meanwhile, in a small bowl, mix together basil, red pepper, oregano, and cilantro, and set aside. 4. Once the crust is cooked, carefully switch the pressure release to Venting. Open the Instant Pot and add the tomatoes in an even layer, followed by the Mozzarella cheese and the spinach. Sprinkle the spice and herb mixture over the top of the pizza. Loosely re-cover dish with aluminum foil. 5. Close the lid to the Instant Pot, set the pressure release to Sealing, and select Manual. Set the Instant Pot to 10 minutes on High Pressure and let cook again. 6. Once cooked, let the pressure naturally disperse from the Instant Pot for about 10 minutes, then carefully switch the pressure release to Venting. 7. Open the Instant Pot, serve, and enjoy!

Baked Eggs and Ham

Prep time: 5 minutes | Cook time: 5 minutes | Serves 2

4 large eggs, beaten	½ cup heavy cream
4 slices ham, diced	½ teaspoon sea salt
½ cup shredded Cheddar cheese	Pinch ground black pepper

1. Grease two ramekins. 2. In a large bowl, whisk together all the ingredients. Divide the egg mixture equally between the ramekins. 3. Set a trivet in the Instant Pot and pour in 1 cup water. Place the ramekins on the trivet. 4. Lock the lid. Select the Manual mode and set the cooking time for 5 minutes on High Pressure. When the timer goes off, perform a quick pressure release. Carefully open the lid. 5. Remove the ramekins from the Instant Pot. 6. Serve immediately.

Poached Eggs

Prep time: 5 minutes | Cook time: 5 minutes | Serves 4

Nonstick cooking spray	4 large eggs

1. Lightly spray 4 cups of a 7-count silicone egg bite mold with nonstick cooking spray. Crack each egg into a sprayed cup. 2. Pour 1 cup of water into the electric pressure cooker. Place the egg bite mold on the wire rack and carefully lower it into the pot. 3. Close and lock the lid of the pressure cooker. Set the valve to sealing. 4. Cook on high pressure for 5 minutes. 5. When the cooking is complete, hit Cancel and quick release the pressure. 6. Once the pin drops, unlock and remove the lid. 7. Run a small rubber spatula or spoon around each egg and carefully remove it from the mold. The white should be cooked, but the yolk should be runny. 8. Serve immediately.

Baked Eggs

Prep time: 15 minutes | Cook time: 20 minutes | Serves 8

1 cup water	2 teaspoons chopped onion
2 tablespoons no-trans-fat tub margarine, melted	1 teaspoon dried parsley
1 cup reduced-fat buttermilk baking mix	½ cup grated reduced-fat cheddar cheese
1½ cups fat-free cottage cheese	1 egg, slightly beaten
	1¼ cups egg substitute
	1 cup fat-free milk

1. Place the steaming rack into the bottom of the inner pot and pour in 1 cup of water. 2. Grease a round springform pan that will fit into the inner pot of the Instant Pot. 3. Pour melted margarine into springform pan. 4. Mix together buttermilk baking mix, cottage cheese, onion, parsley, cheese, egg, egg substitute, and milk in large mixing bowl. 5. Pour mixture over melted margarine. Stir slightly to distribute margarine. 6. Place the springform pan onto the steaming rack, close the lid, and secure to the locking position. Be sure the vent is turned to sealing. Set for 20 minutes on Manual at high pressure. 7. Let the pressure release naturally. 8. Carefully remove the springform pan with the handles of the steaming rack and allow to stand 10 minutes before cutting and serving.

Grain-Free Apple Cinnamon Cake

Prep time: 10 minutes | Cook time: 50 minutes | Serves 8

2 cups almond flour	½ cup plain 2 percent Greek yogurt
½ cup Lakanto Monkfruit Sweetener Golden	2 large eggs
1½ teaspoons ground cinnamon	½ teaspoon pure vanilla extract
1 teaspoon baking powder	1 small apple, chopped into small pieces
½ teaspoon fine sea salt	

1. Pour 1 cup water into the Instant Pot. Line the base of a 7 by 3-inch round cake pan with parchment paper. Butter the sides of the pan and the parchment or coat with nonstick cooking spray. 2. In a medium bowl, whisk together the almond flour, sweetener, cinnamon, baking powder, and salt. In a smaller bowl, whisk together the yogurt, eggs, and vanilla until no streaks of yolk remain. Add the wet mixture to the dry mixture and stir just until the dry ingredients are evenly moistened, then fold in the apple. The batter will be very thick. 3. Transfer the batter to the prepared pan and, using a rubber spatula, spread it in an even layer. Cover the pan tightly with aluminum foil. Place the pan on a long-handled silicone steam rack, then, holding the handles of the steam rack, lower it into the Instant Pot. (If you don't have the long-handled rack, use the wire metal steam rack and a homemade sling) 4. Secure the lid and set the Pressure Release to Sealing. Select the Cake, Pressure Cook, or Manual setting and set the cooking time for 40 minutes at high pressure. (The pot will take about 10 minutes to come up to pressure before the cooking program begins.) 5. When the cooking program ends, let the pressure release naturally for 10 minutes, then move the Pressure Release to Venting to release any remaining steam. Open the pot and, wearing heat-resistant mitts, grasp the handles of the steam rack and lift it out of the pot. Uncover the pan, taking care not to get burned by the steam or to drip condensation onto the cake. Let the cake cool in the pan on a cooling rack for about 5 minutes. 6. Run a butter knife around the edge of the pan to loosen the cake from the pan sides. Invert the cake onto the rack, lift off the pan, and peel off the parchment. Let cool for 15 minutes, then invert the cake onto a serving plate. Cut into eight wedges and serve.

Instant Pot Hard-Boiled Eggs

Prep time: 10 minutes | Cook time: 5 minutes | Serves 7

1 cup water	6 to 8 eggs

1. Pour the water into the inner pot. Place the eggs in a steamer basket or rack that came with pot. 2. Close the lid and secure to the locking position. Be sure the vent is turned to sealing. Set for 5 minutes on Manual at high pressure. (It takes about 5 minutes for pressure to build and then 5 minutes to cook.) 3. Let pressure naturally release for 5 minutes, then do quick pressure release. 4. Place hot eggs into cool water to halt cooking process. You can peel cooled eggs immediately or refrigerate unpeeled.

Keto Cabbage Hash Browns

Prep time: 5 minutes | Cook time: 8 minutes | Serves 3

1 cup shredded white cabbage	½ teaspoon salt
3 eggs, beaten	½ teaspoon onion powder
½ teaspoon ground nutmeg	½ zucchini, grated
	1 tablespoon coconut oil

1. In a bowl, stir together all the ingredients, except for the coconut oil. Form the cabbage mixture into medium hash browns. 2. Press the Sauté button on the Instant Pot and heat the coconut oil. 3. Place the hash browns in the hot coconut oil. Cook for 4 minutes on each side, or until lightly browned. 4. Transfer the hash browns to a plate and serve warm.

Parmesan Baked Eggs

Prep time: 5 minutes | Cook time: 10 minutes | Serves 1

1 tablespoon butter, cut into small pieces	2 tablespoons grated Parmesan cheese
2 tablespoons keto-friendly low-carb Marinara sauce	¼ teaspoon Italian seasoning
3 eggs	1 cup water

1. Place the butter pieces on the bottom of the oven-safe bowl. Spread the marinara sauce over the butter. Crack the eggs on top of the marinara sauce and top with the cheese and Italian seasoning. 2. Cover the bowl with aluminum foil. Pour the water and insert the trivet in the Instant Pot. Put the bowl on the trivet. 3. Set the lid in place. Select the Manual mode and set the cooking time for 10 minutes on Low Pressure. When the timer goes off, do a quick pressure release. Carefully open the lid. 4. Let the eggs cool for 5 minutes before serving.

Classic Coffee Cake

Prep time: 5 minutes | Cook time: 40 minutes | Serves 5 to 6

Base:

2 eggs	¼ cup full-fat cream cheese, softened
2 tablespoons salted grass-fed butter, softened	½ teaspoon salt
1 cup blanched almond flour	½ teaspoon ground cinnamon
1 cup chopped pecans	½ teaspoon ground nutmeg
¼ cup sour cream, at room temperature	¼ teaspoon baking soda

Topping:

1 cup sugar-free chocolate chips	taste
1 cup chopped pecans	½ cup heavy whipping cream
½ cup Swerve, or more to	

1. Pour 1 cup of filtered water into the inner pot of the Instant Pot, then insert the trivet. Using an electric mixer, combine the eggs, butter, flour, pecans, sour cream, cream cheese, salt, cinnamon, nutmeg, and baking soda. Mix thoroughly. Transfer this mixture into a well-greased, Instant Pot-friendly pan (or dish). 2. Using a sling if desired, place the pan onto the trivet, and cover loosely with aluminum foil. Close the lid, set the pressure release to Sealing, and select Manual. Set the Instant Pot to 40 minutes on High Pressure and let cook. 3. While cooking, in a large bowl, mix the chocolate chips, pecans, Swerve, and whipping cream thoroughly. Set aside. 4. Once cooked, let the pressure naturally disperse from the Instant Pot for about 10 minutes, then carefully switch the pressure release to Venting. 5. Open the Instant Pot and remove the pan. Evenly sprinkle the topping mixture over the cake. Let cool, serve, and enjoy!

Breakfast Cereal

Prep time: 5 minutes | Cook time: 5 minutes | Serves 4

2 tablespoons coconut oil	2 tablespoons chopped hazelnuts
1 cup full-fat coconut milk	2 tablespoons chopped macadamia nuts
½ cup chopped cashews	½ teaspoon ground cinnamon
½ cup heavy whipping cream	½ teaspoon ground nutmeg
½ cup chopped pecans	½ teaspoon ground turmeric
⅓ cup Swerve	
¼ cup unsweetened coconut flakes	
2 tablespoons flax seeds	

1. Set the Instant Pot to Sauté and melt the coconut oil. Pour in the coconut milk. 2. Add the cashews, whipping cream, pecans, Swerve, coconut flakes, flax seeds, hazelnuts, macadamia nuts, cinnamon, nutmeg, and turmeric to the Instant Pot. Stir thoroughly. 3. Close the lid, set the pressure release to Sealing, and hit Cancel to stop the current program. Select Manual, set the Instant Pot to 5 minutes on High Pressure, and let cook. 4. Once cooked, let the pressure naturally disperse from the Instant Pot for about 10 minutes, then carefully switch the pressure release to Venting. 5. Open the Instant Pot, serve, and enjoy!

Cheddar Broccoli Egg Bites

Prep time: 10 minutes | Cook time: 10 minutes | Serves 7

5 eggs, beaten	chopped broccoli
3 tablespoons heavy cream	1 ounce (28 g) shredded Cheddar cheese
⅛ teaspoon salt	½ cup water
⅛ teaspoon black pepper	
1 ounce (28 g) finely	

1. In a blender, combine the eggs, heavy cream, salt and pepper and pulse until smooth. 2. Divide the chopped broccoli among the egg cups equally. Pour the egg mixture on top of the broccoli, filling the cups about three-fourths of the way full. Sprinkle the Cheddar cheese on top of each cup. 3. Cover the egg cups tightly with aluminum foil. 4. Pour the water and insert the trivet in the Instant Pot. Put the egg cups on the trivet. 5. Lock the lid. Select the Manual mode and set the cooking time for 10 minutes on High Pressure. Once the timer goes off, perform a natural pressure release for 5 minutes, then release any remaining pressure. Carefully open the lid. 6. Serve immediately.

Shredded Potato Omelet

Prep time: 15 minutes | Cook time: 20 minutes | Serves 6

3 slices bacon, cooked and crumbled	1 cup egg substitute
2 cups shredded cooked potatoes	¼ cup fat-free milk
¼ cup minced onion	¼ teaspoon salt
¼ cup minced green bell pepper	⅛ teaspoon black pepper
	1 cup 75%-less-fat shredded cheddar cheese
	1 cup water

1. With nonstick cooking spray, spray the inside of a round baking dish that will fit in your Instant Pot inner pot. 2. Sprinkle the bacon, potatoes, onion, and bell pepper around the bottom of the baking dish. 3. Mix together the egg substitute, milk, salt, and pepper in mixing bowl. Pour over potato mixture. 4. Top with cheese. 5. Add water, place the steaming rack into the bottom of the inner pot and then place the round baking dish on top. 6. Close the lid and secure to the locking position. Be sure the vent is turned to sealing. Set for 20 minutes on Manual at high pressure. 7. Let the pressure release naturally. 8. Carefully remove the baking dish with the handles of the steaming rack and allow to stand 10 minutes before cutting and serving.

Egg Bites with Sausage and Peppers

Prep time: 5 minutes | Cook time: 15 minutes | Serves 7

4 large eggs	Meat brand), cooked and diced
¼ cup vegan cream cheese (such as Tofutti brand) or cream cheese	½ red bell pepper, seeded and chopped
¼ teaspoon fine sea salt	2 green onions, white and green parts, minced, plus more for garnish (optional)
¼ teaspoon freshly ground black pepper	
3 ounces lean turkey sausage, cooked and crumbled, or 1 vegetarian sausage (such as Beyond	¼ cup vegan cheese shreds or shredded sharp Cheddar cheese

1. In a blender, combine the eggs, cream cheese, salt, and pepper. Blend on medium speed for about 20 seconds, just until combined. Add the sausage, bell pepper, and green onions and pulse for 1 second once or twice. You want to mix in the solid ingredients without grinding them up very much. 2. Pour 1 cup water into the Instant Pot. Generously grease a 7-cup egg-bite mold or seven 2-ounce silicone baking cups with butter or coconut oil, making sure to coat each cup well. Place the prepared mold or cups on a long-handled silicone steam rack. (If you don't have the long-handled rack, use the wire metal steam rack and a homemade sling) 3. Pour ¼ cup of the egg mixture into each prepared mold or cup. Holding the handles of the steam rack, carefully lower the egg bites into the pot. 4. Secure the lid and set the Pressure Release to Sealing. Select the Steam setting and set the cooking time for 8 minutes at low pressure. (The pot will take about 5 minutes to come up to pressure before the cooking program begins.) 5. When the cooking program ends, let the pressure release naturally for 5 minutes, then move the Pressure Release to Venting to release any remaining steam. Open the pot. The egg muffins will have puffed up quite a bit during cooking, but they will deflate and settle as they cool. Wearing heat-resistant mitts, grasp the handles of the steam rack and carefully lift the egg bites out of the pot. Sprinkle the egg bites with the cheese, then let them cool for about 5 minutes, until the cheese has fully melted and you are able to handle the mold or cups comfortably. 6. Pull the sides of the egg mold or cups away from the egg bites, running a butter knife around the edge of each bite to loosen if necessary. Transfer the egg bites to plates, garnish with more green onions (if desired), and serve warm. To store, let cool to room temperature, transfer to an airtight container, and refrigerate for up to 3 days; reheat gently in the microwave for about 1 minute before serving.

Cynthia's Yogurt

Prep time: 10 minutes | Cook time: 8 hours | Serves 16

1 gallon low-fat milk	with active cultures
¼ cup low-fat plain yogurt	

1. Pour milk into the inner pot of the Instant Pot. 2. Lock lid, move vent to sealing, and press the yogurt button. Press Adjust till it reads "boil." 3. When boil cycle is complete (about 1 hour), check the temperature. It should be at 185°F. If it's not, use the Sauté function to warm to 185. 4. After it reaches 185°F, unplug Instant Pot, remove inner pot, and cool. You can place on cooling rack and let it slowly cool. If in a hurry, submerge the base of the pot in cool water. Cool milk to 110°F. 5. When mixture reaches 110, stir in the ¼ cup of yogurt. Lock the lid in place and move vent to sealing. 6. Press Yogurt. Use the Adjust button until the screen says 8:00. This will now incubate for 8 hours. 7. After 8 hours (when the cycle is finished), chill yogurt, or go immediately to straining in step 8. 8. After chilling, or following the 8 hours, strain the yogurt using a nut milk bag. This will give it the consistency of Greek yogurt.

Bacon Egg Cups

Prep time: 5 minutes | Cook time: 7 minutes | Serves 4

6 large eggs
2 strips cooked bacon, sliced in ¼-inch wide pieces
½ cup Cheddar cheese, divided
¼ teaspoon sea salt
¼ teaspoon black pepper
1 cup water
1 tablespoon chopped fresh flat leaf parsley

1. In a small bowl, beat the eggs. Stir in the cooked bacon, ¼ cup of the cheese, sea salt and pepper. Divide the egg mixture equally among four ramekins and loosely cover with aluminum foil. 2. Pour the water and place the trivet in the Instant Pot. Place two ramekins on the trivet and stack the other two on the top. 3. Lock the lid. Select the Manual mode and set the cooking time for 7 minutes at High Pressure. When the timer goes off, use a natural pressure release for 10 minutes, then release any remaining pressure. Carefully open the lid. 4. Top each ramekin with the remaining ¼ cup of the cheese. Lock the lid and melt the cheese for 2 minutes. Garnish with the chopped parsley and serve immediately.

Breakfast Millet with Nuts and Strawberries

Prep time: 0 minutes | Cook time: 30 minutes | Serves 8

2 tablespoons coconut oil or unsalted butter
1½ cups millet
2⅔ cups water
½ teaspoon fine sea salt
1 cup unsweetened almond
milk or other nondairy milk
1 cup chopped toasted pecans, almonds, or peanuts
4 cups sliced strawberries

1. Select the Sauté setting on the Instant Pot and melt the oil. Add the millet and cook for 4 minutes, until aromatic. Stir in the water and salt, making sure all of the grains are submerged in the liquid. 2. Secure the lid and set the Pressure Release to Sealing. Press the Cancel button to reset the cooking program, then select the Porridge, Pressure Cook, or Manual setting and set the cooking time for 12 minutes at high pressure. (The pot will take about 10 minutes to come up to pressure before the cooking program begins.) 3. When the cooking program ends, let the pressure release naturally for 10 minutes, then move the Pressure Release to Venting to release any remaining steam. Open the pot and use a fork to fluff and stir the millet. 4. Spoon the millet into bowls and top each serving with 2 tablespoons of the almond milk, then sprinkle with the nuts and top with the strawberries. Serve warm.

Cheese Egg Muffins

Prep time: 5 minutes | Cook time: 10 minutes | Serves 6

4 eggs
2 tablespoons heavy cream
¼ teaspoon salt
⅛ teaspoon pepper
⅓ cup shredded Cheddar cheese
1 cup water

1. In a large bowl, whisk eggs and heavy cream. Add salt and pepper. 2. Pour mixture into 6 silicone cupcake baking molds. Sprinkle cheese into each cup. 3. Pour water into Instant Pot and place steam rack in bottom of pot. Carefully set filled silicone molds steadily on steam rack. If all do not fit, separate into two batches. 4. Click lid closed. Press the Manual button and adjust time for 10 minutes. When timer beeps, allow a quick release and remove lid. Egg bites will look puffy at first, but will become smaller once they begin to cool. Serve warm.

Pumpkin Mug Muffin

Prep time: 5 minutes | Cook time: 9 minutes | Serves 1

½ cup Swerve
½ cup blanched almond flour
2 tablespoons organic pumpkin purée
1 teaspoon sugar-free chocolate chips
1 tablespoon organic coconut flour
1 egg
1 tablespoon coconut oil
½ teaspoon pumpkin pie spice
½ teaspoon ground nutmeg
½ teaspoon ground cinnamon
⅛ teaspoon baking soda

1. Mix the Swerve, almond flour, pumpkin purée, chocolate chips, coconut flour, egg, coconut oil, pumpkin pie spice, nutmeg, cinnamon, and baking soda in a large bowl. Transfer this mixture into a well-greased, Instant Pot-friendly mug. 2. Pour 1 cup of filtered water into the inner pot of the Instant Pot, and insert the trivet. Cover the mug in foil and place on top of the trivet. 3. Close the lid, set the pressure release to Sealing, and select Manual. Set the Instant Pot to 9 minutes on High Pressure. 4. Once cooked, release the pressure immediately by switching the valve to Venting. Be sure your muffin is done by inserting a toothpick into the cake and making sure it comes out clean, as cook times may vary. 5. Remove mug and enjoy!

Chapter ❷
Stews and Soups

Parmesan Zucchini Soup

Prep time: 10 minutes | Cook time: 1 minute | Serves 2

1 zucchini, grated	1 cup beef broth
1 teaspoon ground paprika	1 tablespoon dried cilantro
½ teaspoon cayenne pepper	1 ounce (28 g) Parmesan, grated
½ cup coconut milk	

1. Put the grated zucchini, paprika, cayenne pepper, coconut milk, beef broth, and dried cilantro in the instant pot. 2. Close and seal the lid. 3. Cook the soup on Manual (High Pressure) for 1 minute. Make a quick pressure release. 4. Ladle the soup in the serving bowls and top with Parmesan.

Pork and Daikon Stew

Prep time: 15 minutes | Cook time: 3 minutes | Serves 6

1 pound (454 g) pork tenderloin, chopped	1 tablespoon heavy cream
1 ounce (28 g) green onions, chopped	1 tablespoon butter
½ cup daikon, chopped	1 teaspoon ground black pepper
1 lemon slice	3 cups water

1. Put all ingredients in the Instant Pot and stir to mix with a spatula. 2. Seal the lid. Set Manual mode and set cooking time for 20 minutes on High Pressure. 3. When cooking is complete, use a natural pressure release for 15 minutes, then release any remaining pressure. Open the lid. 4. Serve warm.

Butternut Squash Soup

Prep time: 30 minutes | Cook time: 15 minutes | Serves 4

2 tablespoons margarine	2 large butternut squash, peeled, seeded, and cubed (about 4 pounds)
1 large onion, chopped	
2 cloves garlic, minced	
1 teaspoon thyme	4 cups low-sodium chicken stock
½ teaspoon sage	
Salt and pepper to taste	

1. In the inner pot of the Instant Pot, melt the margarine using Sauté function. 2. Add onion and garlic and cook until soft, 3 to 5 minutes. 3. Add thyme and sage and cook another minute. Season with salt and pepper. 4. Stir in butternut squash and add chicken stock. 5. Secure the lid and make sure vent is at sealing. Using Manual setting, cook squash and seasonings 10 minutes, using high pressure. 6. When time is up, do a quick release of the pressure. 7. Puree the soup in a food processor or use immersion blender right in the inner pot. If soup is too thick, add more stock. Adjust salt and pepper as needed.

Chicken and Mushroom Soup

Prep time: 5 minutes | Cook time: 15 minutes | Serves 4

1 onion, cut into thin slices	1 teaspoon salt
3 garlic cloves, minced	1 teaspoon freshly ground black pepper
2 cups chopped mushrooms	
1 yellow summer squash, chopped	1 teaspoon Italian seasoning or poultry seasoning
1 pound (454 g) boneless, skinless chicken breast, cut into large chunks	
	1 cup heavy (whipping) cream
2½ cups chicken broth	

1. Put the onion, garlic, mushrooms, squash, chicken, chicken broth, salt, pepper, and Italian seasoning in the inner cooking pot of the Instant Pot. 2. Lock the lid into place. Select Manual and adjust the pressure to High. Cook for 15 minutes. When the cooking is complete, let the pressure release naturally for 10 minutes, then quick-release any remaining pressure. Unlock the lid. 3. Using tongs, transfer the chicken pieces to a bowl and set aside. 4. Tilt the pot slightly. Using an immersion blender, roughly purée the vegetables, leaving a few intact for texture and visual appeal. 5. Shred the chicken and stir it back in to the soup. 6. Add the cream and stir well. Serve.

Italian Vegetable Soup

Prep time: 20 minutes | Cook time: 5 to 9 hours | Serves 6

3 small carrots, sliced	¼ teaspoon pepper
1 small onion, chopped	16-ounce can red kidney beans, undrained
2 small potatoes, diced	
2 tablespoons chopped parsley	3 cups water
1 garlic clove, minced	14½-ounce can stewed tomatoes, with juice
3 teaspoons sodium-free beef bouillon powder	
	1 cup diced, extra-lean, lower-sodium cooked ham
1¼ teaspoons dried basil	

1. In the inner pot of the Instant Pot, layer the carrots, onion, potatoes, parsley, garlic, beef bouillon, basil, pepper, and kidney beans. Do not stir. Add water. 2. Secure the lid and cook on the Low Slow Cook mode for 8–9 hours, or on high 4½–5½ hours, until vegetables are tender. 3. Remove the lid and stir in the tomatoes and ham. Secure the lid again and cook on high Slow Cook mode for 10–15 minutes more.

Chicken Vegetable Soup

Prep time: 12 to 25 minutes | Cook time: 4 minutes | Serves 6

1 to 2 raw chicken breasts, cubed	(bite-sized)
½ medium onion, chopped	¼ to ½ cup chopped savoy cabbage
4 cloves garlic, minced	14½ ounces can low-sodium petite diced tomatoes
½ sweet potato, small cubes	
1 large carrot, peeled and cubed	3 cups low-sodium chicken bone broth
4 stalks celery, chopped, leaves included	½ teaspoon black pepper
½ cup frozen corn	1 teaspoon garlic powder
¼ cup frozen peas	¼ cup chopped fresh parsley
¼ cup frozen lima beans	¼ to ½ teaspoon red pepper flakes
1 cup frozen green beans	

1. Add all of the ingredients, in the order listed, to the inner pot of the Instant Pot. 2. Lock the lid in place, set the vent to sealing, press Manual, and cook at high pressure for 4 minutes. 3. Release the pressure manually as soon as cooking time is finished.

Creamy Sweet Potato Soup

Prep time: 15 minutes | Cook time: 10 minutes | Serves 6

2 tablespoons avocado oil	peeled and cut into 1-inch cubes
1 small onion, chopped	3 cups Vegetable Broth or Chicken Bone Broth
2 celery stalks, chopped	
2 teaspoons minced garlic	
1 teaspoon kosher salt	Plain Greek yogurt, to garnish (optional)
½ teaspoon freshly ground black pepper	Chopped fresh parsley, to garnish (optional)
1 teaspoon ground turmeric	
½ teaspoon ground cinnamon	Pumpkin seeds (pepitas), to garnish (optional)
2 pounds sweet potatoes,	

1. Set the electric pressure cooker to the Sauté setting. When the pot is hot, pour in the avocado oil. 2. Sauté the onion and celery for 3 to 5 minutes or until the vegetables begin to soften. 3. Stir in the garlic, salt, pepper, turmeric, and cinnamon. Hit Cancel. 4. Stir in the sweet potatoes and broth. 5. Close and lock the lid of the pressure cooker. Set the valve to sealing. 6. Cook on high pressure for 10 minutes. 7. When the cooking is complete, hit Cancel and allow the pressure to release naturally. 8. Once the pin drops, unlock and remove the lid. 9. Use an immersion blender to purée the soup right in the pot. If you don't have an immersion blender, transfer the soup to a blender or food processor and purée. (Follow the instructions that came with your machine for blending hot foods.) 10. Spoon into bowls and serve topped with Greek yogurt, parsley, and/or pumpkin seeds (if using).

Chicken and Vegetable Soup

Prep time: 5 minutes | Cook time: 2 minutes | Serves 4

1 pound (454 g) boneless, skinless chicken thighs, diced small	1 tablespoon powdered chicken broth base
1 (10 ounces / 283 g) bag frozen vegetables	1 teaspoon salt
	1 teaspoon freshly ground black pepper
2 cups water	1 cup heavy (whipping) cream
1 teaspoon poultry seasoning	

1. Put the chicken, vegetables, water, poultry seasoning, chicken broth base, salt, and pepper in the inner cooking pot of your Instant Pot. 2. Lock the lid into place. Select Manual and adjust the pressure to High. Cook for 2 minutes. When the cooking is complete, quick-release the pressure (you may want to do this in short bursts so the soup doesn't spurt out). Unlock the lid. 3. Add the cream, stir, and serve. Or, if you prefer, you can mash up the chicken with the back of a wooden spoon to break it into shreds before adding the cream.

Jalapeño Popper Chicken Soup

Prep time: 5 minutes | Cook time: 25 minutes | Serves 4

2 tablespoons butter	4 ounces (113 g) cream cheese
½ medium diced onion	1 teaspoon salt
¼ cup sliced pickled jalapeños	½ teaspoon pepper
¼ cup cooked crumbled bacon	¼ teaspoon garlic powder
	⅓ cup heavy cream
2 cups chicken broth	1 cup shredded sharp Cheddar cheese
2 cups cooked diced chicken	

1. Press the Sauté button. Add butter, onion, and sliced jalapeños to Instant Pot. Sauté for 5 minutes, until onions are translucent. Add bacon and press the Cancel button. 2. Add broth, cooked chicken, cream cheese, salt, pepper, and garlic to Instant Pot. Click lid closed. Press the Soup button and adjust time for 20 minutes. 3. When timer beeps, quick-release the steam. Stir in heavy cream and Cheddar. Continue stirring until cheese is fully melted. Serve warm.

Cauliflower Rice and Chicken Thigh Soup

Prep time: 15 minutes | Cook time: 13 minutes | Serves 5

2 cups cauliflower florets	pepper
1 pound (454 g) boneless, skinless chicken thighs	½ cup sliced zucchini
4½ cups chicken broth	⅓ cup sliced turnips
½ yellow onion, chopped	1 teaspoon dried parsley
2 garlic cloves, minced	3 celery stalks, chopped
1 tablespoon unflavored gelatin powder	1 teaspoon ground turmeric
2 teaspoons sea salt	½ teaspoon dried marjoram
½ teaspoon ground black	1 teaspoon dried thyme
	½ teaspoon dried oregano

1. Add the cauliflower florets to a food processor and pulse until a ricelike consistency is achieved. Set aside. 2. Add the chicken thighs, chicken broth, onions, garlic, gelatin powder, sea salt, and black pepper to the pot. Gently stir to combine. 3. Lock the lid. Select Manual mode and set cooking time for 10 minutes on High Pressure. 4. When cooking is complete, quick release the pressure and open the lid. 5. Transfer the chicken thighs to a cutting board. Chop the chicken into bite-sized pieces and then return the chopped chicken to the pot. 6. Add the cauliflower rice, zucchini, turnips, parsley, celery, turmeric, marjoram, thyme, and oregano to the pot. Stir to combine. 7. Lock the lid. Select Manual mode and set cooking time for 3 minutes on High Pressure. 8. When cooking is complete, quick release the pressure. 9. Open the lid. Ladle the soup into serving bowls. Serve hot.

Garlicky Chicken Soup

Prep time: 5 minutes | Cook time: 20 minutes | Serves 6

10 roasted garlic cloves	1 pound (454 g) boneless, skinless chicken thighs, cubed
½ medium onion, diced	
4 tablespoons butter	
4 cups chicken broth	½ cup heavy cream
½ teaspoon salt	2 ounces (57 g) cream cheese
¼ teaspoon pepper	
1 teaspoon thyme	

1. In small bowl, mash roasted garlic into paste. Press the Sauté button and add garlic, onion, and butter to Instant Pot. Sauté for 2 to 3 minutes until onion begins to soften. Press the Cancel button. 2. Add Chicken Broth, salt, pepper, thyme, and chicken to Instant Pot. Click lid closed. Press the Manual button and adjust time for 20 minutes. 3. When timer beeps, quick-release the pressure. Stir in heavy cream and cream cheese until smooth. Serve warm.

French Onion Soup

Prep time: 10 minutes | Cook time: 20 minutes | Serves 10

½ cup light, soft tub margarine	3 teaspoons sodium-free chicken bouillon powder
8 to 10 large onions, sliced	1½ teaspoons Worcestershire sauce
3 14-ounce cans 98% fat-free, lower-sodium beef broth	3 bay leaves
2½ cups water	10 (1-ounce) slices French bread, toasted

1. Turn the Instant Pot to the Sauté function and add in the margarine and onions. Cook about 5 minutes, or until the onions are slightly soft. Press Cancel. 2. Add the beef broth, water, bouillon powder, Worcestershire sauce, and bay leaves and stir. 3. Secure the lid and make sure vent is set to sealing. Cook on Manual mode for 20 minutes. 4. Let the pressure release naturally for 15 minutes, then do a quick release. Open the lid and discard bay leaves. 5. Ladle into bowls. Top each with a slice of bread and some cheese if you desire.

Favorite Chili

Prep time: 10 minutes | Cook time: 35 minutes | Serves 5

1 pound extra-lean ground beef	1 green pepper, chopped
1 teaspoon salt	2 tablespoons chili powder
½ teaspoons black pepper	½ teaspoons cumin
1 tablespoon olive oil	1 cup water
1 small onion, chopped	16-ounce can chili beans
2 cloves garlic, minced	15 ounces can low-sodium crushed tomatoes

1. Press Sauté button and adjust once to Sauté More function. Wait until indicator says "hot." 2. Season the ground beef with salt and black pepper. 3. Add the olive oil into the inner pot. Coat the whole bottom of the pot with the oil. 4. Add ground beef into the inner pot. The ground beef will start to release moisture. Allow the ground beef to brown and crisp slightly, stirring occasionally to break it up. Taste and adjust the seasoning with more salt and ground black pepper. 5. Add diced onion, minced garlic, chopped pepper, chili powder, and cumin. Sauté for about 5 minutes, until the spices start to release their fragrance. Stir frequently. 6. Add water and 1 can of chili beans, not drained. Mix well. Pour in 1 can of crushed tomatoes. 7. Close and secure lid, making sure vent is set to sealing, and pressure cook on Manual at high pressure for 10 minutes. 8. Let the pressure release naturally when cooking time is up. Open the lid carefully.

Bacon Broccoli Soup

Prep time: 12 minutes | Cook time: 12 minutes | Serves 6

2 large heads broccoli	6 ounces (170 g) extra-sharp Cheddar cheese, shredded (about 1½ cups)
2 strips bacon, chopped	
2 tablespoons unsalted butter	2 ounces (57 g) cream cheese, softened
¼ cup diced onions	
Cloves squeezed from 1 head roasted garlic, or 2 cloves garlic, minced	½ teaspoon fine sea salt
	¼ teaspoon ground black pepper
3 cups chicken broth or beef broth	Pinch of ground nutmeg

1. Cut the broccoli florets off the stems, leaving as much of the stems intact as possible. Reserve the florets for another recipe. Trim the bottom end of each stem so that it is flat. Using a spiral slicer, cut the stems into "noodles." 2. Place the bacon in the Instant Pot and press Sauté. Cook, stirring occasionally, for 4 minutes, or until crisp. Remove the bacon with a slotted spoon and set aside on a paper towel-lined plate to drain, leaving the drippings in the pot. 3. Add the butter and onions to the Instant Pot and cook for 4 minutes, or until the onions are soft. Add the garlic (and, if using raw garlic, sauté for another minute). Add the broth, Cheddar cheese, cream cheese, salt, pepper, and nutmeg and sauté until the cheeses are melted, about 3 minutes. Press Cancel to stop the Sauté. 4. Use a stick blender to purée the soup until smooth. Alternatively, you can pour the soup into a regular blender or food processor and purée until smooth, then return it to the Instant Pot. If using a regular blender, you may need to blend the soup in two batches; if you overfill the blender jar, the soup will not purée properly. 5. Add the broccoli noodles to the puréed soup in the Instant Pot. Seal the lid, press Manual, and set the timer for 1 minute. Once finished, let the pressure release naturally. 6. Remove the lid and stir well. Ladle the soup into bowls and sprinkle some of the bacon on top of each serving.

Beef and Okra Stew

Prep time: 15 minutes | Cook time: 25 minutes | Serves 3

8 ounces (227 g) beef sirloin, chopped	¼ cup coconut cream
	1 cup water
¼ teaspoon cumin seeds	6 ounces (170 g) okra, chopped
1 teaspoon dried basil	
1 tablespoon avocado oil	

1. Sprinkle the beef sirloin with cumin seeds and dried basil and put in the Instant Pot. 2. Add avocado oil and roast the meat on Sauté mode for 5 minutes. Flip occasionally. 3. Add coconut cream, water, and okra. 4. Close the lid and select Manual mode. Set cooking time for 25 minutes on High Pressure. 5. When timer beeps, use a natural pressure release for 10 minutes, the release any remaining pressure. Open the lid. 6. Serve warm.

Chicken Cauliflower Rice Soup

Prep time: 5 minutes | Cook time: 20 minutes | Serves 4

4 tablespoons butter	1 bay leaf
¼ cup diced onion	2 cups chicken broth
2 stalks celery, chopped	2 cups diced cooked chicken
½ cup fresh spinach	
½ teaspoon salt	¾ cup uncooked cauliflower rice
¼ teaspoon pepper	
¼ teaspoon dried thyme	½ teaspoon xanthan gum (optional)
¼ teaspoon dried parsley	

1. Press the Sauté button and add butter to Instant Pot. Add onions and sauté until translucent. Place celery and spinach into Instant Pot and sauté for 2 to 3 minutes until spinach is wilted. Press the Cancel button. 2. Sprinkle seasoning into Instant Pot and add bay leaf, broth, and cooked chicken. Click lid closed. Press the Soup button and adjust time for 10 minutes. 3. When timer beeps, quick-release the pressure and stir in cauliflower rice. Leave Instant Pot on Keep Warm setting to finish cooking cauliflower rice additional 10 minutes. Serve warm. 4. For a thicker soup, stir in xanthan gum.

Ham and Potato Chowder

Prep time: 25 minutes | Cook time: 8 hour s | Serves 5

5 ounces package scalloped potatoes	bouillon powder
	4 cups water
Sauce mix from potato package	1 cup chopped celery
	⅓ cup chopped onions
1 cup extra-lean, reduced-sodium, cooked ham, cut into narrow strips	Pepper to taste
	2 cups fat-free half-and-half
4 teaspoons sodium-free	⅓ cup flour

1. Combine potatoes, sauce mix, ham, bouillon powder, water, celery, onions, and pepper in the inner pot of the Instant Pot. 2. Secure the lid and cook using the Slow Cook function on low for 7 hours. 3. Combine half-and-half and flour. Remove the lid and gradually add to the inner pot, blending well. 4. Secure the lid once more and cook on the low Slow Cook function for up to 1 hour more, stirring occasionally until thickened.

Chicken and Kale Soup

Prep time: 5 minutes | Cook time: 5 minutes | Serves 4

2 cups chopped cooked chicken breast	½ teaspoon ground cinnamon
12 ounces (340 g) frozen kale	Pinch ground cloves
1 onion, chopped	2 teaspoons minced garlic
2 cups water	1 teaspoon freshly ground black pepper
1 tablespoon powdered chicken broth base	1 teaspoon salt
	2 cups full-fat coconut milk

1. Put the chicken, kale, onion, water, chicken broth base, cinnamon, cloves, garlic, pepper, and salt in the inner cooking pot of the Instant Pot. 2. Lock the lid into place. Select Manual and adjust the pressure to High. Cook for 5 minutes. When the cooking is complete, let the pressure release naturally for 10 minutes, then quick-release any remaining pressure. Unlock the lid. 3. Stir in the coconut milk. Taste and adjust any seasonings as needed before serving.

Sicilian Fish Stew

Prep time: 10 minutes | Cook time: 10 minutes | Serves 4 to 6

2 tablespoons extra-virgin olive oil	
2 onions, chopped fine	clam juice
1 teaspoon table salt	¼ cup dry white wine
½ teaspoon pepper	¼ cup golden raisins
1 teaspoon minced fresh thyme or ¼ teaspoon dried	2 tablespoons capers, rinsed
Pinch red pepper flakes	1½ pounds (680 g) skinless
4 garlic cloves, minced, divided	swordfish steak, 1 to 1½ inches thick, cut into 1-inch
1 (28 ounces / 794 g) can whole peeled tomatoes, drained with juice reserved, chopped coarse	pieces
	¼ cup pine nuts, toasted
	¼ cup minced fresh mint
1 (8 ounces / 227 g) bottle	1 teaspoon grated orange zest

1. Using highest sauté function, heat oil in Instant Pot until shimmering. Add onions, salt, and pepper and cook until onions are softened, about 5 minutes. Stir in thyme, pepper flakes, and three-quarters of garlic and cook until fragrant, about 30 seconds. Stir in tomatoes and reserved juice, clam juice, wine, raisins, and capers. Nestle swordfish into pot and spoon some cooking liquid over top. 2. Lock lid in place and close pressure release valve. Select high pressure cook function and cook for 1 minute. Turn off Instant Pot and quick-release pressure. Carefully remove lid, allowing steam to escape away from you. 3. Combine pine nuts, mint, orange zest, and remaining garlic in

bowl. Season stew with salt and pepper to taste. Sprinkle individual portions with pine nut mixture before serving.

All-Purpose Chicken Broth

Prep time: 10 minutes | Cook time: 1 hour 25 minutes | Makes 3 quarts

3 pounds (1.4 kg) chicken wings	crushed and peeled
	12 cups water, divided
1 tablespoon vegetable oil	½ teaspoon table salt
1 onion, chopped	3 bay leaves
3 garlic cloves, lightly	

1. Pat chicken wings dry with paper towels. Using highest sauté function, heat oil in Instant Pot for 5 minutes (or until just smoking). Brown half of chicken wings on all sides, about 10 minutes; transfer to bowl. Repeat with remaining chicken wings; transfer to bowl. 2. Add onion to fat left in pot and cook until softened and well browned, 8 to 10 minutes. Stir in garlic and cook until fragrant, about 30 seconds. Stir in 1 cup water, scraping up any browned bits. Stir in remaining 11 cups water, salt, bay leaves, and chicken and any accumulated juices. 3. Lock lid in place and close pressure release valve. Select high pressure cook function and cook for 1 hour. Turn off Instant Pot and let pressure release naturally for 15 minutes. Quick-release any remaining pressure, then carefully remove lid, allowing steam to escape away from you. 4. Strain broth through fine-mesh strainer into large container, pressing on solids to extract as much liquid as possible; discard solids. Using wide, shallow spoon, skim excess fat from surface of broth. (Broth can be refrigerated for up to 4 days or frozen for up to 2 months.)

Green Chile Corn Chowder

Prep time: 20 minutes | Cook time: 7 to 8 hours | Serves 8

16-ounce can cream-style corn	pimentos, drained
	½ cup chopped cooked ham
3 potatoes, peeled and diced	
	2 10½-ounce cans 100%
2 tablespoons chopped fresh chives	fat-free lower-sodium chicken broth
4-ounce can diced green chilies, drained	Pepper to taste
	Tabasco sauce to taste
2-ounce jar chopped	1 cup fat-free milk

1. Combine all ingredients, except milk, in the inner pot of the Instant Pot. 2. Secure the lid and cook using the Slow Cook function on low 7–8 hours or until potatoes are tender. 3. When cook time is up, remove the lid and stir in the milk. Cover and let simmer another 20 minutes.

Broccoli Cheddar Soup

Prep time: 5 minutes | Cook time: 10 minutes | Serves 4

2 tablespoons butter	1 cup chopped broccoli
⅛ cup onion, diced	1 tablespoon cream cheese, softened
½ teaspoon garlic powder	¼ cup heavy cream
½ teaspoon salt	1 cup shredded Cheddar cheese
¼ teaspoon pepper	
2 cups chicken broth	

1. Press the Sauté button and add butter to Instant Pot. Add onion and sauté until translucent. Press the Cancel button and add garlic powder, salt, pepper, broth, and broccoli to pot. 2. Click lid closed. Press the Soup button and set time for 5 minutes. When timer beeps, stir in heavy cream, cream cheese, and Cheddar.

Creamy Carrot Soup with Warm Spices

Prep time: 15 minutes | Cook time: 10 minutes | Serves 6 to 8

2 tablespoons extra-virgin olive oil	2 cups water
2 onions, chopped	2 pounds (907 g) carrots, peeled and cut into 2-inch pieces
1 teaspoon table salt	½ teaspoon baking soda
1 tablespoon grated fresh ginger	2 tablespoons pomegranate molasses
1 tablespoon ground coriander	½ cup plain Greek yogurt
1 tablespoon ground fennel	½ cup hazelnuts, toasted, skinned, and chopped
1 teaspoon ground cinnamon	½ cup chopped fresh cilantro or mint
4 cups vegetable or chicken broth	

1. Using highest sauté function, heat oil in Instant Pot until shimmering. Add onions and salt and cook until onions are softened, about 5 minutes. Stir in ginger, coriander, fennel, and cinnamon and cook until fragrant, about 30 seconds. Stir in broth, water, carrots, and baking soda. 2. Lock lid in place and close pressure release valve. Select high pressure cook function and cook for 3 minutes. Turn off Instant Pot and quick-release pressure. Carefully remove lid, allowing steam to escape away from you. 3. Working in batches, process soup in blender until smooth, 1 to 2 minutes. Return processed soup to Instant Pot and bring to simmer using highest sauté function. Season with salt and pepper to taste. Drizzle individual portions with pomegranate molasses and top with yogurt, hazelnuts, and cilantro before serving.

Venison and Tomato Stew

Prep time: 12 minutes | Cook time: 42 minutes | Serves 8

1 tablespoon unsalted butter	diced tomatoes
1 cup diced onions	1 teaspoon fine sea salt
2 cups button mushrooms, sliced in half	1 teaspoon ground black pepper
2 large stalks celery, cut into ¼-inch pieces	½ teaspoon dried rosemary, or 1 teaspoon fresh rosemary, finely chopped
Cloves squeezed from 2 heads roasted garlic or 4 cloves garlic, minced	½ teaspoon dried thyme leaves, or 1 teaspoon fresh thyme leaves, finely chopped
2 pounds (907 g) boneless venison or beef roast, cut into 4 large pieces	½ head cauliflower, cut into large florets
5 cups beef broth	Fresh thyme leaves, for garnish
1 (14½ ounces / 411 g) can	

1. Place the butter in the Instant Pot and press Sauté. Once melted, add the onions and sauté for 4 minutes, or until soft. 2. Add the mushrooms, celery, and garlic and sauté for another 3 minutes, or until the mushrooms are golden brown. Press Cancel to stop the Sauté. Add the roast, broth, tomatoes, salt, pepper, rosemary, and thyme. 3. Seal the lid, press Manual, and set the timer for 30 minutes. Once finished, turn the valve to venting for a quick release. 4. Add the cauliflower. Seal the lid, press Manual, and set the timer for 5 minutes. Once finished, let the pressure release naturally. 5. Remove the lid and shred the meat with two forks. Taste the liquid and add more salt, if needed. Ladle the stew into bowls. Garnish with thyme leaves.

Blue Cheese Mushroom Soup

Prep time: 15 minutes | Cook time: 20 minutes | Serves 4

2 cups chopped white mushrooms	1 teaspoon olive oil
3 tablespoons cream cheese	½ teaspoon ground cumin
4 ounces (113 g) scallions, diced	1 teaspoon salt
4 cups chicken broth	2 ounces (57 g) blue cheese, crumbled

1. Combine the mushrooms, cream cheese, scallions, chicken broth, olive oil, and ground cumin in the Instant Pot. 2. Seal the lid. Select Manual mode and set cooking time for 20 minutes on High Pressure. 3. When timer beeps, use a quick pressure release and open the lid. 4. Add the salt and blend the soup with an immersion blender. 5. Ladle the soup in the bowls and top with blue cheese. Serve warm.

Chicken Enchilada Soup

Prep time: 10 minutes | Cook time: 40 minutes | Serves 6

2 (6 ounces / 170 g) boneless, skinless chicken breasts	2 cups chicken broth
½ tablespoon chili powder	⅛ cup pickled jalapeños
½ teaspoon salt	4 ounces (113 g) cream cheese
½ teaspoon garlic powder	1 cup uncooked cauliflower rice
¼ teaspoon pepper	1 avocado, diced
½ cup red enchilada sauce	1 cup shredded mild Cheddar cheese
½ medium onion, diced	½ cup sour cream
1 (4 ounces / 113 g) can green chilies	

1. Sprinkle seasoning over chicken breasts and set aside. Pour enchilada sauce into Instant Pot and place chicken on top. 2. Add onion, chilies, broth, and jalapeños to the pot, then place cream cheese on top of chicken breasts. Click lid closed. Adjust time for 25 minutes. When timer beeps, quick-release the pressure and shred chicken with forks. 3. Mix soup together and add cauliflower rice, with pot on Keep Warm setting. Replace lid and let pot sit for 15 minutes, still on Keep Warm. This will cook cauliflower rice. Serve with avocado, Cheddar, and sour cream.

Thai Shrimp and Mushroom Soup

Prep time: 15 minutes | Cook time: 10 minutes | Serves 6

2 tablespoons unsalted butter, divided	paste
½ pound (227 g) medium uncooked shrimp, shelled and deveined	2 tablespoons lime juice
	1 stalk lemongrass, outer stalk removed, crushed, and finely chopped
½ medium yellow onion, diced	2 tablespoons coconut aminos
2 cloves garlic, minced	1 teaspoon sea salt
1 cup sliced fresh white mushrooms	½ teaspoon ground black pepper
1 tablespoon freshly grated ginger root	13.5 ounces (383 g) can unsweetened, full-fat coconut milk
4 cups chicken broth	3 tablespoons chopped fresh cilantro
2 tablespoons fish sauce	
2½ teaspoons red curry	

1. Select the Instant Pot on Sauté mode. Add 1 tablespoon butter. 2. Once the butter is melted, add the shrimp and sauté for 3 minutes or until opaque. Transfer the shrimp to a medium bowl. Set aside. 3. Add the remaining butter to the pot. Once the butter is melted, add the onions and garlic and sauté for 2 minutes or until the garlic is fragrant and the onions are softened. 4. Add the mushrooms, ginger root, chicken broth, fish sauce, red curry paste, lime juice, lemongrass, coconut aminos, sea salt, and black pepper to the pot. Stir to combine. 5. Lock the lid. Select Manual mode and set cooking time for 5 minutes on High Pressure. 6. When cooking is complete, allow the pressure to release naturally for 5 minutes, then release the remaining pressure. 7. Open the lid. Stir in the cooked shrimp and coconut milk. 8. Select Sauté mode. Bring the soup to a boil and then press Keep Warm / Cancel. Let the soup rest in the pot for 2 minutes. 9. Ladle the soup into bowls and sprinkle the cilantro over top. Serve hot.

Mushroom Pizza Soup

Prep time: 10 minutes | Cook time: 22 minutes | Serves 3

1 teaspoon coconut oil	seasoning
¼ cup cremini mushrooms, sliced	1 teaspoon unsweetened tomato purée
5 ounces (142 g) Italian sausages, chopped	1 cup water
½ jalapeño pepper, sliced	4 ounces (113 g) Mozzarella, shredded
½ teaspoon Italian	

1. Melt the coconut oil in the Instant Pot on Sauté mode. 2. Add the mushrooms and cook for 10 minutes. 3. Add the chopped sausages, sliced jalapeño, Italian seasoning, and unsweetened tomato purée. Pour in the water and stir to mix well. 4. Close the lid and select Manual mode. Set cooking time for 12 minutes on High Pressure. 5. When timer beeps, use a quick pressure release and open the lid. 6. Ladle the soup in the bowls. Top it with Mozzarella. Serve warm.

Buffalo Chicken Soup

Prep time: 7 minutes | Cook time: 10 minutes | Serves 2

1 ounce (28 g) celery stalk, chopped	2 ounces (57 g) Mozzarella, shredded
4 tablespoons coconut milk	6 ounces (170 g) cooked chicken, shredded
¾ teaspoon salt	2 tablespoons keto-friendly Buffalo sauce
¼ teaspoon white pepper	
1 cup water	

1. Place the chopped celery stalk, coconut milk, salt, white pepper, water, and Mozzarella in the Instant Pot. Stir to mix well. 2. Set the Manual mode and set timer for 7 minutes on High Pressure. 3. When timer beeps, use a quick pressure release and open the lid. 4. Transfer the soup on the bowls. Stir in the chicken and Buffalo sauce. Serve warm.

Buttercup Squash Soup

Prep time: 15 minutes | Cook time: 10 minutes | Serves 6

2 tablespoons extra-virgin olive oil	squash, peeled, seeded, and cut into 1-inch chunks
1 medium onion, chopped	½ teaspoon kosher salt
4 to 5 cups Vegetable Broth or Chicken Bone Broth	¼ teaspoon ground white pepper
1½ pounds buttercup	Whole nutmeg, for grating

1. Set the electric pressure cooker to the Sauté setting. When the pot is hot, pour in the olive oil. 2. Add the onion and sauté for 3 to 5 minutes, until it begins to soften. Hit Cancel. 3. Add the broth, squash, salt, and pepper to the pot and stir. (If you want a thicker soup, use 4 cups of broth. If you want a thinner, drinkable soup, use 5 cups.) 4. Close and lock the lid of the pressure cooker. Set the valve to sealing. 5. Cook on high pressure for 10 minutes. 6. When the cooking is complete, hit Cancel and allow the pressure to release naturally. 7. Once the pin drops, unlock and remove the lid. 8. Use an immersion blender to purée the soup right in the pot. If you don't have an immersion blender, transfer the soup to a blender or food processor and purée. (Follow the instructions that came with your machine for blending hot foods.) 9. Pour the soup into serving bowls and grate nutmeg on top.

Vegetable and Chickpea Stew

Prep time: 25 minutes | Cook time: 30 minutes | Serves 6 to 8

¼ cup extra-virgin olive oil, plus extra for drizzling	1 (28 ounces / 794 g) can whole peeled tomatoes, drained with juice reserved, chopped
2 red bell peppers, stemmed, seeded, and cut into 1-inch pieces	1 pound (454 g) Yukon Gold potatoes, peeled and cut into ½-inch pieces
1 onion, chopped fine	2 zucchini, quartered lengthwise and sliced 1 inch thick
½ teaspoon table salt	
½ teaspoon pepper	
1½ tablespoons baharat	
4 garlic cloves, minced	1 (15 ounces / 425 g) can chickpeas, rinsed
1 tablespoon tomato paste	
4 cups vegetable or chicken broth	⅓ cup chopped fresh mint

1. Using highest sauté function, heat oil in Instant Pot until shimmering. Add bell pepper, onion, salt, and pepper and cook until vegetables are softened and lightly browned, 5 to 7 minutes. Stir in baharat, garlic, and tomato paste and cook until fragrant, about 1 minute. Stir in broth and tomatoes and reserved juice, scraping up any browned bits, then stir in potatoes. 2. Lock lid in place and close pressure release valve. Select high pressure cook function and cook for 9 minutes. Turn off Instant Pot and quick-release pressure. Carefully remove lid, allowing steam to escape away from you. 3. Stir zucchini and chickpeas into stew and cook, using highest sauté function, until zucchini is tender, 10 to 15 minutes. Turn off multicooker. Season with salt and pepper to taste. Drizzle individual portions with extra oil, and sprinkle with mint before serving.

Chicken and Zoodles Soup

Prep time: 25 minutes | Cook time: 15 minutes | Serves 2

2 cups water	2 ounces (57 g) zucchini, spiralized
6 ounces (170 g) chicken fillet, chopped	1 tablespoon coconut aminos
1 teaspoon salt	

1. Pour water in the Instant Pot. Add chopped chicken fillet and salt. Close the lid. 2. Select Manual mode and set cooking time for 15 minutes on High Pressure. 3. When cooking is complete, perform a natural pressure release for 10 minutes, then release any remaining pressure. Open the lid. 4. Fold in the zoodles and coconut aminos. 5. Leave the soup for 10 minutes to rest. Serve warm.

Chicken and Asparagus Soup

Prep time: 7 minutes | Cook time: 11 minutes | Serves 8

1 tablespoon unsalted butter (or coconut oil for dairy-free)	paste
	1 teaspoon fine sea salt
¼ cup finely chopped onions	½ teaspoon ground black pepper
2 cloves garlic, minced	2 pounds (907 g) boneless, skinless chicken breasts, cut into ½-inch chunks
1 (14 ounces / 397 g) can full-fat coconut milk	
1 (14 ounces / 397 g) can sugar-free tomato sauce	2 cups asparagus, trimmed and cut into 2-inch pieces
1 cup chicken broth	Fresh cilantro leaves, for garnish
1 tablespoon red curry	Lime wedges, for garnish

1. Place the butter in the Instant Pot and press Sauté. Once melted, add the onions and garlic and sauté for 4 minutes, or until the onions are soft. Press Cancel to stop the Sauté. 2. Add the coconut milk, tomato sauce, broth, curry paste, salt, and pepper and whisk to combine well. Stir in the chicken and asparagus. 3. Seal the lid, press Manual, and set the timer for 7 minutes. Once finished, turn the valve to venting for a quick release. 4. Remove the lid and stir well. Taste and adjust the seasoning to your liking. Ladle the soup into bowls and garnish with cilantro. Serve with lime wedges or a squirt of lime juice.

Nancy's Vegetable Beef Soup

Prep time: 25 minutes | Cook time: 8 hours | Serves 8

2 pounds roast, cubed, or 2 pounds stewing meat	salt stewed tomatoes
15 ounces can corn	5 teaspoons salt-free beef bouillon powder
15 ounces can green beans	Tabasco, to taste
1 pound bag frozen peas	½ teaspoons salt
40 ounces can no-added-	

1. Combine all ingredients in the Instant Pot. Do not drain vegetables. 2. Add water to fill inner pot only to the fill line. 3. Secure the lid, or use the glass lid and set the Instant Pot on Slow Cook mode, Low for 8 hours, or until meat is tender and vegetables are soft.

Beef, Mushroom, and Wild Rice Soup

Prep time: 0 minutes | Cook time: 55 minutes | Serves 6

2 tablespoons extra-virgin olive oil or unsalted butter	1½ pounds beef stew meat, larger pieces halved, or beef chuck, trimmed of fat and cut into ¾-inch pieces
2 garlic cloves, minced	
8 ounces shiitake mushrooms, stems removed and sliced	4 cups low-sodium roasted beef bone broth
1 teaspoon fine sea salt	1 cup wild rice, rinsed
2 carrots, diced	1 tablespoon Worcestershire sauce
2 celery stalks, diced	
1 yellow onion, diced	2 tablespoons tomato paste
1 teaspoon dried thyme	

1. Select the Sauté setting on the Instant Pot and heat the oil and garlic for about 1 minute, until the garlic is bubbling but not browned. Add the mushrooms and salt and sauté for 5 minutes, until the mushrooms have wilted and given up some of their liquid. Add the carrots, celery, and onion and sauté for 4 minutes, until the onion begins to soften. Add the thyme and beef and sauté for 3 minutes more, until the beef is mostly opaque on the outside. Stir in the broth, rice, Worcestershire sauce, and tomato paste, using a wooden spoon to nudge any browned bits from the bottom of the pot. 2. Secure the lid and set the Pressure Release to Sealing. Press the Cancel button to reset the cooking program, then select the Pressure Cook or Manual setting and set the cooking time for 25 minutes at high pressure. (The pot will take about 15 minutes to come up to pressure before the cooking program begins.) 3. When the cooking program ends, let the pressure release naturally for at least 15 minutes, then move the Pressure Release to Venting to release any remaining steam. Open the pot. Ladle the soup into bowls and serve hot.

Turkey and Pinto Chili

Prep time: 0 minutes | Cook time: 60 minutes | Serves 8

2 tablespoons cold-pressed avocado oil	2 teaspoons ground coriander
4 garlic cloves, diced	1 teaspoon dried oregano
1 large yellow onion, diced	1 teaspoon dried sage
4 jalapeño chiles, seeded and diced	1 cup low-sodium chicken broth
2 carrots, diced	3 cups drained cooked pinto beans, or two 15 ounces cans pinto beans, drained and rinsed
4 celery stalks, diced	
2 teaspoons fine sea salt	
2 pounds 93 percent lean ground turkey	Two 14½-ounce cans no-salt petite diced tomatoes and their liquid
Two 4-ounce cans fire-roasted diced green chiles	
4 tablespoons chili powder	¼ cup tomato paste
2 teaspoons ground cumin	

1. Select the Sauté setting on the Instant Pot and heat the oil and garlic for 3 minutes, until the garlic is bubbling but not browned. Add the onion, jalapeños, carrots, celery, and salt and sauté for 5 minutes, until the onion begins to soften. Add the turkey and sauté, using a wooden spoon or spatula to break up the meat as it cooks, for 6 minutes, until cooked through and no streaks of pink remain. Stir in the green chiles, chili powder, cumin, coriander, oregano, sage, and broth, using a wooden spoon or spatula to nudge any browned bits from the bottom of the pot. 2. Pour in the beans in a layer on top of the turkey. Pour in the tomatoes and their liquid and add the tomato paste in a dollop on top. Do not stir in the beans, tomatoes, or tomato paste. 3. Secure the lid and set the Pressure Release to Sealing. Press the Cancel button to reset the cooking program, then select the Pressure Cook or Manual setting and set the cooking time for 15 minutes at high pressure. (The pot will take about 15 minutes to come up to pressure before the cooking program begins.) 4. When the cooking program ends, let the pressure release naturally for at least 20 minutes, then move the Pressure Release to Venting to release any remaining steam. Open the pot and stir the chili to mix all of the ingredients. 5. Press the Cancel button to reset the cooking program, then select the Sauté setting and set the cooking time for 10 minutes. Allow the chili to reduce and thicken. Do not stir the chili while it is cooking, as this will cause it to sputter more. 6. When the cooking program ends, the pot will turn off. Wearing heat-resistant mitts, remove the inner pot from the housing. Wait for about 2 minutes to allow the chili to stop simmering, then give it a final stir. 7. Ladle the chili into bowls and serve hot.

Turkey Barley Vegetable Soup

Prep time: 5 minutes | Cook time: 20 minutes | Serves 8

2 tablespoons avocado oil	frozen chopped carrots (about 2½ cups)
1 pound ground turkey	1 (15 ounces) package frozen peppers and onions (about 2½ cups)
4 cups Chicken Bone Broth, low-sodium store-bought chicken broth, or water	⅓ cup dry barley
1 (28 ounces) carton or can diced tomatoes	1 teaspoon kosher salt
2 tablespoons tomato paste	¼ teaspoon freshly ground black pepper
1 (15 ounces) package	2 bay leaves

1. Set the electric pressure cooker to the Sauté/More setting. When the pot is hot, pour in the avocado oil. 2. Add the turkey to the pot and sauté, stirring frequently to break up the meat, for about 7 minutes or until the turkey is no longer pink. Hit Cancel. 3. Add the broth, tomatoes and their juices, and tomato paste. Stir in the carrots, peppers and onions, barley, salt, pepper, and bay leaves. 4. Close and lock the lid of the pressure cooker. Set the valve to sealing. 5. Cook on high pressure for 20 minutes. 6. When the cooking is complete, hit Cancel and allow the pressure to release naturally for 10 minutes, then quick release any remaining pressure. 7. Once the pin drops, unlock and remove the lid. Discard the bay leaves. 8. Spoon into bowls and serve.

Beef and Mushroom Stew

Prep time: 15 minutes | Cook time: 30 minutes | Serves 4

2 tablespoons coconut oil	½ cup chopped celery
1 pound (454 g) cubed chuck roast	1 tablespoon sugar-free tomato paste
1 cup sliced button mushrooms	1 teaspoon thyme
½ medium onion, chopped	2 garlic cloves, minced
2 cups beef broth	½ teaspoon xanthan gum

1. Press the Sauté button and add coconut oil to Instant Pot. Brown cubes of chuck roast until golden, working in batches if necessary. (If the pan is overcrowded, they will not brown properly.) Set aside after browning is completed. 2. Add mushrooms and onions to pot. Sauté until mushrooms begin to brown and onions are translucent. Press the Cancel button. 3. Add broth to Instant Pot. Use wooden spoon to scrape bits from bottom if necessary. Add celery, tomato paste, thyme, and garlic. Click lid closed. Press the Manual button and adjust time for 35 minutes. When timer beeps, allow a natural release. 4. When pressure valve drops, stir in xanthan gum and

allow to thicken. Serve warm.

French Market Soup

Prep time: 20 minutes | Cook time: 1 hour | Serves 8

2 cups mixed dry beans, washed with stones removed	16-ounce can low-sodium tomatoes
7 cups water	1 large onion, chopped
1 ham hock, all visible fat removed	1 garlic clove, minced
1 teaspoon salt	1 chile, chopped, or 1 teaspoon chili powder
¼ teaspoon pepper	¼ cup lemon juice

1. Combine all ingredients in the inner pot of the Instant Pot. 2. Secure the lid and make sure vent is set to sealing. Using Manual, set the Instant Pot to cook for 60 minutes. 3. When cooking time is over, let the pressure release naturally. When the Instant Pot is ready, unlock the lid, then remove the bone and any hard or fatty pieces. Pull the meat off the bone and chop into small pieces. Add the ham back into the Instant Pot.

Creamy Chicken Wild Rice Soup

Prep time: 15 minutes | Cook time: 15 minutes | Serves 5

2 tablespoons margarine	Fast Cook
½ cup yellow onion, diced	2 14-ounce cans low-sodium chicken broth
¾ cup carrots, diced	1 cup skim milk
¾ cup sliced mushrooms (about 3–4 mushrooms)	1 cup evaporated skim milk
½ pound chicken breast, diced into 1-inch cubes	2 ounces fat-free cream cheese
6.2-ounce box Uncle Ben's Long Grain & Wild Rice	2 tablespoons cornstarch

1. Select the Sauté feature and add the margarine, onion, carrots, and mushrooms to the inner pot. Sauté for about 5 minutes until onions are translucent and soft. 2. Add the cubed chicken and seasoning packet from the Uncle Ben's box and stir to combine. 3. Add the rice and chicken broth. Select Manual, high pressure, then lock the lid and make sure the vent is set to sealing. Set the time for 5 minutes. 4. After the cooking time ends, allow it to stay on Keep Warm for 5 minutes and then quick release the pressure. 5. Remove the lid; change the setting to the Sauté function again. 6. Add the skim milk, evaporated milk, and cream cheese. Stir to melt. 7. In a small bowl, mix the cornstarch with a little bit of water to dissolve, then add to the soup to thicken.

Chicken Noodle Soup

Prep time: 15 minutes | Cook time: 20 minutes | Serves 12

2 tablespoons avocado oil
1 medium onion, chopped
3 celery stalks, chopped
1 teaspoon kosher salt
¼ teaspoon freshly ground black pepper
2 teaspoons minced garlic
5 large carrots, peeled and cut into ¼-inch-thick rounds
3 pounds bone-in chicken breasts (about 3)
4 cups Chicken Bone Broth or low-sodium store-bought chicken broth
4 cups water
2 tablespoons soy sauce
6 ounces whole grain wide egg noodles

1. Set the electric pressure cooker to the Sauté setting. When the pot is hot, pour in the avocado oil. 2. Sauté the onion, celery, salt, and pepper for 3 to 5 minutes or until the vegetables begin to soften. 3. Add the garlic and carrots, and stir to mix well. Hit Cancel. 4. Add the chicken to the pot, meat-side down. Add the broth, water, and soy sauce. Close and lock the lid of the pressure cooker. Set the valve to sealing. 5. Cook on high pressure for 20 minutes. 6. When the cooking is complete, hit Cancel and quick release the pressure. Unlock and remove the lid. 7. Using tongs, remove the chicken breasts to a cutting board. Hit Sauté/More and bring the soup to a boil. 8. Add the noodles and cook for 4 to 5 minutes or until the noodles are al dente. 9. While the noodles are cooking, use two forks to shred the chicken. Add the meat back to the pot and save the bones to make more bone broth. 10. Season with additional pepper, if desired, and serve.

Broccoli and Bacon Cheese Soup

Prep time: 6 minutes | Cook time: 10 minutes | Serves 6

3 tablespoons butter
2 stalks celery, diced
½ yellow onion, diced
3 garlic cloves, minced
3½ cups chicken stock
4 cups chopped fresh broccoli florets
3 ounces (85 g) block-style cream cheese, softened and cubed
½ teaspoon ground nutmeg
½ teaspoon sea salt
1 teaspoon ground black pepper
3 cups shredded Cheddar cheese
½ cup shredded Monterey Jack cheese
2 cups heavy cream
4 slices cooked bacon, crumbled
1 tablespoon finely chopped chives

1. Select Sauté mode. Once the Instant Pot is hot, add the butter and heat until the butter is melted. 2. Add the celery, onions, and garlic. Continue sautéing for 5 minutes or until the vegetables are softened. 3. Add the chicken stock and broccoli florets to the pot. Bring the liquid to a boil. 4. Lock the lid,. Select Manual mode and set cooking time for 5 minutes on High Pressure. 5. When cooking is complete, allow the pressure to release naturally for 10 minutes and then release the remaining pressure. 6. Open the lid and add the cream cheese, nutmeg, sea salt, and black pepper. Stir to combine. 7. Select Sauté mode. Bring the soup to a boil and then slowly stir in the Cheddar and Jack cheeses. Once the cheese has melted, stir in the heavy cream. 8. Ladle the soup into serving bowls and top with bacon and chives. Serve hot.

Beef Stew with Eggplant and Potatoes

Prep time: 15 minutes | Cook time: 50 minutes | Serves 6 to 8

2 pounds (907 g) boneless short ribs, trimmed and cut into 1-inch pieces
1½ teaspoons table salt, divided
2 tablespoons extra-virgin olive oil
1 onion, chopped fine
3 tablespoons tomato paste
¼ cup all-purpose flour
3 garlic cloves, minced
1 tablespoon ground cumin
1 teaspoon ground turmeric
1 teaspoon ground cardamom
¾ teaspoon ground cinnamon
4 cups chicken broth
1 cup water
1 pound (454 g) eggplant, cut into 1-inch pieces
1 pound (454 g) Yukon Gold potatoes, unpeeled, cut into 1-inch pieces
½ cup chopped fresh mint or parsley

1. Pat beef dry with paper towels and sprinkle with 1 teaspoon salt. Using highest sauté function, heat oil in Instant Pot for 5 minutes (or until just smoking). Brown half of beef on all sides, 7 to 9 minutes; transfer to bowl. Set aside remaining uncooked beef. 2. Add onion to fat left in pot and cook, using highest sauté function, until softened, about 5 minutes. Stir in tomato paste, flour, garlic, cumin, turmeric, cardamom, cinnamon, and remaining ½ teaspoon salt. Cook until fragrant, about 1 minute. Slowly whisk in broth and water, scraping up any browned bits. Stir in eggplant and potatoes. Nestle remaining uncooked beef into pot along with browned beef, and add any accumulated juices. 3. Lock lid in place and close pressure release valve. Select high pressure cook function and cook for 30 minutes. Turn off Instant Pot and quick-release pressure. Carefully remove lid, allowing steam to escape away from you. 4. Using wide, shallow spoon, skim excess fat from surface of stew. Stir in mint and season with salt and pepper to taste. Serve.

Beef and Cauliflower Soup

Prep time: 10 minutes | Cook time: 14 minutes | Serves 4

1 cup ground beef
½ cup cauliflower, shredded
1 teaspoon unsweetened tomato purée
¼ cup coconut milk

1 teaspoon minced garlic
1 teaspoon dried oregano
½ teaspoon salt
4 cups water

1. Put all ingredients in the Instant Pot and stir well. 2. Close the lid. Select Manual mode and set cooking time for 14 minutes on High Pressure. 3. When timer beeps, make a quick pressure release and open the lid. 4. Blend with an immersion blender until smooth. 5. Serve warm.

Bacon Curry Soup

Prep time: 10 minutes | Cook time: 20 minutes | Serves 4

3 ounces (85 g) bacon, chopped
1 tablespoon chopped scallions
1 teaspoon curry powder

1 cup coconut milk
3 cups beef broth
1 cup Cheddar cheese, shredded

1. Heat the the Instant Pot on Sauté mode for 3 minutes and add bacon. Cook for 5 minutes. Flip constantly. 2. Add the scallions and curry powder. Sauté for 5 minutes more. 3. Pour in the coconut milk and beef broth. Add the Cheddar cheese and stir to mix well. 4. Select Manual mode and set cooking time for 10 minutes on High Pressure. 5. When timer beeps, use a quick pressure release. Open the lid. 6. Blend the soup with an immersion blender until smooth. Serve warm.

Summer Vegetable Soup

Prep time: 10 minutes | Cook time: 6 minutes | Serves 6

3 cups finely sliced leeks
6 cups chopped rainbow chard, stems and leaves separated
1 cup chopped celery
2 tablespoons minced garlic, divided
1 teaspoon dried oregano
1 teaspoon salt

2 teaspoons freshly ground black pepper
3 cups chicken broth, plus more as needed
2 cups sliced yellow summer squash, ½-inch slices
¼ cup chopped fresh parsley
¾ cup heavy (whipping) cream
4 to 6 tablespoons grated Parmesan cheese

1. Put the leeks, chard, celery, 1 tablespoon of garlic, oregano, salt, pepper, and broth into the inner cooking pot of the Instant Pot. 2. Lock the lid into place. Select Manual and adjust the pressure to High. Cook for 3 minutes. When the cooking is complete, quick-release the pressure. Unlock the lid. 3. Add more broth if needed. 4. Turn the pot to Sauté and adjust the heat to high. Add the yellow squash, parsley, and remaining 1 tablespoon of garlic. 5. Allow the soup to cook for 2 to 3 minutes, or until the squash is softened and cooked through. 6. Stir in the cream and ladle the soup into bowls. Sprinkle with the Parmesan cheese and serve.

Chapter 3
Beef, Pork, and Lamb

Basil and Thyme Pork Loin

Prep time: 10 minutes | Cook time: 17 minutes | Serves 4

1 pound (454 g) pork loin	½ teaspoon salt
1 teaspoon dried basil	2 tablespoons apple cider
1 tablespoon avocado oil	vinegar
1 teaspoon dried thyme	1 cup water, for cooking

1. In the shallow bowl, mix up dried basil, avocado oil, thyme, salt, and apple cider vinegar. 2. Then rub the pork loin with the spice mixture and leave the meat for 10 minutes to marinate. 3. Wrap the meat in foil and put on the steamer rack. 4. Pour water and transfer the steamer rack with meat in the instant pot. 5. Close and seal the lid. Cook the meat on Manual (High Pressure) for 20 minutes. Allow the natural pressure release for 5 minutes. 6. Slice the cooked pork loin.

Shepherd's Pie with Cauliflower-Carrot Mash

Prep time: 10 minutes | Cook time: 35 minutes | Serves 6

1 tablespoon coconut oil	Worcestershire sauce
2 garlic cloves, minced	One 12-ounce bag frozen
1 large yellow onion, diced	baby lima beans, green
1 pound ground lamb	peas, or shelled edamame
1 pound 95 percent lean	3 tablespoons tomato paste
ground beef	1 pound cauliflower florets
½ cup low-sodium	1 pound carrots, halved
vegetable broth	lengthwise and then
1 teaspoons dried thyme	crosswise (or quartered if
1 teaspoon dried sage	very large)
1 teaspoon freshly ground	¼ cup coconut milk or
black pepper	other nondairy milk
1¾ teaspoons fine sea salt	½ cup sliced green onions,
2 tablespoons	white and green parts

1. Select the Sauté setting on the Instant Pot and heat the oil and garlic for 2 minutes, until the garlic is bubbling but not browned. Add the onion and sauté for 3 minutes, until it begins to soften. Add the lamb and beef and sauté, using a wooden spoon or spatula to break up the meat as it cooks, for 6 minutes, until cooked through and no streaks of pink remain. 2. Stir in the broth, using the spoon or spatula to nudge any browned bits from the bottom of the pot. Add the thyme, sage, pepper, ¾ teaspoon of the salt, the Worcestershire sauce, and lima beans and stir to mix. Dollop the tomato paste on top. Do not stir it in. 3. Place a tall steam rack in the pot, then place the cauliflower and carrots on top of the rack. 4. Secure the lid and set the Pressure Release to Sealing. Press the Cancel button to reset the cooking program, then select the Pressure Cook or Manual setting and set the cooking time for 4 minutes at low pressure. (The pot will take about 15 minutes to come up to pressure before the cooking program begins.) 5. Position an oven rack 4 to 6 inches below the heat source and preheat the broiler. 6. When the cooking program ends, perform a quick pressure release by moving the Pressure Release to Venting. Open the pot and, using tongs, transfer the cauliflower and carrots to a bowl. Add the coconut milk and remaining 1 teaspoon salt to the bowl. Using an immersion blender, blend the vegetables until smooth. 7. Wearing heat-resistant mitts, remove the steam rack from the pot. Stir ½ cup of the mashed vegetables into the filling mixture in the pot, incorporating the tomato paste at the same time. Remove the inner pot from the housing. Transfer the mixture to a broiler-safe 9 by 13-inch baking dish, spreading it in an even layer. Dollop the mashed vegetables on top and spread them out evenly with a fork. Broil, checking often, for 5 to 8 minutes, until the mashed vegetables are lightly browned. 8. Spoon the shepherd's pie onto plates, sprinkle with the green onions, and serve hot.

Italian Sausage Stuffed Bell Peppers

Prep time: 15 minutes | Cook time: 17 minutes | Serves 4

4 medium bell peppers,	seasoning blend
tops and seeds removed	½ teaspoon sea salt
1 pound (454 g) ground	¼ teaspoon ground black
pork sausage	pepper
1 large egg	½ teaspoon onion powder
3 tablespoons unsweetened	⅓ cup tomato, puréed
tomato purée	1 cup water
2 garlic cloves, minced	4 slices Mozzarella cheese
½ tablespoon Italian	

1. Using a fork, pierce small holes into the bottoms of the peppers. Set aside. 2. In a large mixing bowl, combine the sausage, egg, tomato purée, garlic, Italian seasoning, sea salt, black pepper, and onion powder. Mix to combine. 3. Stuff each bell pepper with the meat mixture. 4. Place the trivet in the Instant Pot and add the water. 5. Place the stuffed peppers on the trivet. Pour the puréed tomato over. 6. Lock the lid. Select Manual mode and set cooking time for 15 minutes on High Pressure. 7. When cooking is complete, allow the pressure to release naturally for 5 minutes and then release the remaining pressure. 8. Open the lid and top each pepper with 1 slice of the Mozzarella. Secure the lid, select Keep Warm / Cancel, and set cooking time for 2 minutes to melt the cheese. 9. Open the lid and use tongs to carefully transfer the peppers to a large serving platter. Serve warm.

Garlic Butter Italian Sausages

Prep time: 15 minutes | Cook time: 20 minutes | Serves 4

1 teaspoon garlic powder	sausages, chopped
1 cup water	½ teaspoon Italian
1 teaspoon butter	seasoning
12 ounces (340 g) Italian	

1. Sprinkle the chopped Italian sausages with Italian seasoning and garlic powder and place in the instant pot. 2. Add butter and cook the sausages on Sauté mode for 10 minutes. Stir them from time to time with the help of the spatula. 3. Then add water and close the lid. 4. Cook the sausages on Manual mode (High Pressure) for 10 minutes. 5. Allow the natural pressure release for 10 minutes more.

Beef Clod Vindaloo

Prep time: 15 minutes | Cook time: 15 minutes | Serves 2

½ Serrano pepper, chopped	¼ teaspoon ground paprika
¼ teaspoon cumin seeds	1 cup water
¼ teaspoon minced ginger	9 ounces (255 g) beef clod,
¼ teaspoon cayenne pepper	chopped
¼ teaspoon salt	

1. Put Serrano pepper, cumin seeds, minced ginger, cayenne pepper, salt, ground paprika, and water in a food processor. Blend the mixture until smooth. 2. Transfer the mixture in a bowl and add the chopped beef clod. Toss to coat well. 3. Transfer the beef clod and the mixture in the Instant Pot and close the lid. 4. Select Manual mode and set cooking time for 15 minutes on High Pressure. 5. When timer beeps, use a natural pressure release for 10 minutes, then release any remaining pressure. Open the lid. 6. Serve immediately.

Beef Ribs with Radishes

Prep time: 20 minutes | Cook time: 56 minutes | Serves 4

¼ teaspoon ground coriander	in beef short ribs
¼ teaspoon ground cumin	2 tablespoons avocado oil
1 teaspoon kosher salt, plus more to taste	1 cup water
½ teaspoon smoked paprika	2 radishes, ends trimmed, leaves rinsed and roughly chopped
Pinch of ground allspice (optional)	Freshly ground black pepper, to taste
4 (8 ounces / 227 g) bone-	

1. In a small bowl, mix together the coriander, cumin, salt, paprika, and allspice. Rub the spice mixture all over the short ribs. 2. Set the Instant Pot to Sauté mode and add the oil to heat. Add the short ribs, bone side up. Brown for 4 minutes on each side. 3. Pour the water into the Instant Pot. Secure the lid. Press the Manual button and set cooking time for 45 minutes on High Pressure. 4. When timer beeps, allow the pressure to release naturally for 10 minutes, then release any remaining pressure. Open the lid. 5. Remove the short ribs to a serving plate. 6. Add the radishes to the sauce in the pot. Place a metal steaming basket directly on top of the radishes and place the radish leaves in the basket. 7. Secure the lid. Press the Manual button and set cooking time for 3 minutes on High Pressure. 8. When timer beeps, quick release the pressure. Open the lid. Transfer the leaves to a serving bowl. Sprinkle with with salt and pepper. 9. Remove the radishes and place on top of the leaves. Serve hot with the short ribs.

Pork Meatballs with Thyme

Prep time: 15 minutes | Cook time: 16 minutes | Serves 8

2 cups ground pork	1 tablespoon coconut oil
1 teaspoon dried thyme	¼ teaspoon ground ginger
½ teaspoon chili flakes	3 tablespoons almond flour
½ teaspoon garlic powder	¼ cup water

1. In the mixing bowl, mix up ground pork, dried thyme, chili flakes, garlic powder, ground ginger, and almond flour. 2. Make the meatballs. 3. Melt the coconut oil in the instant pot on Sauté mode. 4. Arrange the meatballs in the instant pot in one layer and cook them for 3 minutes from each side. 5. Then add water and cook the meatballs for 10 minutes.

Cinnamon Beef with Blackberries

Prep time: 15 minutes | Cook time: 30 minutes | Serves 2

15 ounces (425 g) beef loin, chopped	cinnamon
1 tablespoon blackberries	⅓ teaspoon ground black pepper
1 cup water	½ teaspoon salt
½ teaspoon ground	1 tablespoon butter

1. Pour water in the instant pot bowl. 2. Add chopped beef loin, blackberries, ground cinnamon, salt, and ground black pepper. Add butter. 3. Close the instant pot lid and set the Meat/Stew mode. 4. Cook the meat for 30 minutes. Then remove the meat from the instant pot. Blend the remaining blackberry mixture. 5. Pour it over the meat.

Braised Pork with Broccoli Rabe and Sage

Prep time: 15 minutes | Cook time: 50 minutes | Serves 4

1½ pounds (680 g) boneless pork butt roast, trimmed and cut into 2-inch pieces
½ teaspoon table salt
½ teaspoon pepper
1 tablespoon extra-virgin olive oil
2 tablespoons minced fresh sage, divided
5 garlic cloves, peeled and smashed
1 tablespoon all-purpose flour
¼ cup chicken broth
¼ cup dry white wine
1 pound (454 g) broccoli rabe, trimmed and cut into 1-inch pieces
½ teaspoon grated orange zest

1. Pat pork dry with paper towels and sprinkle with salt and pepper. Using highest sauté function, heat oil in Instant Pot for 5 minutes (or until just smoking). Brown pork on all sides, 6 to 8 minutes; transfer to plate. 2. Add 1 tablespoon sage, garlic, and flour to fat left in pot and cook, using highest sauté function, until fragrant, about 1 minute. Stir in broth and wine, scraping up any browned bits. Return pork to pot along with any accumulated juices. Lock lid in place and close pressure release valve. Select high pressure cook function and cook for 30 minutes. 3. Turn off Instant Pot and let pressure release naturally for 15 minutes. Quick-release any remaining pressure, then carefully remove lid, allowing steam to escape away from you. Transfer pork to serving dish, tent with aluminum foil, and let rest while preparing broccoli rabe. 4. Whisk sauce until smooth and bring to simmer using highest sauté function. Stir in broccoli rabe and cook, partially covered, until tender and bright green, about 3 minutes. Stir in orange zest and remaining 1 tablespoon sage. Serve pork with broccoli rabe mixture.

Filipino Pork Loin

Prep time: 10 minutes | Cook time: 40 minutes | Serves 4

1 pound (454 g) pork loin, chopped
½ cup apple cider vinegar
1 cup chicken broth
1 chili pepper, chopped
1 tablespoon coconut oil
1 teaspoon salt

1. Melt the coconut oil on Sauté mode. 2. When it is hot, and chili pepper and cook it for 2 minutes. Stir it. 3. Add chopped pork loin and salt. Cook the ingredients for 5 minutes. 4. After this, add apple cider vinegar and chicken broth. 5. Close and seal the lid and cook the Filipino pork for 30 minutes on High Pressure (Manual mode). Then make a quick pressure release.

Beef Shawarma and Veggie Salad Bowls

Prep time: 10 minutes | Cook time: 19 minutes | Serves 4

2 teaspoons olive oil
1½ pounds (680 g) beef flank steak, thinly sliced
Sea salt and freshly ground black pepper, to taste
1 teaspoon cayenne pepper
½ teaspoon ground bay leaf
½ teaspoon ground allspice
½ teaspoon cumin, divided
½ cup Greek yogurt
2 tablespoons sesame oil
1 tablespoon fresh lime juice
2 English cucumbers, chopped
1 cup cherry tomatoes, halved
1 red onion, thinly sliced
½ head romaine lettuce, chopped

1. Press the Sauté button to heat up the Instant Pot. Then, heat the olive oil and cook the beef for about 4 minutes. 2. Add all seasonings, 1½ cups of water, and secure the lid. 3. Choose Manual mode. Set the cook time for 15 minutes on High Pressure. 4. Once cooking is complete, use a natural pressure release. Carefully remove the lid. 5. Allow the beef to cool completely. 6. To make the dressing, whisk Greek yogurt, sesame oil, and lime juice in a mixing bowl. 7. Then, divide cucumbers, tomatoes, red onion, and romaine lettuce among four serving bowls. Dress the salad and top with the reserved beef flank steak. Serve warm.

Bone Broth Brisket with Tomatoes

Prep time: 5 minutes | Cook time: 75 minutes | Serves 4 to 5

2 tablespoons coconut oil
½ teaspoon garlic salt
½ teaspoon crushed red pepper
½ teaspoon dried basil
½ teaspoon kosher salt
½ teaspoon freshly ground black pepper
1 (14 ounces / 397 g) can sugar-free or low-sugar diced tomatoes
1 cup grass-fed bone broth
1 pound (454 g) beef brisket, chopped

1. Set the Instant Pot to Sauté and melt the oil. Mix the garlic salt, red pepper, basil, kosher salt, black pepper, and tomatoes in a medium bowl. 2. Pour bone broth into the Instant Pot, then add the brisket, and top with the premixed sauce. Close the lid, set the pressure release to Sealing, and hit Cancel to stop the current program. Select Manual, set the Instant Pot to 75 minutes on High Pressure, and let cook. 3. Once cooked, carefully switch the pressure release to Venting. Open the Instant Pot, and serve. You can pour remaining sauce over brisket, if desired.

Cider-Herb Pork Tenderloin

Prep time: 15 minutes | Cook time: 18 minutes | Serves 4

¼ teaspoon ground cumin
½ teaspoon ground nutmeg
½ teaspoon dried thyme
½ teaspoon ground coriander
1 tablespoon sesame oil
1 pound (454 g) pork tenderloin
2 tablespoons apple cider vinegar
1 cup water

1. In the mixing bowl, mix up ground cumin, ground nutmeg, thyme, ground coriander, and apple cider vinegar. 2. Then rub the meat with the spice mixture. 3. Heat up sesame oil on Sauté mode for 2 minutes. 4. Put the pork tenderloin in the hot oil and cook it for 5 minutes from each side or until meat is light brown. 5. Add water. 6. Close and seal the lid. Cook the meat on Manual mode (High Pressure) for 5 minutes. 7. When the time is finished, allow the natural pressure release for 15 minutes.

Beef Tenderloin with Red Wine Sauce

Prep time: 30 minutes | Cook time: 10 minutes | Serves 5

2 pounds (907 g) beef tenderloin
Salt and black pepper, to taste
2 tablespoons avocado oil
½ cup beef broth
½ cup dry red wine
2 cloves garlic, minced
1 teaspoon Worcestershire sauce
1½ teaspoons dried rosemary
¼ teaspoon xanthan gum
Chopped fresh rosemary, for garnish (optional)

1. Thirty minutes prior to cooking, take the tenderloin out of the fridge and let it come to room temperature. Crust the outside of the tenderloin in salt and pepper. 2. Turn the pot to Sauté mode and add the avocado oil. Once hot, add the tenderloin and sear on all sides, about 5 minutes. Press Cancel. 3. Add the broth, wine, garlic, Worcestershire sauce, and rosemary to the pot around the beef. 4. Close the lid and seal the vent. Cook on High Pressure for 8 minutes. Quick release the steam. 5. Remove the tenderloin to a platter, tent with aluminum foil, and let it rest for 10 minutes. Press Cancel. 6. Turn the pot to Sauté mode. Once the broth has begun a low boil, add the xanthan gum and whisk until a thin sauce has formed, 2 to 3 minutes. 7. Slice the tenderloin against the grain into thin rounds. Top each slice with the red wine glaze. Garnish with rosemary, if desired.

Beef Burgers with Kale and Cheese

Prep time: 6 minutes | Cook time: 6 minutes | Serves 6

1 pound (454 g) ground beef
½ pound (227 g) beef sausage, crumbled
1½ cups chopped kale
¼ cup chopped scallions
2 garlic cloves, minced
½ cup grated Romano cheese
⅓ cup crumbled blue cheese
Salt and ground black pepper, to taste
1 teaspoon crushed dried sage
½ teaspoon oregano
½ teaspoon dried basil
1 tablespoon olive oil

1. Place 1½ cups of water and a steamer basket in your Instant Pot. 2. Mix all ingredients until everything is well incorporated. 3. Shape the mixture into 6 equal sized patties. Place the burgers on the steamer basket. 4. Secure the lid. Choose Manual mode and High Pressure; cook for 6 minutes. Once cooking is complete, use a quick pressure release; carefully remove the lid. Bon appétit!

Albóndigas Sinaloenses

Prep time: 15 minutes | Cook time: 10 minutes | Serves 6

1 pound (454 g) ground pork
½ pound (227 g) Italian sausage, crumbled
2 tablespoons yellow onion, finely chopped
½ teaspoon dried oregano
1 sprig fresh mint, finely minced
½ teaspoon ground cumin
2 garlic cloves, finely minced
¼ teaspoon fresh ginger, grated
Seasoned salt and ground black pepper, to taste
1 tablespoon olive oil
½ cup yellow onions, finely chopped
2 chipotle chilies in adobo
2 tomatoes, puréed
2 tablespoons tomato passata
1 cup chicken broth

1. In a mixing bowl, combine the pork, sausage, 2 tablespoons of yellow onion, oregano, mint, cumin, garlic, ginger, salt, and black pepper. 2. Roll the mixture into meatballs and reserve. 3. Press the Sauté button to heat up the Instant Pot. Heat the olive oil and cook the meatballs for 4 minutes, stirring continuously. 4. Stir in ½ cup of yellow onions, chilies in adobo, tomatoes passata, and broth. Add reserved meatballs. 5. Secure the lid. Choose the Manual mode and set cooking time for 6 minutes at High pressure. 6. Once cooking is complete, use a quick pressure release. Carefully remove the lid. 7. Serve immediately.

Cilantro Lime Shredded Pork

Prep time: 5 minutes | Cook time: 30 minutes | Serves 4

1 tablespoon chili adobo sauce	1 (2½ to 3 pounds / 1.1 to 1.4 kg) cubed pork butt
1 tablespoon chili powder	1 tablespoon coconut oil
2 teaspoons salt	2 cups beef broth
1 teaspoon garlic powder	1 lime, cut into wedges
1 teaspoon cumin	¼ cup chopped cilantro
½ teaspoon pepper	

1. In a small bowl, mix adobo sauce, chili powder, salt, garlic powder, cumin, and pepper. 2. Press the Sauté button on Instant Pot and add coconut oil to pot. Rub spice mixture onto cubed pork butt. Place pork into pot and sear for 3 to 5 minutes per side. Add broth. 3. Press the Cancel button. Lock Lid. Press the Manual button and adjust time to 30 minutes. 4. When timer beeps, let pressure naturally release until the float valve drops, and unlock lid. 5. Shred pork with fork. Pork should easily fall apart. For extra-crispy pork, place single layer in skillet on stove over medium heat. Cook for 10 to 15 minutes or until water has cooked out and pork becomes brown and crisp. Serve warm with fresh lime wedges and cilantro garnish.

Korean Short Rib Lettuce Wraps

Prep time: 7 minutes | Cook time: 25 minutes | Serves 4

¼ cup coconut aminos, or 1 tablespoon wheat-free tamari	½ teaspoon fine sea salt
2 tablespoons coconut vinegar	½ teaspoon red pepper flakes, plus more for garnish
2 tablespoons sesame oil	1 pound (454 g) boneless beef short ribs, sliced ½ inch thick
3 green onions, thinly sliced, plus more for garnish	For Serving:
2 teaspoons peeled and grated fresh ginger	1 head radicchio, thinly sliced
2 teaspoons minced garlic	Butter lettuce leaves

1. Place the coconut aminos, vinegar, sesame oil, green onions, ginger, garlic, salt, and red pepper flakes in the Instant Pot and stir to combine. Add the short ribs and toss to coat well. 2. Seal the lid, press Manual, and set the timer for 20 minutes. Once finished, let the pressure release naturally. 3. Remove the ribs from the Instant Pot and set aside on a warm plate, leaving the sauce in the pot. 4. Press Sauté and cook the sauce, whisking often, until thickened to your liking, about 5 minutes. 5. Put the sliced radicchio on a serving platter, then lay the short ribs on top. Pour the thickened sauce over the ribs. Garnish with more sliced green onions and red pepper flakes. Serve wrapped in lettuce leaves.

Beef and Cauliflower Burgers

Prep time: 15 minutes | Cook time: 15 minutes | Serves 2

½ cup shredded cauliflower	1 tablespoon scallions, diced
5 ounces (142 g) ground beef	1 egg, beaten
1 teaspoon garlic salt	1 tablespoon coconut oil
¼ teaspoon ground cumin	¼ cup hot water

1. In the mixing bowl, mix up shredded cauliflower, ground beef, garlic salt, ground cumin, and diced scallions. 2. When the meat mixture is homogenous, add egg and stir it well. 3. Make the burgers from the cauliflower and meat mixture. 4. After this, heat up the coconut oil on Sauté mode. 5. Place the burgers in the hot oil in one layer and cook them for 5 minutes from each side. 6. Then add water and close the lid. Cook the meal on Sauté mode for 5 minutes more.

Pork Butt Roast

Prep time: 10 minutes | Cook time: 9 minutes | Serves 6 to 8

3 to 4 pounds pork butt roast	favorite rub
2 to 3 tablespoons of your	2 cups water

1. Place pork in the inner pot of the Instant Pot. 2. Sprinkle in the rub all over the roast and add the water, being careful not to wash off the rub. 3. Secure the lid and set the vent to sealing. Cook for 9 minutes on the Manual setting. 4. Let the pressure release naturally.

Nutmeg Pork Tenderloin

Prep time: 10 minutes | Cook time: 20 minutes | Serves 6

1 pound (454 g) pork tenderloin, sliced	1 teaspoon ground nutmeg
½ cup apple cider vinegar	1 tablespoon butter
	½ cup water

1. Mix up the sliced pork tenderloin with ground nutmeg and put it in the instant pot. 2. Add water, butter, and apple cider vinegar. 3. Close and seal the lid and cook the meat on Manual mode (High Pressure) for 20 minutes. 4. When the time is finished, make a quick pressure release and open the lid.

French Dip Chuck Roast

Prep time: 5 minutes | Cook time: 70 minutes | Serves 6

2 tablespoons avocado oil	3 cloves garlic, minced
2 to 2½ pounds (907 g to 1.1 kg) chuck roast	1 teaspoon salt
2 cups beef broth	½ teaspoon black pepper
2 tablespoons dried rosemary	¼ teaspoon dried thyme
	½ onion, quartered
	2 bay leaves

1. Turn the pot to Sauté mode. Once hot, add the avocado oil. Add the roast and sear it on each side. This should take about 5 minutes. Press Cancel. 2. Add the broth to the pot. 3. Add the rosemary, garlic, salt, pepper, and thyme to the top of the roast. Add the onion and bay leaves. 4. Close the lid and seal the vent. Cook on High Pressure for 50 minutes. Let the steam naturally release for 15 minutes before Manually releasing. 5. Remove the roast to a plate and shred with two forks. Strain the jus though a fine-mesh sieve. Serve the roast au jus for dipping.

Pork Cubes with Fennel

Prep time: 8 minutes | Cook time: 30 minutes | Serves 2

1 teaspoon lemon juice	1 ounce (28 g) fennel, chopped
10 ounces (283 g) pork loin, chopped	1 teaspoon salt
½ cup water	½ teaspoon peppercorns

1. Sprinkle the chopped pork loin with the lemon juice. 2. Then strew the meat with the salt. 3. Place the meat in the meat mold. 4. Insert the meat mold in the instant pot. 5. Add water, fennel, and peppercorns. 6. Close the lid and lock it. 7. Set the Meat/Stew mode and put a timer on 30 minutes. 8. Serve the pork cubes with hot gravy.

Moroccan Lamb Stew

Prep time: 5 minutes | Cook time: 50 minutes | Serves 3

½ cup coconut milk	coriander
1 teaspoon butter	13 ounces (369 g) lamb shoulder, chopped
½ teaspoon dried rosemary	1 teaspoon ground anise
¼ teaspoon salt	¾ cup water
½ teaspoon ground	

1. Slice the mushrooms and place them in the instant pot bowl. 2. Add all remaining ingredients. Close and seal the lid. 3. Set Manual mode for 45 minutes. 4. When the time is over, make natural pressure release for 10 minutes.

Garlic Lamb Vindaloo

Prep time: 10 minutes | Cook time: 34 minutes | Serves 4

1 tablespoon unsalted butter (or coconut oil for dairy-free)	½ teaspoon cayenne pepper
¼ cup diced onions	2 pounds (907 g) boneless lamb shoulder, cut into 1½-inch cubes
6 cloves garlic, minced	1 (14 ounces / 397 g) can full-fat coconut milk
3 tablespoons grainy mustard	1 tablespoon lime juice
2 teaspoons ground cumin	Fresh cilantro leaves, for garnish
2 teaspoons turmeric powder	

1. Place the butter in the Instant Pot and press Sauté. Once melted, add the onions and garlic and cook, stirring often, for 4 minutes, or until the onions are soft. Press Cancel to stop the Sauté. 2. Place the mustard, cumin, turmeric, and cayenne in a small bowl and stir well. Place the lamb in the Instant Pot and cover with the mustard mixture. Pour in the coconut milk. 3. Seal the lid, press Manual, and set the timer for 30 minutes. Once finished, let the pressure release naturally. 4. Remove the lid and stir in the lime juice. Garnish with cilantro and serve.

Beef Back Ribs with Barbecue Glaze

Prep time: 10 minutes | Cook time: 35 minutes | Serves 4

½ cup water	¼ teaspoon garlic powder
1 (3-pound / 1.4-kg) rack beef back ribs, prepared with rub of choice	2 teaspoons apple cider vinegar
¼ cup unsweetened tomato purée	¼ teaspoon liquid smoke
¼ teaspoon Worcestershire sauce	¼ teaspoon smoked paprika
	3 tablespoons Swerve
	Dash of cayenne pepper

1. Pour the water in the pot and place the trivet inside. 2. Arrange the ribs on top of the trivet. 3. Close the lid. Select Manual mode and set cooking time for 25 minutes on High Pressure. 4. Meanwhile, prepare the glaze by whisking together the tomato purée, Worcestershire sauce, garlic powder, vinegar, liquid smoke, paprika, Swerve, and cayenne in a medium bowl. Heat the broiler. 5. When timer beeps, quick release the pressure. Open the lid. Remove the ribs and place on a baking sheet. 6. Brush a layer of glaze on the ribs. Put under the broiler for 5 minutes. 7. Remove from the broiler and brush with glaze again. Put back under the broiler for 5 more minutes, or until the tops are sticky. 8. Serve immediately.

Coconut Pork Muffins

Prep time: 5 minutes | Cook time: 9 minutes | Serves 2

1 egg, beaten	cream
2 tablespoons coconut flour	4 ounces (113 g) ground
1 teaspoon parsley	pork, fried
¼ teaspoon salt	1 cup water
1 tablespoon coconut	

1. Whisk together the egg, coconut flour, parsley, salt, and coconut cream. Add the fried ground pork. Mix the the mixture until homogenous. 2. Pour the mixture into a muffin pan. 3. Pour the water in the Instant Pot and place in the trivet. 4. Lower the muffin pan on the trivet and close the Instant Pot lid. 5. Set the Manual mode and set cooking time for 4 minutes on High Pressure. 6. When timer beeps, perform a natural pressure release for 5 minutes, then release any remaining pressure. Open the lid. 7. Serve warm.

Cuban Pork Shoulder

Prep time: 20 minutes | Cook time: 35 minutes | Serves 3

9 ounces (255 g) pork shoulder, boneless, chopped	½ teaspoon ground black pepper
1 tablespoon avocado oil	¼ cup apple cider vinegar
1 teaspoon ground cumin	1 cup water

1. In the mixing bowl, mix up avocado oil, ground cumin, ground black pepper, and apple cider vinegar. 2. Mix up pork shoulder and spice mixture together and transfer on the foil. Wrap the meat mixture. 3. Pour water and insert the steamer rack in the instant pot. 4. Put the wrapped pork shoulder on the rack. Close and seal the lid. 5. Cook the Cuban pork for 35 minutes. 6. Then allow the natural pressure release for 10 minutes.

Lamb Sirloin Masala

Prep time: 10 minutes | Cook time: 25 minutes | Serves 3

12 ounces (340 g) lamb sirloin, sliced	1 tablespoon lemon juice
1 tablespoon garam masala	1 tablespoon olive oil
	¼ cup coconut cream

1. Sprinkle the sliced lamb sirloin with garam masala, lemon juice, olive oil, and coconut cream in a large bowl. Toss to mix well. 2. Transfer the mixture in the Instant Pot. Cook on Sauté mode for 25 minutes. Flip the lamb for every 5 minutes. 3. When cooking is complete, allow to cool for 10 minutes, then serve warm.

Beef Shami Kabob

Prep time: 15 minutes | Cook time: 35 minutes | Serves 4

1 pound (454 g) beef chunks, chopped	2 cups water
1 teaspoon ginger paste	¼ cup almond flour
½ teaspoon ground cumin	1 egg, beaten
	1 tablespoon coconut oil

1. Put the beef chunks, ginger paste, ground cumin, and water in the Instant Pot. 2. Select Manual mode and set cooking time for 30 minutes on High Pressure. 3. When timer beeps, make a quick pressure release. Open the lid. 4. Drain the water from the meat. Transfer the beef in the blender. Add the almond flour and beaten egg. Blend until smooth. Shape the mixture into small meatballs. 5. Heat the coconut oil on Sauté mode and put the meatballs inside. 6. Cook for 2 minutes on each side or until golden brown. 7. Serve immediately.

Pork Taco Casserole

Prep time: 15 minutes | Cook time: 30 minutes | Serves 6

½ cup water	pork
2 eggs	½ cup tomatoes, puréed
3 ounces (85 g) Cottage cheese, at room temperature	1 tablespoon taco seasoning
¼ cup heavy cream	3 ounces (85 g) chopped green chilies
1 teaspoon taco seasoning	6 ounces (170 g) Queso Manchego cheese, shredded
6 ounces (170 g) Cotija cheese, crumbled	
¾ pound (340 g) ground	

1. Add the water in the Instant Pot and place in the trivet. 2. In a mixing bowl, combine the eggs, Cottage cheese, heavy cream, and taco seasoning. 3. Lightly grease a casserole dish. Spread the Cotija cheese over the bottom. Stir in the egg mixture. 4. Lower the casserole dish onto the trivet. 5. Secure the lid. Choose Manual mode and set cooking time for 20 minutes on High Pressure. 6. Once cooking is complete, use a quick pressure release. Carefully remove the lid. 7. In the meantime, heat a skillet over a medium-high heat. Brown the ground pork, crumbling with a fork. 8. Add the tomato purée, taco seasoning, and green chilies. Spread the mixture over the prepared cheese crust. 9. Top with shredded Queso Manchego. 10. Secure the lid. Choose Manual mode and set cooking time for 10 minutes on High Pressure. 11. Once cooking is complete, use a quick pressure release. Carefully remove the lid. Serve immediately.

Garlic Beef Roast

Prep time: 2 minutes | Cook time: 70 minutes | Serves 6

2 pounds (907 g) top round roast
½ cup beef broth
2 teaspoons salt
1 teaspoon black pepper
3 whole cloves garlic
1 bay leaf

1. Add the roast, broth, salt, pepper, garlic, and bay leaf to the pot. 2. Close the lid and seal the vent. Cook on High Pressure for 15 minutes. Let the steam naturally release for 15 minutes before Manually releasing. 3. Remove the beef from the pot and slice or shred it. Store it in an airtight container in the fridge or freezer.

Greek Lamb Leg

Prep time: 10 minutes | Cook time: 50 minutes | Serves 4

1 pound (454 g) lamb leg
½ teaspoon dried thyme
1 teaspoon paprika powder
¼ teaspoon cumin seeds
1 tablespoon softened butter
2 garlic cloves
¼ cup water

1. Rub the lamb leg with dried thyme, paprika powder, and cumin seeds on a clean work surface. 2. Brush the leg with softened butter and transfer to the Instant Pot. Add garlic cloves and water. 3. Close the lid. Select Manual mode and set cooking time for 50 minutes on High Pressure. 4. When timer beeps, use a quick pressure release. Open the lid. 5. Serve warm.

Zesty Swiss Steak

Prep time: 35 minutes | Cook time: 35 minutes | Serves 6

3 to 4 tablespoons flour
½ teaspoon salt
¼ teaspoon pepper
1½ teaspoons dry mustard
1½ to 2 pounds round steak, trimmed of fat
1 tablespoon canola oil
1 cup sliced onions
1 pound carrots, sliced
14½ ounces can whole tomatoes
⅓ cup water
1 tablespoon brown sugar
1½ tablespoons Worcestershire sauce

1. Combine flour, salt, pepper, and dry mustard. 2. Cut steak in serving pieces. Dredge in flour mixture. 3. Set the Instant Pot to Sauté and add in the oil. Brown the steak pieces on both sides in the oil. Press Cancel. 4. Add onions and carrots into the Instant Pot. 5. Combine the tomatoes, water, brown sugar, and Worcestershire sauce. Pour into the Instant Pot. 6. Secure the lid and make sure the vent is set to sealing. Press Manual and set the time for 35 minutes. 7. When cook time is up, let the pressure release naturally for 15 minutes, then perform a quick release.

Turmeric Pork Loin

Prep time: 10 minutes | Cook time: 22 minutes | Serves 4

1 pound (454 g) pork loin
1 teaspoon ground turmeric
1 teaspoon coconut oil
½ teaspoon salt
½ cup organic almond milk

1. Cut the pork loin into the strips and sprinkle with salt and ground turmeric. 2. Heat up the coconut oil on Sauté mode for 1 minute and add pork strips. 3. Sauté them for 6 minutes. Stir the meat from time to time. 4. After this, add almond milk and close the lid. 5. Sauté the pork for 15 minutes.

Blue Pork

Prep time: 5 minutes | Cook time: 20 minutes | Serves 2

1 teaspoon coconut oil
2 pork chops
2 ounces (57 g) blue cheese, crumbled
1 teaspoon lemon juice
¼ cup heavy cream

1. Heat the coconut oil in the Instant Pot on Sauté mode. 2. Put the pork chops in the Instant Pot and cook on Sauté mode for 5 minutes on each side. 3. Add the lemon juice and crumbled cheese. Stir to mix well. 4. Add heavy cream and close the lid. 5. Select Manual mode and set cooking time for 10 minutes on High Pressure. 6. When timer beeps, perform a natural pressure release for 5 minutes, then release any remaining pressure. Open the lid. 7. Serve immediately.

Chili Pork Loin

Prep time: 10 minutes | Cook time: 20 minutes | Serves 2

10 ounces (283 g) pork loin
¼ cup water
1 teaspoon chili paste
½ teaspoon ground black pepper
½ teaspoon salt

1. Chop the pork loin into the medium pieces. 2. Sprinkle the meat with the salt and ground black pepper. 3. add chili paste in the meat. 4. Mix up the meat mixture with the help of the hands. 5. Pour water in the instant pot bowl and add meat mixture. 6. Close the lid and set the Meat/Stew mode. Cook the meal for 25 minutes. 7. Then chill the meat until warm.

Salisbury Steaks with Seared Cauliflower

Prep time: 5 minutes | Cook time: 30 minutes | Serves 4

Salisbury Steaks	½ teaspoon fine sea salt
1 pound 95 percent lean ground beef	2 tablespoons tomato paste
⅓ cup almond flour	1½ teaspoons yellow mustard
1 large egg	1 cup low-sodium roasted beef bone broth
½ teaspoon fine sea salt	
¼ teaspoon freshly ground black pepper	Seared Cauliflower
2 tablespoons cold-pressed avocado oil	1 tablespoon olive oil
1 small yellow onion, sliced	1 head cauliflower, cut into bite-size florets
1 garlic clove, chopped	2 tablespoons chopped fresh flat-leaf parsley
8 ounces cremini or button mushrooms, sliced	¼ teaspoon fine sea salt
	2 teaspoons cornstarch
	2 teaspoons water

1. To make the steaks: In a bowl, combine the beef, almond flour, egg, salt, and pepper and mix with your hands until all of the ingredients are evenly distributed. Divide the mixture into four equal portions, then shape each portion into an oval patty about ½ inch thick. 2. Select the Sauté setting on the Instant Pot and heat the oil for 2 minutes. Swirl the oil to coat the bottom of the pot, then add the patties and sear for 3 minutes, until browned on one side. Using a thin, flexible spatula, flip the patties and sear the second side for 2 to 3 minutes, until browned. Transfer the patties to a plate. 3. Add the onion, garlic, mushrooms, and salt to the pot and sauté for 4 minutes, until the onion is translucent and the mushrooms have begun to give up their liquid. Add the tomato paste, mustard, and broth and stir with a wooden spoon, using it to nudge any browned bits from the bottom of the pot. Return the patties to the pot in a single layer and spoon a bit of the sauce over each one. 4. Secure the lid and set the Pressure Release to Sealing. Press the Cancel button to reset the cooking program, then select the Pressure Cook or Manual setting and set the cooking time for 10 minutes at high pressure. (The pot will take about 5 minutes to come up to pressure before the cooking program begins.) 5. When the cooking program ends, let the pressure release naturally for at least 10 minutes, then move the Pressure Release to Venting to release any remaining steam. 6. To make the cauliflower: While the pressure is releasing, in a large skillet over medium heat, warm the oil. Add the cauliflower and stir or toss to coat with the oil, then cook, stirring every minute or two, until lightly browned, about 8 minutes. Turn off the heat, sprinkle in the parsley and salt, and stir to combine. Leave in the skillet, uncovered, to keep warm. 7. Open the pot and, using a slotted spatula, transfer the patties to a serving plate. In a small bowl, stir together the cornstarch and water. Press the Cancel button to reset the cooking program, then select the Sauté setting. When the sauce comes to a simmer, stir in the cornstarch mixture and let the sauce boil for about 1 minute, until thickened. Press the Cancel button to turn off the Instant Pot. 8. Spoon the sauce over the patties. Serve right away, with the cauliflower.

Peppercorn Pork with Salsa Verde

Prep time: 10 minutes | Cook time: 40 minutes | Serves 3

12 ounces (340 g) pork shoulder, sliced	½ cup water
½ cup salsa verde	¾ teaspoon peppercorns
	½ teaspoon salt

1. Toss the butter in the instant pot and sauté it for 1 minute or until it is melted. 2. After this, add pork shoulder, salt, and peppercorns; sauté the ingredients for 10 minutes. 3. After this, add water and salsa verde. 4. Set the Bean/Chili mode and set the timer on 30 minutes (High Pressure). 5. When the time is over, make a natural pressure release.

Bacon-Wrapped Pork Bites

Prep time: 15 minutes | Cook time: 20 minutes | Serves 4

3 tablespoons butter	sliced
10 ounces (283 g) pork tenderloin, cubed	½ teaspoon white pepper
6 ounces (170 g) bacon,	¾ cup chicken stock

1. Melt the butter on Sauté mode in the Instant Pot. 2. Meanwhile, wrap the pork tenderloin cubes in the sliced bacon and sprinkle with white pepper. Secure with toothpicks, if necessary. 3. Put the wrapped pork tenderloin in the melted butter and cook for 3 minutes on each side. 4. Add the chicken stock and close the lid. 5. Select Manual mode and set cooking time for 14 minutes on High Pressure. 6. When timer beeps, use a natural pressure release for 5 minutes, then release any remaining pressure. Open the lid. 7. Discard the toothpicks and serve immediately.

Chapter 4
Fish and Seafood

Foil-Packet Salmon

Prep time: 2 minutes | Cook time: 7 minutes | Serves 2

2 (3-ounce / 85-g) salmon fillets	¼ teaspoon pepper
¼ teaspoon garlic powder	¼ teaspoon dried dill
1 teaspoon salt	½ lemon
	1 cup water

1. Place each filet of salmon on a square of foil, skin-side down. 2. Season with garlic powder, salt, and pepper and squeeze the lemon juice over the fish. 3. Cut the lemon into four slices and place two on each filet. Close the foil packets by folding over edges. 4. Add the water to the Instant Pot and insert a trivet. Place the foil packets on the trivet. 5. Secure the lid. Select the Steam mode and set the cooking time for 7 minutes at Low Pressure. 6. Once cooking is complete, do a quick pressure release. Carefully open the lid. 7. Check the internal temperature with a meat thermometer to ensure the thickest part of the filets reached at least 145ºF (63ºC). Salmon should easily flake when fully cooked. Serve immediately.

Coconut Shrimp Curry

Prep time: 10 minutes | Cook time: 4 minutes | Serves 5

15 ounces (425 g) shrimp, peeled

1 teaspoon chili powder	1 teaspoon olive oil
1 teaspoon garam masala	½ teaspoon minced garlic
1 cup coconut milk	

1. Heat up the instant pot on Sauté mode for 2 minutes. 2. Then add olive oil. Cook the ingredients for 1 minute. 3. Add shrimp and sprinkle them with chili powder, garam masala, minced garlic, and coconut milk. 4. Carefully stir the ingredients and close the lid. 5. Cook the shrimp curry on Manual mode for 1 minute. Make a quick pressure release.

Tuna Spinach Cakes

Prep time: 15 minutes | Cook time: 8 minutes | Serves 4

10 ounces (283 g) tuna, shredded	1 teaspoon ground coriander
1 cup spinach	2 tablespoon coconut flakes
1 egg, beaten	1 tablespoon avocado oil

1. Blend the spinach in the blender until smooth. 2. Then transfer it in the mixing bowl and add tuna, egg, and ground coriander. 3. Add coconut flakes and stir the mass with the help of the spoon. 4. Heat up avocado oil in the instant pot on Sauté mode for 2 minutes. 5. Then make the medium size cakes from the tuna mixture and place them in the hot oil. 6. Cook the tuna cakes on Sauté mode for 3 minutes. Then flip the on another side and cook for 3 minutes more or until they are light brown.

Basil Cod Fillets

Prep time: 5 minutes | Cook time: 12 minutes | Serves 4

½ cup water	softened
4 frozen cod fillets (about 6 ounces / 170 g each)	1 ounce (28 g) cream cheese, softened
1 teaspoon dried basil	2 teaspoons lemon juice
Pinch of salt	1½ teaspoons chopped fresh basil, plus more for garnish (optional)
Pinch of black pepper	
4 lemon slices	
¼ cup heavy cream	Lemon wedges, for garnish (optional)
2 tablespoons butter,	

1. Place the trivet inside the pot and add the water. Lay a piece of aluminum foil on top of the trivet and place the cod on top. 2. Sprinkle the fish with the dried basil, salt, and pepper. Set a lemon slice on top of each fillet. 3. Close the lid and seal the vent. Cook on High Pressure for 9 minutes. Quick release the steam. Press Cancel. 4. Remove the trivet and fish from the pot. Rinse the pot if needed and turn to Sauté mode. 5. Add the cream and butter and whisk as the butter melts and the cream warms up. Add the cream cheese and whisk until thickened, 2 to 3 minutes. Add the lemon juice and another pinch of salt and pepper. Once the sauce is thickened and well combined, 1 to 2 minutes, press Cancel and add the fresh basil. 6. Pour the sauce over the fish. Garnish with fresh basil or a lemon wedge, if desired.

Clam Chowder with Bacon and Celery

Prep time: 10 minutes | Cook time: 4 minutes | Serves 2

5 ounces (142 g) clams	chopped
1 ounce (28 g) bacon, chopped	½ cup water
3 ounces (85 g) celery,	½ cup heavy cream

1. Cook the bacon on Sauté mode for 1 minute. 2. Then add clams, celery, water, and heavy cream. 3. Close and seal the lid. 4. Cook the seafood on steam mode (High Pressure) for 3 minutes. Make a quick pressure release. 5. Ladle the clams with the heavy cream mixture in the bowls.

Rosemary Baked Haddock

Prep time: 7 minutes | Cook time: 10 minutes | Serves 2

2 eggs, beaten	¾ teaspoon dried rosemary
12 ounces (340 g) haddock fillet, chopped	2 ounces (57 g) Parmesan, grated
1 tablespoon cream cheese	1 teaspoon butter

1. Whisk the beaten eggs until homogenous. Add the cream cheese, dried rosemary, and dill. 2. Grease the springform with the butter and place the haddock inside. 3. Pour the egg mixture over the fish and add sprinkle with Parmesan. 4. Set the Manual mode (High Pressure) and cook for 5 minutes. Then make a natural release pressure for 5 minutes.

Fish Tagine

Prep time: 25 minutes | Cook time: 12 minutes | Serves 4

2 tablespoons extra-virgin olive oil, plus extra for drizzling	1¼ teaspoons paprika
1 large onion, halved and sliced ¼ inch thick	1 teaspoon ground cumin
1 pound (454 g) carrots, peeled, halved lengthwise, and sliced ¼ inch thick	¼ teaspoon red pepper flakes
2 (2-inch) strips orange zest, plus 1 teaspoon grated zest	¼ teaspoon saffron threads, crumbled
¾ teaspoon table salt, divided	1 (8 ounces / 227 g) bottle clam juice
2 tablespoons tomato paste	1½ pounds (680 g) skinless halibut fillets, 1½ inches thick, cut into 2-inch pieces
4 garlic cloves, minced, divided	¼ cup pitted oil-cured black olives, quartered
	2 tablespoons chopped fresh parsley
	1 teaspoon sherry vinegar

1. Using highest sauté function, heat oil in Instant Pot until shimmering. Add onion, carrots, orange zest strips, and ¼ teaspoon salt, and cook until vegetables are softened and lightly browned, 10 to 12 minutes. Stir in tomato paste, three-quarters of garlic, paprika, cumin, pepper flakes, and saffron and cook until fragrant, about 30 seconds. Stir in clam juice, scraping up any browned bits. 2. Sprinkle halibut with remaining ½ teaspoon salt. Nestle halibut into onion mixture and spoon some of cooking liquid on top of pieces. Lock lid in place and close pressure release valve. Select high pressure cook function and set cook time for 0 minutes. Once Instant Pot has reached pressure, immediately turn off pot and quick-release pressure. 3. Discard orange zest. Gently stir in olives, parsley, vinegar, grated orange zest, and remaining garlic. Season with salt and pepper to taste. Drizzle extra oil over individual portions before serving.

Salmon Steaks with Garlicky Yogurt

Prep time: 2 minutes | Cook time: 4 minutes | Serves 4

1 cup water	1 (8 ounces / 227 g) container full-fat Greek yogurt
2 tablespoons olive oil	
4 salmon steaks	2 cloves garlic, minced
Coarse sea salt and ground black pepper, to taste	2 tablespoons mayonnaise
Garlicky Yogurt:	⅓ teaspoon Dijon mustard

1. Pour the water into the Instant Pot and insert a trivet. 2. Rub the olive oil into the fish and sprinkle with the salt and black pepper on all sides. Put the fish on the trivet. 3. Lock the lid. Select the Manual mode and set the cooking time for 4 minutes at High Pressure. 4. When the timer beeps, perform a quick pressure release. Carefully remove the lid. 5. Meanwhile, stir together all the ingredients for the garlicky yogurt in a bowl. 6. Serve the salmon steaks alongside the garlicky yogurt.

Lemon Salmon with Tomatoes

Prep time: 7 minutes | Cook time: 21 minutes | Serves 4

1 tablespoon unsalted butter	for garnish
3 cloves garlic, minced	¼ teaspoon ground black pepper
¼ cup lemon juice	4 (6 ounces / 170 g) skinless salmon fillets
1¼ cups fresh or canned diced tomatoes	1 teaspoon fine sea salt
1 tablespoon chopped fresh flat-leaf parsley, plus more	Lemon wedges, for garnish

1. Add the butter to your Instant Pot and select the Sauté mode. Once melted, add the garlic (if using) and sauté for 1 minute. 2. Add the roasted garlic, lemon juice, tomatoes, parsley, and pepper. Let simmer for 5 minutes, or until the liquid has reduced a bit. 3. Meanwhile, rinse the salmon and pat dry with a paper towel. Sprinkle on all sides with the salt. 4. Using a spatula, push the reduced sauce to one side of the pot and place the salmon on the other side. Spoon the sauce over the salmon. 5. Sauté uncovered for another 15 minutes, or until the salmon flakes easily with a fork. The timing will depend on the thickness of the fillets. 6. Transfer the salmon to a serving plate. Serve with the sauce and garnish with the parsley and lemon wedges.

Chunky Fish Soup with Tomatoes

Prep time: 10 minutes | Cook time: 8 minutes | Serves 4

2 teaspoons olive oil	fillets
1 yellow onion, chopped	1 cup shrimp
1 bell pepper, sliced	1 tablespoon sweet
1 celery, diced	Hungarian paprika
2 garlic cloves, minced	1 teaspoon hot Hungarian
3 cups fish stock	paprika
2 ripe tomatoes, crushed	½ teaspoon caraway seeds
¾ pound (340 g) haddock	

1. Set the Instant Pot to Sauté. Add and heat the oil. Once hot, add the onions and sauté until soft and fragrant. 2. Add the pepper, celery, and garlic and continue to sauté until soft. 3. Stir in the remaining ingredients. 4. Lock the lid. Select the Manual mode and set the cooking time for 5 minutes at High Pressure. 5. When the timer beeps, perform a quick pressure release. Carefully remove the lid. 6. Divide into serving bowls and serve hot.

Shrimp and Asparagus Risotto

Prep time: 15 minutes | Cook time: 20 minutes | Serves 4

¼ cup extra-virgin olive oil, divided	broth, plus extra as needed
8 ounces (227 g) asparagus, trimmed and cut on bias into 1-inch lengths	1 pound (454 g) large shrimp (26 to 30 per pound), peeled and deveined
½ onion, chopped fine	2 ounces (57 g) Parmesan cheese, grated (1 cup)
¼ teaspoon table salt	1 tablespoon lemon juice
1½ cups Arborio rice	1 tablespoon minced fresh chives
3 garlic cloves, minced	
½ cup dry white wine	
3 cups chicken or vegetable	

1. Using highest sauté function, heat 1 tablespoon oil in Instant Pot until shimmering. Add asparagus, partially cover, and cook until just crisp-tender, about 4 minutes. Using slotted spoon, transfer asparagus to bowl; set aside. 2. Add onion, 2 tablespoons oil, and salt to now-empty pot and cook, using highest sauté function, until onion is softened, about 5 minutes. Stir in rice and garlic and cook until grains are translucent around edges, about 3 minutes. Stir in wine and cook until nearly evaporated, about 1 minute. 3. Stir in broth, scraping up any rice that sticks to bottom of pot. Lock lid in place and close pressure release valve. Select high pressure cook function and cook for 7 minutes. 4. Turn off Instant Pot and quick-release

pressure. Carefully remove lid, allowing steam to escape away from you. Stir shrimp and asparagus into risotto, cover, and let sit until shrimp are opaque throughout, 5 to 7 minutes. Add Parmesan and remaining 1 tablespoon oil, and stir vigorously until risotto becomes creamy. Adjust consistency with extra hot broth as needed. Stir in lemon juice and season with salt and pepper to taste. Sprinkle individual portions with chives before serving.

Cod Fillet with Olives

Prep time: 15 minutes | Cook time: 10 minutes | Serves 2

8 ounces (227 g) cod fillet	¼ teaspoon salt
¼ cup sliced olives	1 cup water, for cooking
1 teaspoon olive oil	

1. Pour water and insert the steamer rack in the instant pot. 2. Then cut the cod fillet into 2 servings and sprinkle with salt and olive oil. 3. Then place the fish on the foil and top with the sliced olives. Wrap the fish and transfer it in the steamer rack. 4. Close and seal the lid. Cook the fish on Manual mode (High Pressure) for 10 minutes. 5. Allow the natural pressure release for 5 minutes.

Fish Packets with Pesto and Cheese

Prep time: 8 minutes | Cook time: 6 minutes | Serves 4

1½ cups cold water.	1 (4 ounces / 113 g) jar pesto
4 (4 ounces / 113 g) white fish fillets, such as cod or haddock	½ cup shredded Parmesan cheese (about 2 ounces / 57 g)
1 teaspoon fine sea salt	Halved cherry tomatoes, for garnish
½ teaspoon ground black pepper	

1. Pour the water into your Instant Pot and insert a steamer basket. 2. Sprinkle the fish on all sides with the salt and pepper. Take four sheets of parchment paper and place a fillet in the center of each sheet. 3. Dollop 2 tablespoons of the pesto on top of each fillet and sprinkle with 2 tablespoons of the Parmesan cheese. 4. Wrap the fish in the parchment by folding in the edges and folding down the top like an envelope to close tightly. 5. Stack the packets in the steamer basket, seam-side down. 6. Lock the lid. Select the Manual mode and set the cooking time for 6 minutes at Low Pressure. 7. Once cooking is complete, do a natural pressure release for 10 minutes, then release any remaining pressure. Carefully open the lid. 8. Remove the fish packets from the pot. Transfer to a serving plate and garnish with the cherry tomatoes. 9. Serve immediately.

Shrimp Louie Salad with Thousand Island Dressing

Prep time: 5 minutes | Cook time: 20 minutes | Serves 4

2 cups water	Freshly ground black
1½ teaspoons fine sea salt	pepper
1 pound medium shrimp,	2 green onions, white and
peeled and deveined	green parts, sliced thinly
4 large eggs	2 hearts romaine lettuce
Thousand island Dressing	or 1 head iceberg lettuce,
¼ cup no-sugar-added	shredded
ketchup	1 English cucumber, sliced
¼ cup mayonnaise	8 radishes, sliced
1 tablespoon fresh lemon	1 cup cherry tomatoes,
juice	sliced
1 teaspoon Worcestershire	1 large avocado, pitted,
sauce	peeled, and sliced
⅛ teaspoon cayenne pepper	

1. Combine the water and salt in the Instant Pot and stir to dissolve the salt. 2. Secure the lid and set the Pressure Release to Sealing. Select the Steam setting and set the cooking time for 0 (zero) minutes at low pressure. (The pot will take about 10 minutes to come up to pressure before the cooking program begins.) 3. Meanwhile, prepare an ice bath. 4. When the cooking program ends, perform a quick release by moving the Pressure Release to Venting. Open the pot and stir in the shrimp, using a wooden spoon to nudge them all down into the water. Cover the pot and leave the shrimp for 2 minutes on the Keep Warm setting. The shrimp will gently poach and cook through. Uncover the pot and, wearing heat-resistant mitts, lift out the inner pot and drain the shrimp in a colander. Transfer them to the ice bath to cool for 5 minutes, then drain them in the colander and set aside in the refrigerator. 5. Rinse out the inner pot and return it to the housing. Pour in 1 cup water and place the wire metal steam rack into the pot. Place the eggs on top of the steam rack. 6. Secure the lid and set the Pressure Release to Sealing. Press the Cancel button to reset the cooking program, then select the Egg, Pressure Cook, or Manual setting and set the cooking time for 5 minutes at high pressure. (The pot will take about 5 minutes to come up to pressure before the cooking program begins.) 7. While the eggs are cooking, prepare another ice bath. 8. When the cooking program ends, let the pressure release naturally for 5 minutes, then move the Pressure Release to Venting to release any remaining steam. Using tongs, transfer the eggs to the ice bath and let cool for 5 minutes. 9. To make the dressing: In a small bowl, stir together the ketchup, mayonnaise, lemon juice, Worcestershire sauce, cayenne, ¼ teaspoon black pepper, and green onions. 10. Arrange the lettuce, cucumber, radishes, tomatoes, and avocado on individual plates or in large, shallow individual bowls. Mound the cooked shrimp in the center of each salad. Peel the eggs, quarter them lengthwise, and place the quarters around the shrimp. 11. Spoon the dressing over the salads and top with additional black pepper. Serve right away.

Salmon Fillets and Bok Choy

Prep time: 5 minutes | Cook time: 8 minutes | Serves 4

1½ cups water	pepper, to taste
2 tablespoons unsalted	2 cups Bok choy, sliced
butter	1 cup chicken broth
4 (1-inch thick) salmon	3 cloves garlic, minced
fillets	1 teaspoon grated lemon
½ teaspoon cayenne pepper	zest
Sea salt and freshly ground	½ teaspoon dried dill weed

1. Pour the water into your Instant Pot and insert a trivet. 2. Brush the salmon with the melted butter and season with the cayenne pepper, salt, and black pepper on all sides. 3. Lock the lid. Select the Manual mode and set the cooking time for 3 minutes at Low Pressure. 4. When the timer beeps, perform a quick pressure release. Carefully remove the lid. 5. Add the remaining ingredients. 6. Lock the lid. Select the Manual mode and set the cooking time for 5 minutes at High Pressure. 7. When the timer beeps, perform a quick pressure release. Carefully remove the lid. 8. Serve the poached salmon with the veggies on the side.

Haddock and Veggie Foil Packets

Prep time: 5 minutes | Cook time: 10 minutes | Serves 4

1½ cups water	2 sprigs rosemary
1 lemon, sliced	4 haddock fillets
2 bell peppers, sliced	Sea salt, to taste
1 brown onion, sliced into	⅓ teaspoon ground black
rings	pepper, or more to taste
4 sprigs parsley	2 tablespoons extra-virgin
2 sprigs thyme	olive oil

1. Pour the water and lemon into your Instant Pot and insert a steamer basket. 2. Assemble the packets with large sheets of heavy-duty foil. 3. Place the peppers, onion rings, parsley, thyme, and rosemary in the center of each foil. Place the fish fillets on top of the veggies. 4. Sprinkle with the salt and black pepper and drizzle the olive oil over the fillets. Place the packets in the steamer basket. 5. Lock the lid. Select the Manual mode and set the cooking time for 10 minutes at Low Pressure. 6. When the timer beeps, perform a quick pressure release. Carefully remove the lid. 7. Serve warm.

Steamed Halibut with Lemon

Prep time: 10 minutes | Cook time: 9 minutes | Serves 3

3 halibut fillet	coriander
½ lemon, sliced	1 tablespoon avocado oil
½ teaspoon white pepper	1 cup water, for cooking
½ teaspoon ground	

1. Pour water and insert the steamer rack in the instant pot. 2. Rub the fish fillets with white pepper, ground coriander, and avocado oil. 3. Place the fillets in the steamer rack. 4. Then top the halibut with sliced lemon. Close and seal the lid. 5. Cook the meal on High Pressure for 9 minutes. Make a quick pressure release.

Ahi Tuna and Cherry Tomato Salad

Prep time: 5 minutes | Cook time: 4 minutes | Serves 4

1 cup water	1 head lettuce
2 sprigs thyme	1 cup cherry tomatoes, halved
2 sprigs rosemary	1 red bell pepper, julienned
2 sprigs parsley	2 tablespoons extra-virgin olive oil
1 lemon, sliced	
1 pound (454 g) ahi tuna	1 teaspoon Dijon mustard
⅓ teaspoon ground black pepper	Sea salt, to taste

1. Pour the water into your Instant Pot. Add the thyme, rosemary, parsley, and lemon and insert a trivet. 2. Lay the fish on the trivet and season with the ground black pepper. 3. Lock the lid. Select the Manual mode and set the cooking time for 4 minutes at High Pressure. 4. When the timer beeps, perform a quick pressure release. Carefully remove the lid. 5. In a salad bowl, place the remaining ingredients and toss well. Add the flaked tuna and toss again. 6. Serve chilled.

Tuna Stuffed Poblano Peppers

Prep time: 15 minutes | Cook time: 12 minutes | Serves 4

7 ounces (198 g) canned tuna, shredded	2 ounces (57 g) Provolone cheese, grated
1 teaspoon cream cheese	4 poblano pepper
¼ teaspoon minced garlic	1 cup water, for cooking

1. Remove the seeds from poblano peppers. 2. In the mixing bowl, mix up shredded tuna, cream cheese, minced garlic, and grated cheese. 3. Then fill the peppers with tuna mixture and put it in the baking pan. 4. Pour water and insert the baking pan in the instant pot. 5. Cook the meal on Manual mode (High Pressure) for 12 minutes. Then make a quick pressure release.

Rosemary Catfish

Prep time: 10 minutes | Cook time: 20 minutes | Serves 4

16 ounces (454 g) catfish fillet	1 teaspoon garlic powder
	1 tablespoon avocado oil
1 tablespoon dried rosemary	1 teaspoon salt
	1 cup water, for cooking

1. Cut the catfish fillet into 4 steaks. 2. Then sprinkle them with dried rosemary, garlic powder, avocado oil, and salt. 3. Place the fish steak in the baking mold in one layer. 4. After this, pour water and insert the steamer rack in the instant pot. 5. Put the baking mold with fish on the rack. Close and seal the lid. 6. Cook the meal on Manual (High Pressure) for 20 minutes. Make a quick pressure release.

Cayenne Cod

Prep time: 10 minutes | Cook time: 10 minutes | Serves 2

2 cod fillets	½ teaspoon dried oregano
¼ teaspoon chili powder	1 tablespoon lime juice
½ teaspoon cayenne pepper	2 tablespoons avocado oil

1. Rub the cod fillets with chili powder, cayenne pepper, dried oregano, and sprinkle with lime juice. 2. Then pour the avocado oil in the instant pot and heat it up on Sauté mode for 2 minutes. 3. Put the cod fillets in the hot oil and cook for 5 minutes. 4. Then flip the fish on another side and cook for 5 minutes more.

Lemon Shrimp Skewers

Prep time: 10 minutes | Cook time: 2 minutes | Serves 4

1 tablespoon lemon juice	peeled
1 teaspoon coconut aminos	1 teaspoon olive oil
12 ounces (340 g) shrimp,	1 cup water

1. Put the shrimp in the mixing bowl. 2. Add lemon juice, coconut aminos, and olive oil. 3. Then string the shrimp on the skewers. 4. Pour water in the instant pot. 5. Then insert the trivet. 6. Put the shrimp skewers on the trivet. 7. Close the lid and cook the seafood on Manual mode (High Pressure) for 2 minutes. 8. When the time is finished, make a quick pressure release.

Baked Flounder with Artichoke

Prep time: 10 minutes | Cook time: 10 minutes | Serves 2

8 ounces (227 g) flounder fillet	¼ teaspoon salt
1 lemon slice, chopped	½ large artichoke, chopped
1 teaspoon ground black pepper	1 tablespoon sesame oil
	1 cup water, for cooking

1. Brush the round baking pan with sesame oil. 2. Then place the chopped artichoke in the baking pan and flatten it. 3. Sprinkle the flounder fillet with ground black pepper and salt and put over the artichoke. 4. Add chopped lemon. 5. Pour water and insert the steamer rack in the instant pot. 6. Place the pan with fish in the steamer. Close and seal the lid. 7. Cook the meal on Manual (High Pressure) for 10 minutes. Make a quick pressure release.

Mediterranean Salmon with Whole-Wheat Couscous

Prep time: 5 minutes | Cook time: 30 minutes | Serves 4

Couscous	1 pound skinless salmon fillet
1 cup whole-wheat couscous	
1 cup water	2 teaspoons extra-virgin olive oil
1 tablespoon extra-virgin olive oil	1 tablespoon fresh lemon juice
1 teaspoon dried basil	1 garlic clove, minced
¼ teaspoon fine sea salt	¼ teaspoon dried oregano
1 pint cherry or grape tomatoes, halved	¼ teaspoon fine sea salt
8 ounces zucchini, halved lengthwise, then sliced crosswise ¼ inch thick	¼ teaspoon freshly ground black pepper
	1 tablespoon capers, drained
Salmon	Lemon wedges for serving

1. Pour 1 cup water into the Instant Pot. Have ready two-tier stackable stainless-steel containers. 2. To make the couscous: In one of the containers, stir together the couscous, water, oil, basil, and salt. Sprinkle the tomatoes and zucchini over the top. 3. To make the salmon: Place the salmon fillet in the second container. In a small bowl, whisk together the oil, lemon juice, garlic, oregano, salt, pepper, and capers. Spoon the oil mixture over the top of the salmon. 4. Place the container with the couscous and vegetables on the bottom and the salmon container on top. Cover the top container with its lid and then latch the containers together. Grasping the handle, lower the containers into the Instant Pot. 5. Secure the lid and set the Pressure Release to Sealing. Select the Pressure Cook or Manual setting and set the cooking time for 20 minutes at high pressure. (The pot will take about 10 minutes to come up to pressure before the cooking program begins.) 6. When the cooking program ends, let the pressure release naturally for 5 minutes, then move the Pressure Release to Venting to release any remaining steam. Open the pot and, wearing heat-resistant mitts, lift out the stacked containers. Unlatch, unstack, and open the containers, taking care not to get burned by the steam. 7. Using a fork, fluff the couscous and mix in the vegetables. Spoon the couscous onto plates, then use a spatula to cut the salmon into four pieces and place a piece on top of each couscous serving. Serve right away, with lemon wedges on the side.

Salmon with Lemon-Garlic Mashed Cauliflower

Prep time: 15 minutes | Cook time: 10 minutes | Serves 4

2 tablespoons extra-virgin olive oil	cut into 2-inch florets
4 garlic cloves, peeled and smashed	4 (6 ounces / 170 g) skinless salmon fillets, 1½ inches thick
½ cup chicken or vegetable broth	½ teaspoon ras el hanout
¾ teaspoon table salt, divided	½ teaspoon grated lemon zest
1 large head cauliflower (3 pounds / 1.4 kg), cored and	3 scallions, sliced thin
	1 tablespoon sesame seeds, toasted

1. Using highest sauté function, cook oil and garlic in Instant Pot until garlic is fragrant and light golden brown, about 3 minutes. Turn off Instant Pot, then stir in broth and ¼ teaspoon salt. Arrange cauliflower in pot in even layer. 2. Fold sheet of aluminum foil into 16 by 6-inch sling. Sprinkle flesh side of salmon with ras el hanout and remaining ½ teaspoon salt, then arrange skinned side down in center of sling. Using sling, lower salmon into Instant Pot on top of cauliflower; allow narrow edges of sling to rest along sides of insert. Lock lid in place and close pressure release valve. Select high pressure cook function and cook for 2 minutes. 3. Turn off Instant Pot and quick-release pressure. Carefully remove lid, allowing steam to escape away from you. Using sling, transfer salmon to large plate. Tent with foil and let rest while finishing cauliflower. 4. Using potato masher, mash cauliflower mixture until no large chunks remain. Using highest sauté function, cook cauliflower, stirring often, until slightly thickened, about 3 minutes. Stir in lemon zest and season with salt and pepper to taste. Serve salmon with cauliflower, sprinkling individual portions with scallions and sesame seeds.

Foil-Pack Haddock with Spinach

Prep time: 15 minutes | Cook time: 15 minutes | Serves 4

12 ounces (340 g) haddock fillet	1 teaspoon minced garlic
1 cup spinach	½ teaspoon ground coriander
1 tablespoon avocado oil	1 cup water, for cooking

1. Blend the spinach until smooth and mix up with avocado oil, ground coriander, and minced garlic. 2. Then cut the haddock into 4 fillets and place on the foil. 3. Top the fish fillets with spinach mixture and place them on the rack. 4. Pour water and insert the rack in the instant pot. 5. Close and seal the lid and cook the haddock on Manual (High Pressure) for 15 minutes. 6. Do a quick pressure release.

Braised Striped Bass with Zucchini and Tomatoes

Prep time: 20 minutes | Cook time: 16 minutes | Serves 4

2 tablespoons extra-virgin olive oil, divided, plus extra for drizzling	flakes
	1 (28 ounces / 794 g) can whole peeled tomatoes, drained with juice reserved, halved
3 zucchini (8 ounces / 227 g each), halved lengthwise and sliced ¼ inch thick	
1 onion, chopped	1½ pounds (680 g) skinless striped bass, 1½ inches thick, cut into 2-inch pieces
¾ teaspoon table salt, divided	
3 garlic cloves, minced	¼ teaspoon pepper
1 teaspoon minced fresh oregano or ¼ teaspoon dried	2 tablespoons chopped pitted kalamata olives
¼ teaspoon red pepper	2 tablespoons shredded fresh mint

1. Using highest sauté function, heat 1 tablespoon oil in Instant Pot for 5 minutes (or until just smoking). Add zucchini and cook until tender, about 5 minutes; transfer to bowl and set aside. 2. Add remaining 1 tablespoon oil, onion, and ¼ teaspoon salt to now-empty pot and cook, using highest sauté function, until onion is softened, about 5 minutes. Stir in garlic, oregano, and pepper flakes and cook until fragrant, about 30 seconds. Stir in tomatoes and reserved juice. 3. Sprinkle bass with remaining ½ teaspoon salt and pepper. Nestle bass into tomato mixture and spoon some of cooking liquid on top of pieces. Lock lid in place and close pressure release valve. Select high pressure cook function and set cook time for 0 minutes. Once Instant Pot has reached pressure, immediately turn off pot and quick-release pressure. Carefully remove lid, allowing steam to escape away from you. 4. Transfer bass to plate, tent with aluminum foil, and let rest while finishing vegetables. Stir zucchini into pot and let sit until heated through, about 5 minutes. Stir in olives and season with salt and pepper to taste. Serve bass with vegetables, sprinkling individual portions with mint and drizzling with extra oil.

Cod with Warm Tabbouleh Salad

Prep time: 10 minutes | Cook time: 6 minutes | Serves 4

1 cup medium-grind bulgur, rinsed	3 tablespoons extra-virgin olive oil, divided, plus extra for drizzling
1 teaspoon table salt, divided	¼ teaspoon pepper
1 lemon, sliced ¼ inch thick, plus 2 tablespoons juice	1 small shallot, minced
	10 ounces (283 g) cherry tomatoes, halved
4 (6 ounces / 170 g) skinless cod fillets, 1½ inches thick	1 cup chopped fresh parsley
	½ cup chopped fresh mint

1. Arrange trivet included with Instant Pot in base of insert and add ½ cup water. Fold sheet of aluminum foil into 16 by 6-inch sling, then rest 1½-quart round soufflé dish in center of sling. Combine 1 cup water, bulgur, and ½ teaspoon salt in dish. Using sling, lower soufflé dish into pot and onto trivet; allow narrow edges of sling to rest along sides of insert. 2. Lock lid in place and close pressure release valve. Select high pressure cook function and cook for 3 minutes. Turn off Instant Pot and quick-release pressure. Carefully remove lid, allowing steam to escape away from you. Using sling, transfer soufflé dish to wire rack; set aside to cool. Remove trivet; do not discard sling or water in pot. 3. Arrange lemon slices widthwise in 2 rows across center of sling. Brush cod with 1 tablespoon oil and sprinkle with remaining ½ teaspoon salt and pepper. Arrange cod skinned side down in even layer on top of lemon slices. Using sling, lower cod into Instant Pot; allow narrow edges of sling to rest along sides of insert. Lock lid in place and close pressure release valve. Select high pressure cook function and cook for 3 minutes. 4. Meanwhile, whisk remaining 2 tablespoons oil, lemon juice, and shallot together in large bowl. Add bulgur, tomatoes, parsley, and mint, and gently toss to combine. Season with salt and pepper to taste. 5. Turn off Instant Pot and quick-release pressure. Carefully remove lid, allowing steam to escape away from you. Using sling, transfer cod to large plate. Gently lift and tilt fillets with spatula to remove lemon slices. Serve cod with salad, drizzling individual portions with extra oil.

Chili and Turmeric Haddock

Prep time: 10 minutes | Cook time: 5 minutes | Serves 4

1 chili pepper, minced	turmeric
1 pound (454 g) haddock, chopped	½ cup fish stock
½ teaspoon ground	1 cup water

1. In the mixing bowl mix up chili pepper, ground turmeric, and fish stock. 2. Then add chopped haddock and transfer the mixture in the baking mold. 3. Pour water in the instant pot and insert the trivet. 4. Place the baking mold with fish on the trivet and close the lid. 5. Cook the meal on Manual (High Pressure) for 5 minutes. Make a quick pressure release.

Perch Fillets with Red Curry

Prep time: 5 minutes | Cook time: 6 minutes | Serves 4

1 cup water	Sea salt and ground black pepper, to taste
2 sprigs rosemary	
1 large-sized lemon, sliced	1 tablespoon red curry paste
1 pound (454 g) perch fillets	
1 teaspoon cayenne pepper	1 tablespoons butter

1. Add the water, rosemary, and lemon slices to the Instant Pot and insert a trivet. 2. Season the perch fillets with the cayenne pepper, salt, and black pepper. Spread the red curry paste and butter over the fillets. 3. Arrange the fish fillets on the trivet. 4. Lock the lid. Select the Manual mode and set the cooking time for 6 minutes at Low Pressure. 5. When the timer beeps, perform a quick pressure release. Carefully remove the lid. Serve with your favorite keto sides.

Ginger Cod

Prep time: 10 minutes | Cook time: 20 minutes | Serves 2

1 teaspoon ginger paste	1 tablespoon coconut oil
8 ounces (227 g) cod fillet, chopped	¼ cup coconut milk

1. Melt the coconut oil in the instant pot on Sauté mode. 2. Then add ginger paste and coconut milk and bring the mixture to boil. 3. Add chopped cod and sauté the meal for 12 minutes. Stir the fish cubes with the help of the spatula from time to time.

Snapper in Spicy Tomato Sauce

Prep time: 5 minutes | Cook time: 5 minutes | Serves 6

2 teaspoons coconut oil, melted	¾ cup vegetable broth
1 teaspoon celery seeds	1 (4 ounces / 113 g) can fire-roasted diced tomatoes
½ teaspoon fresh grated ginger	1 bell pepper, sliced
½ teaspoon cumin seeds	1 jalapeño pepper, minced
1 yellow onion, chopped	Sea salt and ground black pepper, to taste
2 cloves garlic, minced	¼ teaspoon chili flakes
1½ pounds (680 g) snapper fillets	½ teaspoon turmeric powder

1. Set the Instant Pot to Sauté. Add and heat the sesame oil until hot. Sauté the celery seeds, fresh ginger, and cumin seeds. 2. Add the onion and continue to sauté until softened and fragrant. 3. Mix in the minced garlic and continue to cook for 30 seconds. Add the remaining ingredients and stir well. 4. Lock the lid. Select the Manual mode and set the cooking time for 3 minutes at Low Pressure. 5. When the timer beeps, perform a quick pressure release. Carefully remove the lid. 6. Serve warm

Garam Masala Fish

Prep time: 10 minutes | Cook time: 10 minutes | Serves 4

2 tablespoons sesame oil	powder
½ teaspoon cumin seeds	1 tablespoon chopped fresh dill leaves
½ cup chopped leeks	
1 teaspoon ginger-garlic paste	1 tablespoon chopped fresh curry leaves
1 pound (454 g) cod fillets, boneless and sliced	1 tablespoon chopped fresh parsley leaves
2 ripe tomatoes, chopped	Coarse sea salt, to taste
1½ tablespoons fresh lemon juice	½ teaspoon smoked cayenne pepper
½ teaspoon garam masala	¼ teaspoon ground black pepper, or more to taste
½ teaspoon turmeric	

1. Set the Instant Pot to Sauté. Add and heat the sesame oil until hot. Sauté the cumin seeds for 30 seconds. 2. Add the leeks and cook for another 2 minutes until translucent. Add the ginger-garlic paste and cook for an additional 40 seconds. 3. Stir in the remaining ingredients. 4. Lock the lid. Select the Manual mode and set the cooking time for 6 minutes at Low Pressure. 5. When the timer beeps, perform a quick pressure release. Carefully remove the lid. 6. Serve immediately.

Caprese Salmon

Prep time: 10 minutes | Cook time: 15 minutes | Serves 2

10 ounces (283 g) salmon fillet (2 fillets)	½ teaspoon ground black pepper
4 ounces (113 g) Mozzarella, sliced	1 tablespoon apple cider vinegar
4 cherry tomatoes, sliced	1 tablespoon butter
1 teaspoon erythritol	1 cup water, for cooking
1 teaspoon dried basil	

1. Grease the mold with butter and put the salmon inside. 2. Sprinkle the fish with erythritol, dried basil, ground black pepper, and apple cider vinegar. 3. Then top the salmon with tomatoes and Mozzarella. 4. Pour water and insert the steamer rack in the instant pot. 5. Put the fish on the rack. 6. Close and seal the lid. 7. Cook the meal on Manual mode at High Pressure for 15 minutes. Make a quick pressure release.

Lemon Pepper Tilapia with Broccoli and Carrots

Prep time: 0 minutes | Cook time: 15 minutes | Serves 4

1 pound tilapia fillets	½ cup low-sodium vegetable broth
1 teaspoon lemon pepper seasoning	2 tablespoons fresh lemon juice
¼ teaspoon fine sea salt	
2 tablespoons extra-virgin olive oil	1 pound broccoli crowns, cut into bite-size florets
2 garlic cloves, minced	8 ounces carrots, cut into ¼-inch thick rounds
1 small yellow onion, sliced	

1. Sprinkle the tilapia fillets all over with the lemon pepper seasoning and salt. 2. Select the Sauté setting on the Instant Pot and heat the oil and garlic for 2 minutes, until the garlic is bubbling but not browned. Add the onion and sauté for about 3 minutes more, until it begins to soften. 3. Pour in the broth and lemon juice, then use a wooden spoon to nudge any browned bits from the bottom of the pot. Using tongs, add the fish fillets to the pot in a single layer; it's fine if they overlap slightly. Place the broccoli and carrots on top. 4. Secure the lid and set the Pressure Release to Sealing. Press the Cancel button to reset the cooking program, then select the Pressure Cook or Manual setting and set the cooking time for 1 minute at low pressure. (The pot will take about 10 minutes to come up to pressure before the cooking program begins.) 5. When the cooking program ends, let the pressure release naturally for 10 minutes (don't open the pot before the 10 minutes are up, even if the float valve has gone down), then move the Pressure Release to Venting to release any remaining steam. Open the pot. Use a fish spatula to transfer the vegetables and fillets to plates. Serve right away.

Flounder Meuniere

Prep time: 15 minutes | Cook time: 10 minutes | Serves 4

16 ounces (454 g) flounder fillet	½ cup almond flour
½ teaspoon ground black pepper	2 tablespoons olive oil
	1 tablespoon lemon juice
½ teaspoon salt	1 teaspoon chopped fresh parsley

1. Cut the fish fillets into 4 servings and sprinkle with salt, ground black pepper, and lemon juice. 2. Heat up the instant pot on Sauté mode for 2 minutes and add olive oil. 3. Coat the flounder fillets in the almond flour and put them in the hot olive oil. 4. Sauté the fish fillets for 4 minutes and then flip on another side. 5. Cook the meal for 3 minutes more or until it is golden brown. 6. Sprinkle the cooked flounder with the fresh parsley.

Greek Shrimp with Tomatoes and Feta

Prep time: 10 minutes | Cook time: 2 minutes | Serves 6

3 tablespoons unsalted butter	1 teaspoon dried oregano
1 tablespoon garlic	1 teaspoon salt
½ teaspoon red pepper flakes, or more as needed	1 pound (454 g) frozen shrimp, peeled
1½ cups chopped onion	1 cup crumbled feta cheese
1 (14½ ounces / 411 g) can diced tomatoes, undrained	½ cup sliced black olives
	¼ cup chopped parsley

1. Preheat the Instant Pot by selecting Sauté and adjusting to high heat. When the inner cooking pot is hot, add the butter and heat until it foams. Add the garlic and red pepper flakes, and cook just until fragrant, about 1 minute. 2. Add the onion, tomatoes, oregano, and salt, and stir to combine. 3. Add the frozen shrimp. 4. Lock the lid into place. Select Manual and adjust the pressure to Low. Cook for 1 minute. When the cooking is complete, quick-release the pressure. Unlock the lid. 5. Mix the shrimp in with the lovely tomato broth. 6. Allow the mixture to cool slightly. Right before serving, sprinkle with the feta cheese, olives, and parsley. This dish makes a soupy broth, so it's great over mashed cauliflower.

Parmesan Salmon Loaf

Prep time: 15 minutes | Cook time: 25 minutes | Serves 6

12 ounces (340 g) salmon, boiled and shredded
3 eggs, beaten
½ cup almond flour
1 teaspoon garlic powder

¼ cup grated Parmesan
1 teaspoon butter, softened
1 cup water, for cooking

1. Pour water in the instant pot. 2. Mix up the rest of the ingredients in the mixing bowl and stir until smooth. 3. After this, transfer the salmon mixture in the loaf pan and flatten; insert the pan in the instant pot. Close and seal the lid. 4. Cook the meal on Manual mode (High Pressure) for 25 minutes. 5. When the cooking time is finished, make a quick pressure release and cool the loaf well before serving.

Almond Milk Curried Fish

Prep time: 10 minutes | Cook time: 3 minutes | Serves 2

8 ounces (227 g) cod fillet, chopped
1 teaspoon curry paste

1 cup organic almond milk

1. Mix up curry paste and almond milk and pour the liquid in the instant pot. 2. Add chopped cod fillet and close the lid. 3. Cook the fish curry on Manual mode (High Pressure) for 3 minutes. 4. Then make the quick pressure release for 5 minutes.

Dill Salmon Cakes

Prep time: 15 minutes | Cook time: 10 minutes | Serves 4

1 pound (454 g) salmon fillet, chopped
1 tablespoon chopped dill
2 eggs, beaten

½ cup almond flour
1 tablespoon coconut oil

1. Put the chopped salmon, dill, eggs, and almond flour in the food processor. 2. Blend the mixture until it is smooth. 3. Then make the small balls (cakes) from the salmon mixture. 4. After this, heat up the coconut oil on Sauté mode for 3 minutes. 5. Put the salmon cakes in the instant pot in one layer and cook them on Sauté mode for 2 minutes from each side or until they are light brown.

Chapter 5
Poultry

Greek Chicken

Prep time: 25 minutes | Cook time: 20 minutes | Serves 6

4 potatoes, unpeeled, quartered	minced
2 pounds chicken pieces, trimmed of skin and fat	3 teaspoons dried oregano
2 large onions, quartered	¾ teaspoons salt
1 whole bulb garlic, cloves	½ teaspoons pepper
	1 tablespoon olive oil
	1 cup water

1. Place potatoes, chicken, onions, and garlic into the inner pot of the Instant Pot, then sprinkle with seasonings. Top with oil and water. 2. Secure the lid and make sure vent is set to sealing. Cook on Manual mode for 20 minutes. 3. When cook time is over, let the pressure release naturally for 5 minutes, then release the rest manually.

Thai Yellow Curry with Chicken Meatballs

Prep time: 5 minutes | Cook time: 30 minutes | Serves 4

1 pound 95 percent lean ground chicken	very large)
⅓ cup gluten-free panko (Japanese bread crumbs)	8 ounces zucchini, quartered lengthwise, then cut crosswise into 1-inch lengths (or cut into halves, then thirds if large)
1 egg white	
1 tablespoon coconut oil	
1 yellow onion, cut into 1-inch pieces	
One 14-ounce can light coconut milk	8 ounces cremini mushrooms, quartered
3 tablespoons yellow curry paste	Fresh Thai basil leaves for serving (optional)
¾ cup water	Fresno or jalapeño chile, thinly sliced, for serving (optional)
8 ounces carrots, halved lengthwise, then cut crosswise into 1-inch lengths (or quartered if	1 lime, cut into wedges
	Cooked cauliflower "rice" for serving

1. In a medium bowl, combine the chicken, panko, and egg white and mix until evenly combined. Set aside. 2. Select the Sauté setting on the Instant Pot and heat the oil for 2 minutes. Add the onion and sauté for 5 minutes, until it begins to soften and brown. Add ½ cup of the coconut milk and the curry paste and sauté for 1 minute more, until bubbling and fragrant. Press the Cancel button to turn off the pot, then stir in the water. 3. Using a 1½-tablespoon cookie scoop, shape and drop meatballs into the pot in a single layer. 4. Secure the lid and set the Pressure Release to Sealing. Select the Pressure Cook or Manual setting and set the cooking time for 5 minutes at high pressure. (The pot will take about 5 minutes to come up to pressure before the cooking program begins.) 5. When the cooking program ends, perform a quick pressure release by moving the Pressure Release to Venting, or let the pressure release naturally. Open the pot and stir in the carrots, zucchini, mushrooms, and remaining 1¼ cups coconut milk. 6. Press the Cancel button to reset the cooking program, then select the Sauté setting. Bring the curry to a simmer (this will take about 2 minutes), then let cook, uncovered, for about 8 minutes, until the carrots are fork-tender. Press the Cancel button to turn off the pot. 7. Ladle the curry into bowls. Serve piping hot, topped with basil leaves and chile slices, if desired, and the lime wedges and cauliflower "rice" on the side.

Speedy Chicken Cacciatore

Prep time: 5 minutes | Cook time: 30 minutes | Serves 6

2 pounds boneless, skinless chicken thighs	sliced
1½ teaspoons fine sea salt	½ cup dry red wine
½ teaspoon freshly ground black pepper	1½ teaspoons Italian seasoning
2 tablespoons extra-virgin olive oil	½ teaspoon red pepper flakes (optional)
3 garlic cloves, chopped	One 14½ ounces can diced tomatoes and their liquid
2 large red bell peppers, seeded and cut into ¼ by 2-inch strips	2 tablespoons tomato paste
2 large yellow onions,	Cooked brown rice or whole-grain pasta for serving

1. Season the chicken thighs on both sides with 1 teaspoon of the salt and the black pepper. 2. Select the Sauté setting on the Instant Pot and heat the oil and garlic for 2 minutes, until the garlic is bubbling but not browned. Add the bell peppers, onions, and remaining ½ teaspoon salt and sauté for 3 minutes, until the onions begin to soften. Stir in the wine, Italian seasoning, and pepper flakes (if using). Using tongs, add the chicken to the pot, turning each piece to coat it in the wine and spices and nestling them in a single layer in the liquid. Pour the tomatoes and their liquid on top of the chicken and dollop the tomato paste on top. Do not stir them in. 3. Secure the lid and set the Pressure Release to Sealing. Press the Cancel button to reset the cooking program, then select the Poultry, Pressure Cook, or Manual setting and set the cooking time for 12 minutes at high pressure. (The pot will take about 15 minutes to come up to pressure before the cooking program begins.) 4. When the cooking program ends, perform a quick pressure release by moving the Pressure Release to Venting, or let the pressure release naturally. Open the pot and, using tongs, transfer the chicken and vegetables to a serving dish. 5. Spoon some of the sauce over the chicken and serve hot, with the rice on the side.

Herbed Whole Turkey Breast

Prep time: 10 minutes | Cook time:30 minutes | Serves 12

3 tablespoons extra-virgin olive oil	(from 1 small lemon)
1½ tablespoons herbes de Provence or poultry seasoning	1 tablespoon kosher salt
	1½ teaspoons freshly ground black pepper
2 teaspoons minced garlic	1 (6 pounds) bone-in, skin-on whole turkey breast,
1 teaspoon lemon zest	rinsed and patted dry

1. In a small bowl, whisk together the olive oil, herbes de Provence, garlic, lemon zest, salt, and pepper. 2. Rub the outside of the turkey and under the skin with the olive oil mixture. 3. Pour 1 cup of water into the electric pressure cooker and insert a wire rack or trivet. 4. Place the turkey on the rack, skin-side up. 5. Close and lock the lid of the pressure cooker. Set the valve to sealing. 6. Cook on high pressure for 30 minutes. 7. When the cooking is complete, hit Cancel. Allow the pressure to release naturally for 20 minutes, then quick release any remaining pressure. 8. Once the pin drops, unlock and remove the lid. 9. Carefully transfer the turkey to a cutting board. Remove the skin, slice, and serve.

Pulled BBQ Chicken and Texas-Style Cabbage Slaw

Prep time: 5 minutes | Cook time: 20 minutes | Serves 6

Chicken	1 large Fuji or Gala apple, julienned
1 cup water	
¼ teaspoon fine sea salt	½ cup chopped fresh cilantro
3 garlic cloves, peeled	
2 bay leaves	3 tablespoons fresh lime juice
2 pounds boneless, skinless chicken thighs (see Note)	
Cabbage Slaw	3 tablespoons extra-virgin olive oil
½ head red or green cabbage, thinly sliced	
	½ teaspoon ground cumin
1 red bell pepper, seeded and thinly sliced	¼ teaspoon fine sea salt
2 jalapeño chiles, seeded and cut into narrow strips	¾ cup low-sugar or unsweetened barbecue sauce
2 carrots, julienned	Cornbread, for serving

1. To make the chicken: Combine the water, salt, garlic, bay leaves, and chicken thighs in the Instant Pot, arranging the chicken in a single layer. 2. Secure the lid and set the Pressure Release to Sealing. Select the Poultry, Pressure Cook, or Manual setting and set the cooking time for 10 minutes at high pressure. (The pot will take about 10 minutes to come up to pressure before the cooking program begins.) 3. To make the slaw: While the chicken is cooking, in a large bowl, combine the cabbage, bell pepper, jalapeños, carrots, apple, cilantro, lime juice, oil, cumin, and salt and toss together until the vegetables and apples are evenly coated. 4. When the cooking program ends, perform a quick pressure release by moving the Pressure Release to Venting, or let the pressure release naturally. Open the pot and, using tongs, transfer the chicken to a cutting board. Using two forks, shred the chicken into bite-size pieces. Wearing heat-resistant mitts, lift out the inner pot and discard the cooking liquid. Return the inner pot to the housing. 5. Return the chicken to the pot and stir in the barbecue sauce. You can serve it right away or heat it for a minute or two on the Sauté setting, then return the pot to its Keep Warm setting until ready to serve. 6. Divide the chicken and slaw evenly among six plates. Serve with wedges of cornbread on the side.

Thanksgiving Turkey

Prep time: 5 minutes | Cook time: 60 minutes | Serves 8

1 turkey breast (7 pounds / 3.2 kg), giblets removed	2 teaspoons black pepper
	½ onion, quartered
4 tablespoons butter, softened	1 rib celery, cut into 3 or 4 pieces
2 teaspoons ground sage	1 cup chicken broth
2 teaspoons garlic powder	2 or 3 bay leaves
2 teaspoons salt	1 teaspoon xanthan gum

1. Pat the turkey dry with a paper towel. 2. In a small bowl, combine the butter with the sage, garlic powder, salt, and pepper. Rub the butter mixture all over the top of the bird. Place the onion and celery inside the cavity. 3. Place the trivet in the pot. Add the broth and bay leaves to the pot. 4. Place the turkey on the trivet. If you need to remove the trivet to make the turkey fit, you can. The turkey will be near the top of the pot, which is fine. 5. Close the lid and seal the vent. Cook on High Pressure for 35 minutes. It is normal if it takes your pot a longer time to come to pressure. 6. Let the steam naturally release for 20 minutes before Manually releasing. Press Cancel. 7. Heat the broiler. 8. Carefully remove the turkey to a sheet pan. Place under the broiler for 5 to 10 minutes to crisp up the skin. 9. While the skin is crisping, use the juices to make a gravy. Pour the juices through a mesh sieve, reserving 2 cups of broth. Return the reserved broth to the pot. Turn the pot to Sauté mode. When the broth starts to boil, add the xanthan gum and whisk until the desired consistency is reached. Add more xanthan gum if you like a thicker gravy. 10. Remove the turkey from the broiler and place on a platter. Carve as desired and serve with the gravy.

Chicken Casserole

Prep time: 15 minutes | Cook time: 15 minutes | Serves 4

1 cup broccoli florets	¼ teaspoon pepper
1½ cups Alfredo sauce	1 pound (454 g) thin-sliced
½ cup chopped fresh spinach	deli chicken
¼ cup whole-milk ricotta cheese	1 cup shredded whole-milk Mozzarella cheese
½ teaspoon salt	1 cup water

1. Put the broccoli florets in a large bowl. Add the Alfredo sauce, spinach, ricotta, salt, and pepper to the bowl and stir to mix well. Using a spoon, separate the veggie mix into three sections. 2. Layer the chicken into the bottom of a 7-cup glass bowl. Place one section of the veggie mix on top in an even layer and top with a layer of shredded Mozzarella cheese. Repeat until all veggie mix has been used and finish with a layer of Mozzarella cheese. Cover the dish with aluminum foil. 3. Pour the water into the Instant Pot and insert the trivet. Place the dish on the trivet. 4. Secure the lid. Select the Manual mode and set the cooking time for 15 minutes at High Pressure. 5. Once cooking is complete, do a quick pressure release. Carefully open the lid. 6. If desired, broil in oven for 3 to 5 minutes until golden. Serve warm.

Chicken Casablanca

Prep time: 20 minutes | Cook time: 12 minutes | Serves 8

2 large onions, sliced	½ teaspoon salt
1 teaspoon ground ginger	½ teaspoon pepper
3 garlic cloves, minced	¼ teaspoon cinnamon
2 tablespoons canola oil, divided	2 tablespoons raisins
3 pounds skinless chicken pieces	14½-ounce can chopped tomatoes
3 large carrots, diced	3 small zucchini, sliced
2 large potatoes, unpeeled, diced	15 ounces can garbanzo beans, drained
½ teaspoon ground cumin	2 tablespoons chopped parsley

1. Using the Sauté function of the Instant Pot, cook the onions, ginger, and garlic in 1 tablespoon of the oil for 5 minutes, stirring constantly. Remove onions, ginger, and garlic from pot and set aside. 2. Brown the chicken pieces with the remaining oil, then add the cooked onions, ginger and garlic back in as well as all of the remaining ingredients, except the parsley. 3. Secure the lid and make sure vent is in the sealing position. Cook on Manual mode for 12 minutes. 4. When cook time is up, let the pressure release naturally for 5 minutes and then release the rest of

the pressure manually.

Turmeric Chicken Nuggets

Prep time: 10 minutes | Cook time: 9 minutes | Serves 5

8 ounces (227 g) chicken fillet	coriander
1 teaspoon ground turmeric	½ cup almond flour
½ teaspoon ground	2 eggs, beaten
	½ cup butter

1. Chop the chicken fillet roughly into the medium size pieces. 2. In the mixing bowl, mix up ground turmeric, ground coriander, and almond flour. 3. Then dip the chicken pieces in the beaten egg and coat in the almond flour mixture. 4. Toss the butter in the instant pot and melt it on Sauté mode for 4 minutes. 5. Then put the coated chicken in the hot butter and cook for 5 minutes or until the nuggets are golden brown.

Cheesy Stuffed Cabbage

Prep time: 30 minutes | Cook time: 18 minutes | Serves 6 to 8

1 to 2 heads savoy cabbage	pepper
1 pound ground turkey	¼ cup finely diced mushrooms
1 egg	1 teaspoon salt
1 cup reduced-fat shredded cheddar cheese	½ teaspoon black pepper
2 tablespoons evaporated skim milk	1 teaspoon garlic powder
¼ cup reduced-fat shredded Parmesan cheese	6 basil leaves, fresh and cut chiffonade
¼ cup reduced-fat shredded mozzarella cheese	1 tablespoon fresh parsley, chopped
¼ cup finely diced onion	1 quart of your favorite pasta sauce
¼ cup finely diced bell	

1. Remove the core from the cabbages. 2. Boil pot of water and place 1 head at a time into the water for approximately 10 minutes. 3. Allow cabbage to cool slightly. Once cooled, remove the leaves carefully and set aside. You'll need about 15 or 16. 4. Mix together the meat and all remaining ingredients except the pasta sauce. 5. One leaf at a time, put a heaping tablespoon of meat mixture in the center. 6. Tuck the sides in and then roll tightly. 7. Add ½ cup sauce to the bottom of the inner pot of the Instant Pot. 8. Place the rolls, fold-side down, into the pot and layer them, putting a touch of sauce between each layer and finally on top. (You may want to cook the rolls in two batches.) 9. Lock lid and make sure vent is at sealing. Set timer on 18 minutes on Manual at high pressure, then manually release the pressure when cook time is over.

Chicken Tacos with Fried Cheese Shells

Prep time: 5 minutes | Cook time: 25 minutes | Serves 6

Chicken:

4 (6 ounces / 170 g) boneless, skinless chicken breasts	¼ teaspoon pepper
	1 tablespoon chili powder
	2 teaspoons garlic powder
1 cup chicken broth	2 teaspoons cumin
1 teaspoon salt	

Cheese Shells:

1½ cups shredded whole-milk Mozzarella cheese

1. Combine all ingredients for the chicken in the Instant Pot. 2. Secure the lid. Select the Manual mode and set the cooking time for 20 minutes at High Pressure. 3. Once cooking is complete, do a quick pressure release. Carefully open the lid. 4. Shred the chicken and serve in bowls or cheese shells. 5. Make the cheese shells: Heat a nonstick skillet over medium heat. 6. Sprinkle ¼ cup of Mozzarella cheese in the skillet and fry until golden. Flip and turn off the heat. Allow the cheese to get brown. Fill with chicken and fold. The cheese will harden as it cools. Repeat with the remaining cheese and filling. 7. Serve warm.

Chicken in Mushroom Gravy

Prep time: 10 minutes | Cook time: 10 minutes | Serves 6

6 (5 ounces each) boneless, skinless chicken-breast halves	low-sodium chicken broth
	10¾-ounce can 98% fat-free, reduced-sodium cream of mushroom soup
Salt and pepper to taste	
¼ cup dry white wine or	4 ounces sliced mushrooms

1. Place chicken in the inner pot of the Instant Pot. Season with salt and pepper. 2. Combine wine and soup in a bowl, then pour over the chicken. Top with the mushrooms. 3. Secure the lid and make sure the vent is set to sealing. Set on Manual mode for 10 minutes. 4. When cooking time is up, let the pressure release naturally.

Marjoram Chicken Wings with Cream Cheese

Prep time: 7 minutes | Cook time: 10 minutes | Serves 2

1 teaspoon marjoram	½ teaspoon ground black pepper
1 teaspoon cream cheese	
½ green pepper	14 ounces (397 g) chicken wings
½ teaspoon salt	

¾ cup water | 1 teaspoon coconut oil

1. Rub the chicken wings with the marjoram, salt, and ground black pepper. 2. Blend the green pepper until you get a purée. 3. Rub the chicken wings in the green pepper purée. 4. Then toss the coconut oil in the instant pot bowl and preheat it on the Sauté mode. 5. Add the chicken wings and cook them for 3 minutes from each side or until light brown. 6. Then add cream cheese and water. 7. Cook the meal on Manual mode for 4 minutes at High Pressure. 8. When the time is over, make a quick pressure release. 9. Let the cooked chicken wings chill for 1 to 2 minutes and serve them!

Mexican Turkey Tenderloin

Prep time: 5 minutes | Cook time: 8 minutes | Serves 6

1 cup Low-Sodium Salsa or bottled salsa	boneless turkey breast, cut into 6 pieces
1 teaspoon chili powder	Freshly ground black pepper
½ teaspoon ground cumin	
¼ teaspoon dried oregano	½ cup shredded Monterey Jack cheese or Mexican cheese blend
1½ pounds unseasoned turkey tenderloin or	

1. In a small bowl or measuring cup, combine the salsa, chili powder, cumin, and oregano. Pour half of the mixture into the electric pressure cooker. 2. Nestle the turkey into the sauce. Grind some pepper onto each piece of turkey. Pour the remaining salsa mixture on top. 3. Close and lock the lid of the pressure cooker. Set the valve to sealing. 4. Cook on high pressure for 8 minutes. 5. When the cooking is complete, hit Cancel. Allow the pressure to release naturally for 10 minutes, then quick release any remaining pressure. 6. Once the pin drops, unlock and remove the lid. 7. Sprinkle the cheese on top, and put the lid back on for a few minutes to let the cheese melt. 8. Serve immediately.

Sage Chicken Thighs

Prep time: 10 minutes | Cook time: 16 minutes | Serves 4

1 teaspoon dried sage	4 skinless chicken thighs
1 teaspoon ground turmeric	1 cup water
2 teaspoons avocado oil	1 teaspoon sesame oil

1. Rub the chicken thighs with dried sage, ground turmeric, sesame oil, and avocado oil. 2. Then pour water in the instant pot and insert the steamer rack. 3. Place the chicken thighs on the rack and close the lid. 4. Cook the meal on Manual (High Pressure) for 16 minutes. 5. Then make a quick pressure release and open the lid. 6. Let the cooked chicken thighs cool for 10 minutes before serving.

BLT Chicken Salad

Prep time: 15 minutes | Cook time: 17 minutes | Serves 4

4 slices bacon
2 (6 ounces / 170 g) chicken breasts
1 teaspoon salt
½ teaspoon garlic powder
¼ teaspoon dried parsley
Sauce:
⅓ cup mayonnaise
1 ounce (28 g) chopped pecans
½ cup diced Roma
¼ teaspoon pepper
¼ teaspoon dried thyme
1 cup water
2 cups chopped romaine lettuce

tomatoes
½ avocado, diced
1 tablespoon lemon juice

1. Press the Sauté button to heat your Instant Pot. 2. Add the bacon and cook for about 7 minutes, flipping occasionally, until crisp. Remove and place on a paper towel to drain. When cool enough to handle, crumble the bacon and set aside. 3. Sprinkle the chicken with salt, garlic powder, parsley, pepper, and thyme. 4. Pour the water into the Instant Pot. Use a wooden spoon to ensure nothing is stuck to the bottom of the pot. Add the trivet to the pot and place the chicken on top of the trivet. 5. Secure the lid. Select the Manual mode and set the cooking time for 10 minutes at High Pressure. 6. Meanwhile, whisk together all the ingredients for the sauce in a large salad bowl. 7. Once cooking is complete, do a quick pressure release. Carefully open the lid. 8. Remove the chicken and let sit for 10 minutes. Cut the chicken into cubes and transfer to the salad bowl, along with the cooked bacon. Gently stir until the chicken is thoroughly coated. Mix in the lettuce right before serving.

Crack Chicken Breasts

Prep time: 5 minutes | Cook time: 15 minutes | Serves 2

½ pound (227 g) boneless, skinless chicken breasts
2 ounces (57 g) cream cheese, softened
½ cup grass-fed bone broth
¼ cup tablespoons keto-
friendly ranch dressing
½ cup shredded full-fat Cheddar cheese
3 slices bacon, cooked and chopped into small pieces

1. Combine all the ingredients except the Cheddar cheese and bacon in the Instant Pot. 2. Secure the lid. Select the Manual mode and set the cooking time for 15 minutes at High Pressure. 3. Once cooking is complete, do a quick pressure release. Carefully open the lid. 4. Add the Cheddar cheese and bacon and stir well, then serve.

Paprika Chicken Wings

Prep time: 10 minutes | Cook time: 13 minutes | Serves 4

1 pound (454 g) boneless chicken wings
1 teaspoon ground paprika
1 teaspoon avocado oil
¼ teaspoon minced garlic
¾ cup beef broth

1. Pour the avocado oil in the instant pot. 2. Rub the chicken wings with ground paprika and minced garlic and put them in the instant pot. 3. Cook the chicken on Sauté mode for 4 minutes from each side. 4. Then add beef broth and close the lid. 5. Sauté the meal for 5 minutes more.

Braised Chicken with Mushrooms and Tomatoes

Prep time: 20 minutes | Cook time: 25 minutes | Serves 4

1 tablespoon extra-virgin olive oil
1 pound (454 g) portobello mushroom caps, gills removed, caps halved and sliced ½ inch thick
1 onion, chopped fine
¾ teaspoon salt, divided
4 garlic cloves, minced
1 tablespoon tomato paste
1 tablespoon all-purpose flour
2 teaspoons minced fresh
sage
½ cup dry red wine
1 (14½ ounces / 411 g) can diced tomatoes, drained
4 (5 to 7 ounces / 142 to 198 g) bone-in chicken thighs, skin removed, trimmed
¼ teaspoon pepper
2 tablespoons chopped fresh parsley
Shaved Parmesan cheese

1. Using highest sauté function, heat oil in Instant Pot until shimmering. Add mushrooms, onion, and ¼ teaspoon salt. Partially cover and cook until mushrooms are softened and have released their liquid, about 5 minutes. Stir in garlic, tomato paste, flour, and sage and cook until fragrant, about 1 minute. Stir in wine, scraping up any browned bits, then stir in tomatoes. 2. Sprinkle chicken with remaining ½ teaspoon salt and pepper. Nestle chicken skinned side up into pot and spoon some of sauce on top. Lock lid in place and close pressure release valve. Select high pressure cook function and cook for 15 minutes. 3. Turn off Instant Pot and quick-release pressure. Carefully remove lid, allowing steam to escape away from you. Transfer chicken to serving dish, tent with aluminum foil, and let rest while finishing sauce. 4. Using highest sauté function, bring sauce to simmer and cook until thickened slightly, about 5 minutes. Season sauce with salt and pepper to taste. Spoon sauce over chicken and sprinkle with parsley and Parmesan. Serve.

Ann's Chicken Cacciatore

Prep time: 25 minutes | Cook time: 3 to 9 minutes | Serves 8

1 large onion, thinly sliced	¼ cup dry white wine
3 pound chicken, cut up, skin removed, trimmed of fat	¼ teaspoons pepper
	1 to 2 garlic cloves, minced
2 6-ounce cans tomato paste	1 to 2 teaspoons dried oregano
4-ounce can sliced mushrooms, drained	½ teaspoon dried basil
	½ teaspoon celery seed, optional
1 teaspoon salt	1 bay leaf

1. In the inner pot of the Instant Pot, place the onion and chicken. 2. Combine remaining ingredients and pour over the chicken. 3. Secure the lid and make sure vent is at sealing. Cook on Slow Cook mode, low 7 to 9 hours, or high 3 to 4 hours.

Chicken with Spiced Sesame Sauce

Prep time: 20 minutes | Cook time: 8 minutes | Serves 5

2 tablespoons tahini (sesame sauce)	2 teaspoons minced garlic
¼ cup water	1 teaspoon shredded ginger root (Microplane works best)
1 tablespoon low-sodium soy sauce	
¼ cup chopped onion	2 pounds chicken breast, chopped into 8 portions
1 teaspoon red wine vinegar	

1. Place first seven ingredients in bottom of the inner pot of the Instant Pot. 2. Add coarsely chopped chicken on top. 3. Secure the lid and make sure vent is at sealing. Set for 8 minutes using Manual setting. When cook time is up, let the pressure release naturally for 10 minutes, then perform a quick release. 4. Remove ingredients and shred chicken with fork. Combine with other ingredients in pot for a tasty sandwich filling or sauce.

Paprika Chicken with Tomato

Prep time: 10 minutes | Cook time: 20 minutes | Serves 2

8 ounces (227 g) chicken fillet, sliced	1 teaspoon ground paprika
1 tomato, chopped	½ teaspoon ground turmeric
2 tablespoons mascarpone	1 tablespoon butter
1 teaspoon coconut oil	

1. Rub the chicken fillet with ground paprika, ground turmeric, and paprika. 2. Put the sliced chicken in the instant pot. 3. Add tomato, mascarpone, coconut oil, and butter. 4. Close the lid and cook the meal on Sauté mode for 20 minutes. 5. Stir it every 5 minutes to avoid burning.

Broccoli Chicken Divan

Prep time: 15 minutes | Cook time: 10 minutes | Serves 4

1 cup chopped broccoli	
2 tablespoons cream cheese	½ cup grated Cheddar cheese
½ cup heavy cream	
1 tablespoon curry powder	6 ounces (170 g) chicken fillet, cooked and chopped
¼ cup chicken broth	

1. Mix up broccoli and curry powder and put the mixture in the instant pot. 2. Add heavy cream and cream cheese. 3. Then add chicken and mix up the ingredients. 4. Then add chicken broth and heavy cream. 5. Top the mixture with Cheddar cheese. Close and seal the lid. 6. Cook the meal on Manual mode (High Pressure) for 10 minutes. Allow the natural pressure release for 5 minutes, open the lid and cool the meal for 10 minutes.

Chicken and Scallions Stuffed Peppers

Prep time: 5 minutes | Cook time: 20 minutes | Serves 5

1 tablespoon butter, at room temperature	¼ teaspoon shallot powder
½ cup scallions, chopped	6 ounces (170 g) goat cheese, crumbled
1 pound (454 g) ground chicken	1½ cups water
½ teaspoon sea salt	5 bell peppers, tops, membrane, and seeds removed
½ teaspoon chili powder	
⅓ teaspoon paprika	½ cup sour cream
⅓ teaspoon ground cumin	

1. Set your Instant Pot to Sauté and melt the butter. 2. Add the scallions and chicken and sauté for 2 to 3 minutes. 3. Stir in the sea salt, chili powder, paprika, cumin, and shallot powder. Add the crumbled goat cheese, stir, and reserve the mixture in a bowl. 4. Clean your Instant Pot. Pour the water into the Instant Pot and insert the trivet. 5. Stuff the bell peppers with enough of the chicken mixture, and don't pack the peppers too tightly. Put the peppers on the trivet. 6. Lock the lid. Select the Poultry mode and set the cooking time for 15 minutes at High Pressure. 7. When the timer beeps, perform a natural pressure release for 10 minutes, then release any remaining pressure. Carefully remove the lid. 8. Remove from the Instant Pot and serve with the sour cream.

Mexican Chicken with Red Salsa

Prep time: 10 minutes | Cook time: 20 minutes | Serves 8

2 pounds (907 g) boneless, skinless chicken thighs, cut into bite-size pieces	diced tomatoes, undrained
1½ tablespoons ground cumin	1 (5 ounces / 142 g) can sugar-free tomato paste
1½ tablespoons chili powder	1 small onion, chopped
1 tablespoon salt	3 garlic cloves, minced
2 tablespoons vegetable oil	2 ounces (57 g) pickled jalapeños from a can, with juice
1 (14½ ounces / 411 g) can	½ cup sour cream

1. Preheat the Instant Pot by selecting Sauté and adjusting to high heat. 2. In a medium bowl, coat the chicken with the cumin, chili powder, and salt. 3. Put the oil in the inner cooking pot. When it is shimmering, add the coated chicken pieces. (This step lets the spices bloom a bit to get their full flavor.) Cook the chicken for 4 to 5 minutes. 4. Add the tomatoes, tomato paste, onion, garlic, and jalapeños. 5. Lock the lid into place. Select Manual and adjust the pressure to High. Cook for 15 minutes. When the cooking is complete, let the pressure release naturally for 10 minutes, then quick-release any remaining pressure. Unlock and remove the lid. 6. Use two forks to shred the chicken. Serve topped with the sour cream. This dish is good with mashed cauliflower, steamed vegetables, or a salad.

Classic Chicken Salad

Prep time: 5 minutes | Cook time: 12 minutes | Serves 8

2 pounds (907 g) chicken breasts	pepper
1 cup vegetable broth	1 cup mayonnaise
2 sprigs fresh thyme	2 stalks celery, chopped
1 teaspoon granulated garlic	2 tablespoons chopped fresh chives
1 teaspoon onion powder	1 teaspoon fresh lemon juice
1 bay leaf	1 teaspoon Dijon mustard
½ teaspoon ground black	½ teaspoon coarse sea salt

1. Combine the chicken, broth, thyme, garlic, onion powder, bay leaf, and black pepper in the Instant Pot. 2. Lock the lid. Select the Poultry mode and set the cooking time for 12 minutes at High Pressure. 3. When the timer beeps, perform a natural pressure release for 10 minutes, then release any remaining pressure. Carefully remove the lid. 4. Remove the chicken from the Instant Pot and

let rest for a few minutes until cooled slightly. 5. Slice the chicken breasts into strips and place in a salad bowl. Add the remaining ingredients and gently stir until well combined. Serve immediately.

Mild Chicken Curry with Coconut Milk

Prep time: 10 minutes | Cook time: 14 minutes | Serves 4 to 6

1 large onion, diced	flavor)
6 cloves garlic, crushed	½ teaspoon chili powder
¼ cup coconut oil	24 ounces can of low-sodium diced or crushed tomatoes
½ teaspoon black pepper	
½ teaspoon turmeric	
½ teaspoon paprika	13½ ounces can of light coconut milk (I prefer a brand that has no unwanted ingredients, like guar gum or sugar)
¼ teaspoon cinnamon	
¼ teaspoon cloves	
¼ teaspoon cumin	
¼ teaspoon ginger	4 pounds boneless skinless chicken breasts, cut into chunks
½ teaspoon salt	
1 tablespoon curry powder (more if you like more	

1. Sauté onion and garlic in the coconut oil, either with Sauté setting in the inner pot of the Instant Pot or on stove top, then add to pot. 2. Combine spices in a small bowl, then add to the inner pot. 3. Add tomatoes and coconut milk and stir. 4. Add chicken, and stir to coat the pieces with the sauce. 5. Secure the lid and make sure vent is at sealing. Set to Manual mode (or Pressure Cook on newer models) for 14 minutes. 6. Let pressure release naturally (if you're crunched for time, you can do a quick release). 7. Serve with your favorite sides, and enjoy!

Pecorino Chicken

Prep time: 10 minutes | Cook time: 15 minutes | Serves 3

2 ounces (57 g) Pecorino cheese, grated	1 tablespoon butter
10 ounces (283 g) chicken breast, skinless, boneless	¾ cup heavy cream
	½ teaspoon salt
	½ teaspoon red hot pepper

1. Chop the chicken breast into the cubes. 2. Toss butter in the instant pot and preheat it on the Sauté mode. 3. Add the chicken cubes. 4. Sprinkle the poultry with the salt and red hot pepper. 5. Add cream and mix up together all the ingredients. 6. Close the lid of the instant pot and seal it. 7. Set Poultry mode and put a timer on 15 minutes. 8. When the time is over, let the chicken rest for 5 minutes more. 9. Transfer the meal on the plates and sprinkle with the grated cheese. The cheese shouldn't melt immediately.

Chicken and Mixed Greens Salad

Prep time: 5 minutes | Cook time: 20 minutes | Serves 4

Chicken:

2 tablespoons avocado oil	½ teaspoon dried parsley
1 pound (454 g) chicken breast, cubed	½ teaspoon dried basil
½ cup filtered water	½ teaspoon kosher salt
½ teaspoon ground turmeric	½ teaspoon freshly ground black pepper

Salad:

1 avocado, mashed	½ cup chopped spinach
1 cup chopped arugula	2 tablespoons pine nuts, toasted
1 cup chopped Swiss chard	
1 cup chopped kale	

1. Combine all the chicken ingredients in the Instant Pot. 2. Secure the lid. Select the Manual mode and set the cooking time for 20 minutes at High Pressure. 3. Meanwhile, toss all the salad ingredients in a large salad bowl. 4. Once cooking is complete, do a quick pressure release. Carefully open the lid. 5. Remove the chicken to the salad bowl and serve.

Garlic Galore Rotisserie Chicken

Prep time: 5 minutes | Cook time: 3 minutes | Serves 4

3 pounds whole chicken	stock, broth, or water
2 tablespoons olive oil, divided	2 tablespoons garlic powder
Salt to taste	2 teaspoons onion powder
Pepper to taste	½ teaspoon basil
20 to 30 cloves fresh garlic, peeled and left whole	½ teaspoon cumin
1 cup low-sodium chicken	½ teaspoon chili powder

1. Rub chicken with one tablespoon of the olive oil and sprinkle with salt and pepper. 2. Place the garlic cloves inside the chicken. Use butcher's twine to secure the legs. 3. Press the Sauté button on the Instant Pot, then add the rest of the olive oil to the inner pot. 4. When the pot is hot, place the chicken inside. You are just trying to sear it, so leave it for about 4 minutes on each side. 5. Remove the chicken and set aside. Place the trivet at the bottom of the inner pot and pour in the chicken stock. 6. Mix together the remaining seasonings and rub them all over the entire chicken. 7. Place the chicken back inside the inner pot, breast-side up, on top of the trivet and secure the lid to the sealing position. 8. Press the Manual button and use the +/- to set it for 25 minutes. 9. When the timer beeps, allow the pressure to release naturally for 15 minutes. If the lid will not open at this point, quick release the remaining pressure and remove the chicken. 10. Let the chicken rest for 5–10 minutes before serving.

Chicken Meatballs with Green Cabbage

Prep time: 15 minutes | Cook time: 4 minutes | Serves 4

1 pound (454 g) ground chicken	ground black pepper, divided
¼ cup heavy (whipping) cream	¼ teaspoon ground allspice
2 teaspoons salt, divided	4 to 6 cups thickly chopped green cabbage
½ teaspoon ground caraway seeds	½ cup coconut milk
1½ teaspoons freshly	2 tablespoons unsalted butter

1. To make the meatballs, put the chicken in a bowl. Add the cream, 1 teaspoon of salt, the caraway, ½ teaspoon of pepper, and the allspice. Mix thoroughly. Refrigerate the mixture for 30 minutes. Once the mixture has cooled, it is easier to form the meatballs. 2. Using a small scoop, form the chicken mixture into small-to medium-size meatballs. Place half the meatballs in the inner cooking pot of your Instant Pot and cover them with half the cabbage. Place the remaining meatballs on top of the cabbage, then cover them with the rest of the cabbage. 3. Pour in the milk, place pats of the butter here and there, and sprinkle with the remaining 1 teaspoon of salt and 1 teaspoon of pepper. 4. Lock the lid into place. Select Manual and adjust the pressure to High. Cook for 4 minutes. When the cooking is complete, quick-release the pressure. Unlock the lid. Serve the meatballs on top of the cabbage.

Cheese Stuffed Chicken

Prep time: 15 minutes | Cook time: 20 minutes | Serves 4

12 ounces (340 g) chicken fillet	1 tablespoon cream cheese
4 ounces (113 g) provolone cheese, sliced	½ teaspoon dried cilantro
	½ teaspoon smoked paprika
	1 cup water, for cooking

1. Beat the chicken fillet well and rub it with dried cilantro and smoked paprika. 2. Then spread it with cream cheese and top with Provolone cheese. 3. Roll the chicken fillet into the roll and wrap in the foil. 4. Pour water and insert the rack in the instant pot. 5. Place the chicken roll on the rack. Close and seal the lid. 6. Cook it on Manual mode (High Pressure) for 20 minutes. 7. Make a quick pressure release and slice the chicken roll into the servings.

Chicken Alfredo with Bacon

Prep time: 10 minutes | Cook time: 27 minutes | Serves 4

2 (6 ounces / 170 g) boneless, skinless chicken breasts, butterflied	1 cup water
½ teaspoon garlic powder	1 stick butter
¼ teaspoon dried parsley	2 cloves garlic, finely minced
¼ teaspoon dried thyme	¼ cup heavy cream
¼ teaspoon salt	½ cup grated Parmesan cheese
⅛ teaspoon pepper	¼ cup cooked crumbled bacon
2 tablespoons coconut oil	

1. Sprinkle the chicken breasts with the garlic powder, parsley, thyme, salt, and pepper. 2. Set your Instant Pot to Sauté and melt the coconut oil. 3. Add the chicken and sear for 3 to 5 minutes until golden brown on both sides. 4. Remove the chicken with tongs and set aside. 5. Pour the water into the Instant Pot and insert the trivet. Place the chicken on the trivet. 6. Secure the lid. Select the Manual mode and set the cooking time for 20 minutes at High Pressure. 7. Once cooking is complete, do a quick pressure release. Carefully open the lid. 8. Remove the chicken from the pot to a platter and set aside. 9. Pour the water out of the Instant Pot, reserving ½ cup; set aside. 10. Set your Instant Pot to Sauté again and melt the butter. 11. Add the garlic, heavy cream, cheese, and reserved water to the Instant Pot. Cook for 3 to 4 minutes until the sauce starts to thicken, stirring frequently. 12. Stir in the crumbled bacon and pour the mixture over the chicken. Serve immediately.

Shredded Buffalo Chicken

Prep time: 10 minutes | Cook time: 20 minutes | Serves 8

2 tablespoons avocado oil	as Frank's RedHot)
½ cup finely chopped onion	½ tablespoon apple cider vinegar
1 celery stalk, finely chopped	¼ teaspoon garlic powder
1 large carrot, chopped	2 bone-in, skin-on chicken breasts (about 2 pounds)
⅓ cup mild hot sauce (such	

1. Set the electric pressure cooker to the Sauté setting. When the pot is hot, pour in the avocado oil. 2. Sauté the onion, celery, and carrot for 3 to 5 minutes or until the onion begins to soften. Hit Cancel. 3. Stir in the hot sauce, vinegar, and garlic powder. Place the chicken breasts in the sauce, meat-side down. 4. Close and lock the lid of the pressure cooker. Set the valve to sealing. 5. Cook on high pressure for 20 minutes. 6. When cooking is complete, hit Cancel and quick release the pressure. Once the pin drops,

unlock and remove the lid. 7. Using tongs, transfer the chicken breasts to a cutting board. When the chicken is cool enough to handle, remove the skin, shred the chicken and return it to the pot. Let the chicken soak in the sauce for at least 5 minutes. 8. Serve immediately.

Chicken Enchilada Bowl

Prep time: 10 minutes | Cook time: 35 minutes | Serves 4

2 (6 ounces / 170 g) boneless, skinless chicken breasts	1 (4 ounces / 113 g) can green chilies
2 teaspoons chili powder	¼ cup diced onion
½ teaspoon garlic powder	2 cups cooked cauliflower rice
½ teaspoon salt	1 avocado, diced
¼ teaspoon pepper	½ cup sour cream
2 tablespoons coconut oil	1 cup shredded Cheddar cheese
¾ cup red enchilada sauce	
¼ cup chicken broth	

1. Sprinkle the chili powder, garlic powder, salt, and pepper on chicken breasts. 2. Set your Instant Pot to Sauté and melt the coconut oil. Add the chicken breasts and sear each side for about 5 minutes until golden brown. 3. Pour the enchilada sauce and broth over the chicken. Using a wooden spoon or rubber spatula, scrape the bottom of pot to make sure nothing is sticking. Stir in the chilies and onion. 4. Secure the lid. Select the Manual mode and set the cooking time for 25 minutes at High Pressure. 5. Once cooking is complete, do a quick pressure release. Carefully open the lid. 6. Remove the chicken and shred with two forks. Serve the chicken over the cauliflower rice and place the avocado, sour cream, and Cheddar cheese on top.

Chicken Thighs with Feta

Prep time: 7 minutes | Cook time: 15 minutes | Serves 2

4 lemon slices	4 ounces (113 g) feta, crumbled
2 chicken thighs	1 teaspoon butter
1 tablespoon Greek seasoning	½ cup water

1. Rub the chicken thighs with Greek seasoning. 2. Then spread the chicken with butter. 3. Pour water in the instant pot and place the trivet. 4. Place the chicken on the foil and top with the lemon slices. Top it with feta. 5. Wrap the chicken in the foil and transfer on the trivet. 6. Cook on the Sauté mode for 10 minutes. Then make a quick pressure release for 5 minutes. 7. Discard the foil from the chicken thighs and serve!

Chicken Escabèche

Prep time: 5 minutes | Cook time: 15 minutes | Serves 4

1 cup filtered water	½ teaspoon coriander
1 pound (454 g) chicken, mixed pieces	½ teaspoon ground cumin
3 garlic cloves, smashed	½ teaspoon mint, finely chopped
2 bay leaves	½ teaspoon kosher salt
1 onion, chopped	½ teaspoon freshly ground black pepper
½ cup red wine vinegar	

1. Pour the water into the Instant Pot and insert the trivet. 2. Thoroughly combine the chicken, garlic, bay leaves, onion, vinegar, coriander, cumin, mint, salt, and black pepper in a large bowl. 3. Put the bowl on the trivet and cover loosely with aluminum foil. 4. Secure the lid. Select the Manual mode and set the cooking time for 15 minutes at High Pressure. 5. Once cooking is complete, do a natural pressure release for 10 minutes, then release any remaining pressure. Carefully open the lid. 6. Remove the dish from the Instant Pot and cool for 5 to 10 minutes before serving.

Lemony Chicken with Fingerling Potatoes and Olives

Prep time: 20 minutes | Cook time: 21 minutes | Serves 4

4 (5- to 7-ounce / 142- to 198-g) bone-in chicken thighs, trimmed	½ cup chicken broth
½ teaspoon table salt	1 small lemon, sliced thin
¼ teaspoon pepper	1½ pounds (680 g) fingerling potatoes, unpeeled
2 teaspoons extra-virgin olive oil, plus extra for drizzling	¼ cup pitted brine-cured green or black olives, halved
4 garlic cloves, peeled and smashed	2 tablespoons coarsely chopped fresh parsley

1. Pat chicken dry with paper towels and sprinkle with salt and pepper. Using highest sauté function, heat oil in Instant Pot for 5 minutes (or until just smoking). Place chicken skin side down in pot and cook until well browned on first side, about 5 minutes; transfer to plate. 2. Add garlic to fat left in pot and cook, using highest sauté function, until golden and fragrant, about 2 minutes. Stir in broth and lemon, scraping up any browned bits. Return chicken skin side up to pot and add any accumulated juices. Arrange potatoes on top. Lock lid in place and close pressure release valve. Select high pressure cook function and cook for 9 minutes. 3. Turn off Instant Pot and quick-release pressure. Carefully remove lid, allowing steam to escape away from you. Transfer chicken to serving dish and discard skin, if desired. Stir olives and parsley into potatoes and season with salt and pepper to taste. Serve chicken with potatoes.

Bacon-Wrapped Chicken Tenders

Prep time: 15 minutes | Cook time: 15 minutes | Serves 2

4 ounces (113 g) chicken fillet	¼ teaspoon salt
2 bacon slices	1 teaspoon olive oil
½ teaspoon ground paprika	1 cup water, for cooking

1. Cut the chicken fillet on 2 tenders and sprinkle them with salt, ground paprika, and olive oil. 2. Wrap the chicken tenders in the bacon and transfer in the steamer rack, 3. Pour water and insert the steamer rack with the chicken tenders in the instant pot. 4. Close and seal the lid and cook the meal on Manual mode (High Pressure) for 15 minutes. 5. When the time is finished, allow the natural pressure release for 10 minutes.

Simple Chicken Masala

Prep time: 10 minutes | Cook time: 17 minutes | Serves 3

12 ounces (340 g) chicken fillet
1 tablespoon masala spices
1 tablespoon avocado oil
3 tablespoons organic almond milk

1. Heat up avocado oil in the instant pot on Sauté mode for 2 minutes. 2. Meanwhile, chop the chicken fillet roughly and mix it up with masala spices. 3. Add almond milk and transfer the chicken in the instant pot. 4. Cook the chicken bites on Sauté mode for 15 minutes. Stir the meal occasionally.

Chapter 6
Vegetables and Sides

Spaghetti Squash Noodles with Tomatoes

Prep time: 15 minutes | Cook time: 14 to 16 minutes | Serves 4

1 medium spaghetti squash	1 teaspoon kosher salt
1 cup water	½ teaspoon freshly ground
2 tablespoons olive oil	black pepper
1 small yellow onion, diced	1 (14½ ounces / 411 g)
6 garlic cloves, minced	can sugar-free crushed
2 teaspoons crushed red	tomatoes
pepper flakes	¼ cup capers
2 teaspoons dried oregano	1 tablespoon caper brine
1 cup sliced cherry	½ cup sliced olives
tomatoes	

1. With a sharp knife, halve the spaghetti squash crosswise. Using a spoon, scoop out the seeds and sticky gunk in the middle of each half. 2. Pour the water into the Instant Pot and place the trivet in the pot with the handles facing up. Arrange the squash halves, cut side facing up, on the trivet. 3. Lock the lid. Select the Manual mode and set the cooking time for 7 minutes on High Pressure. When the timer goes off, use a quick pressure release. Carefully open the lid. 4. Remove the trivet and pour out the water that has collected in the squash cavities. Using the tines of a fork, separate the cooked strands into spaghetti-like pieces and set aside in a bowl. 5. Pour the water out of the pot. Select the Sauté mode and heat the oil. 6. Add the onion to the pot and sauté for 3 minutes. Add the garlic, pepper flakes and oregano to the pot and sauté for 1 minute. 7. Stir in the cherry tomatoes, salt and black pepper and cook for 2 minutes, or until the tomatoes are tender. 8. Pour in the crushed tomatoes, capers, caper brine and olives and bring the mixture to a boil. Continue to cook for 2 to 3 minutes to allow the flavors to meld. 9. Stir in the spaghetti squash noodles and cook for 1 to 2 minutes to warm everything through. 10. Transfer the dish to a serving platter and serve.

Almond Butter Zucchini Noodles

Prep time: 10 minutes | Cook time: 4 minutes | Serves 4

2 tablespoons coconut oil	2 tablespoons almond
1 yellow onion, chopped	butter
2 zucchini, julienned	Sea salt and freshly ground
1 cup shredded Chinese	black pepper, to taste
cabbage	1 teaspoon cayenne pepper
2 garlic cloves, minced	

1. Press the Sauté button to heat up your Instant Pot.

Heat the coconut oil and sweat the onion for 2 minutes. 2. Add the other ingredients. 3. Secure the lid. Choose Manual mode and High Pressure; cook for 2 minutes. Once cooking is complete, use a quick pressure release; carefully remove the lid. Bon appétit!

Braised Cabbage with Ginger

Prep time: 10 minutes | Cook time: 8 minutes | Serves 6

1 tablespoon avocado oil	1 clove garlic, minced
1 tablespoon butter or ghee	1-inch piece fresh ginger,
(or more avocado oil)	grated
½ medium onion, diced	1 pound (454 g) green or
1 medium bell pepper (any	red cabbage, cored and
color), diced	leaves chopped
1 teaspoon sea salt	½ cup bone broth or
½ teaspoon ground black	vegetable broth
pepper	

1. Set the Instant Pot to Sauté and heat the oil and butter together. When the butter has stopped foaming, add the onion, bell pepper, salt, and black pepper. Sauté, stirring frequently, until just softened, about 3 minutes. Add the garlic and ginger and cook 1 minute longer. Add the cabbage and stir to combine. Pour in the broth. 2. Secure the lid and set the steam release valve to Sealing. Press the Manual button and set the cook time to 2 minutes. 3. When the Instant Pot beeps, carefully switch the steam release valve to Venting to quick-release the pressure. When fully released, open the lid. Stir the cabbage and transfer it to a serving dish. Serve warm.

Asparagus with Copoundy Cheese

Prep time: 5 minutes | Cook time: 1 minute | Serves 4

1½ pounds (680 g) fresh	Sea salt, to taste
asparagus	¼ teaspoon ground black
1 cup water	pepper
2 tablespoons olive oil	½ cup shredded Copoundy
4 garlic cloves, minced	cheese

1. Pour the water into the Instant Pot and put the steamer basket in the pot. 2. Place the asparagus in the steamer basket. Drizzle the asparagus with the olive oil and sprinkle with the garlic on top. Season with salt and black pepper. 3. Close and secure the lid. Select the Manual mode and set the cooking time for 1 minute at High Pressure. Once cooking is complete, do a quick pressure release. Carefully open the lid. 4. Transfer the asparagus to a platter and served topped with the shredded cheese.

Wild Rice Salad with Cranberries and Almonds

Prep time: 10 minutes | Cook time: 25 minutes | Serves 18

For the rice

2 cups wild rice blend, rinsed	2½ cups Vegetable Broth or Chicken Bone Broth
1 teaspoon kosher salt	

For the dressing

¼ cup extra-virgin olive oil	Juice of 1 medium orange (about ¼ cup)
¼ cup white wine vinegar	
1½ teaspoons grated orange zest	1 teaspoon honey or pure maple syrup

For the salad

¾ cup unsweetened dried cranberries	toasted
½ cup sliced almonds,	Freshly ground black pepper

Make the Rice 1. In the electric pressure cooker, combine the rice, salt, and broth. 2. Close and lock the lid. Set the valve to sealing. 3. Cook on high pressure for 25 minutes. 4. When the cooking is complete, hit Cancel and allow the pressure to release naturally for 15 minutes, then quick release any remaining pressure. 5. Once the pin drops, unlock and remove the lid. 6. Let the rice cool briefly, then fluff it with a fork. Make the Dressing 7. While the rice cooks, make the dressing: In a small jar with a screw-top lid, combine the olive oil, vinegar, zest, juice, and honey. (If you don't have a jar, whisk the ingredients together in a small bowl.) Shake to combine. Make the Salad 8. In a large bowl, combine the rice, cranberries, and almonds. 9. Add the dressing and season with pepper. 10. Serve warm or refrigerate.

Broccoli and Mushroom Bake

Prep time: 10 minutes | Cook time: 3 minutes | Serves 4

½ cup sunflower seeds, soaked overnight	broken into florets
2 tablespoons sesame seeds	½ cup chopped spring onions
1 cup water	10 ounces (283 g) white fresh mushrooms, sliced
1 cup unsweetened almond milk	Sea salt and white pepper, to taste
¼ teaspoon grated nutmeg	
½ teaspoon sea salt	1 tablespoon cayenne pepper
1 tablespoon nutritional yeast	
2 tablespoons rice vinegar	¼ teaspoon dried dill
1 pound (454 g) broccoli,	¼ teaspoon ground bay leaf

1. Add sunflower seeds, sesame seeds, water, milk, nutmeg, ½ teaspoon of sea salt, nutritional yeast, and vinegar to your blender. 2. Blend until smooth and uniform. 3. Spritz a casserole dish with a nonstick cooking spray. Add broccoli, spring onions and mushrooms. 4. Sprinkle with salt, white pepper, cayenne pepper, dill, and ground bay leaf. Pour the prepared vegan béchamel over your casserole. 5. Add 1 cup of water and a metal rack to your Instant Pot. Place the dish on the rack. 6. Secure the lid. Choose Manual mode and High Pressure; cook for 3 minutes. Once cooking is complete, use a quick pressure release; carefully remove the lid. 7. Allow the dish to stand for 5 to 10 minutes before slicing and serving. Bon appétit!

Curried Cauliflower and Tomatoes

Prep time: 10 minutes | Cook time: 2 minutes | Serves 4 to 6

1 medium head cauliflower, cut into bite-size pieces	2 tablespoons red curry paste
1 (14 ounces / 397 g) can sugar-free diced tomatoes, undrained	1 teaspoon salt
	1 teaspoon garlic powder
1 bell pepper, thinly sliced	½ teaspoon onion powder
1 (14 ounces / 397 g) can full-fat coconut milk	½ teaspoon ground ginger
	¼ teaspoon chili powder
½ to 1 cup water	Freshly ground black pepper, to taste

1. Add all the ingredients, except for the black pepper, to the Instant Pot and stir to combine. 2. Lock the lid. Select the Manual setting and set the cooking time for 2 minutes at High Pressure. Once the timer goes off, use a quick pressure release. Carefully open the lid. 3. Sprinkle the black pepper and stir well. Serve immediately.

Vegetable Medley

Prep time: 20 minutes | Cook time: 2 minutes | Serves 8

2 medium parsnips	1 teaspoon salt
4 medium carrots	3 tablespoons sugar
1 turnip, about 4½ inches diameter	2 tablespoons canola or olive oil
1 cup water	½ teaspoon salt

1. Clean and peel vegetables. Cut in 1-inch pieces. 2. Place the cup of water and 1 teaspoon salt into the Instant Pot's inner pot with the vegetables. 3. Secure the lid and make sure vent is set to sealing. Press Manual and set for 2 minutes. 4. When cook time is up, release the pressure manually and press Cancel. Drain the water from the inner pot. 5. Press Sauté and stir in sugar, oil, and salt. Cook until sugar is dissolved. Serve.

Spicy Cauliflower Head

Prep time: 5 minutes | Cook time: 7 minutes | Serves 4

13 ounces (369 g) cauliflower head	1 tablespoon avocado oil
1 cup water	1 teaspoon ground paprika
1 tablespoon coconut cream	1 teaspoon ground turmeric
	½ teaspoon ground cumin
	½ teaspoon salt

1. Pour the water in the Instant Pot and insert the trivet. 2. In the mixing bowl, stir together the coconut cream, avocado oil, paprika, turmeric, cumin and salt. 3. Carefully brush the cauliflower head with the coconut cream mixture. Sprinkle the remaining coconut cream mixture over the cauliflower. 4. Transfer the cauliflower head onto the trivet. 5. Lock the lid. Select the Manual mode and set the cooking time for 7 minutes at High Pressure. When the timer goes off, use a natural pressure release for 10 minutes, then release any remaining pressure. Carefully open the lid. 6. Serve immediately.

Braised Radishes with Sugar Snap Peas and Dukkah

Prep time: 20 minutes | Cook time: 5 minutes | Serves 4

¼ cup extra-virgin olive oil, divided	8 ounces (227 g) sugar snap peas, strings removed, sliced thin on bias
1 shallot, sliced thin	8 ounces (227 g) cremini mushrooms, trimmed and sliced thin
3 garlic cloves, sliced thin	
1½ pounds (680 g) radishes, 2 cups greens reserved, radishes trimmed and halved if small or quartered if large	2 teaspoons grated lemon zest plus 1 teaspoon juice
	1 cup plain Greek yogurt
½ cup water	½ cup fresh cilantro leaves
½ teaspoon table salt	3 tablespoons dukkah

1. Using highest sauté function, heat 2 tablespoons oil in Instant Pot until shimmering. Add shallot and cook until softened, about 2 minutes. Stir in garlic and cook until fragrant, about 30 seconds. Stir in radishes, water, and salt. Lock lid in place and close pressure release valve. Select high pressure cook function and cook for 1 minute. 2. Turn off Instant Pot and quick-release pressure. Carefully remove lid, allowing steam to escape away from you. Stir in snap peas, cover, and let sit until heated through, about 3 minutes. Add radish greens, mushrooms, lemon zest and juice, and remaining 2 tablespoons oil and gently toss to combine. Season with salt and pepper to taste. 3. Spread ¼ cup yogurt over bottom of 4 individual serving plates. Using slotted spoon, arrange vegetable mixture on top and sprinkle with cilantro and dukkah. Serve.

Cauliflower Mac and Cheese

Prep time: 6 minutes | Cook time: 3 minutes | Serves 6

1 cup water	Mozzarella cheese
1 large cauliflower, chopped into bite-size florets	2½ cups shredded sharp Cheddar cheese
	1 teaspoon ground mustard
1 cup heavy whipping cream	1 teaspoon ground turmeric
	Sea salt, to taste
½ cup sour cream	Pinch of cayenne pepper (optional)
1 cup shredded Gruyère or	

1. Pour the water into the Instant Pot. Place a metal steaming basket inside. Put the cauliflower florets in the basket. Secure the lid and set the steam release valve to Sealing. Press the Manual button and set the cook time to 3 minutes. When the Instant Pot beeps, carefully switch the steam release valve to Venting to quick-release the pressure. When fully released, open the lid. 2. Meanwhile, prepare the cheese sauce. In a large skillet, gently bring the cream to a simmer over medium to medium-low heat. Whisk in the sour cream until smooth, then gradually whisk in the Gruyère and 2 cups of the Cheddar until melted. Stir in the ground mustard and turmeric. Taste and adjust the salt. 3. Remove the cauliflower from the pot and toss it in the cheese sauce to coat. Serve warm, topped with the remaining Cheddar and a sprinkling of cayenne (if using).

Asparagus and Mushroom Soup

Prep time: 10 minutes | Cook time: 7 minutes | Serves 4

2 tablespoons coconut oil	4 cups vegetable broth
½ cup chopped shallots	2 tablespoons balsamic vinegar
2 cloves garlic, minced	Himalayan salt, to taste
1 pound (454 g) asparagus, washed, trimmed, and chopped	¼ teaspoon ground black pepper
4 ounces (113 g) button mushrooms, sliced	¼ teaspoon paprika
	¼ cup vegan sour cream

1. Press the Sauté button to heat up your Instant Pot. Heat the oil and cook the shallots and garlic for 2 to 3 minutes. 2. Add the remaining ingredients, except for sour cream, to the Instant Pot. 3. Secure the lid. Choose Manual mode and High Pressure; cook for 4 minutes. Once cooking is complete, use a quick pressure release; carefully remove the lid. 4. Spoon into four soup bowls; add a dollop of sour cream to each serving and serve immediately. Bon appétit!

Vinegary Broccoli with Cheese

Prep time: 5 minutes | Cook time: 5 minutes | Serves 4

1 pound (454 g) broccoli, cut into florets	2 tablespoons balsamic vinegar
1 cup water	1 teaspoon cumin seeds
2 garlic cloves, minced	1 teaspoon mustard seeds
1 cup crumbled Cottage cheese	Salt and pepper, to taste

1. Pour the water into the Instant Pot and put the steamer basket in the pot. Place the broccoli in the steamer basket. 2. Close and secure the lid. Select the Manual setting and set the cooking time for 5 minutes at High Pressure. Once the timer goes off, do a quick pressure release. Carefully open the lid. 3. Stir in the remaining ingredients. 4. Serve immediately.

Braised Whole Cauliflower with North African Spices

Prep time: 15 minutes | Cook time: 10 minutes | Serves 4

2 tablespoons extra-virgin olive oil	drained with juice reserved, chopped coarse
6 garlic cloves, minced	1 large head cauliflower (3 pounds / 1.4 kg)
3 anchovy fillets, rinsed and minced (optional)	½ cup pitted brine-cured green olives, chopped coarse
2 teaspoons ras el hanout	
⅛ teaspoon red pepper flakes	¼ cup golden raisins
1 (28 ounces / 794 g) can whole peeled tomatoes,	¼ cup fresh cilantro leaves
	¼ cup pine nuts, toasted

1. Using highest sauté function, cook oil, garlic, anchovies (if using), ras el hanout, and pepper flakes in Instant Pot until fragrant, about 3 minutes. Turn off Instant Pot, then stir in tomatoes and reserved juice. 2. Trim outer leaves of cauliflower and cut stem flush with bottom florets. Using paring knife, cut 4-inch-deep cross in stem. Nestle cauliflower stem side down into pot and spoon some of sauce over top. Lock lid in place and close pressure release valve. Select high pressure cook function and cook for 3 minutes. 3. Turn off Instant Pot and quick-release pressure. Carefully remove lid, allowing steam to escape away from you. Using tongs and slotted spoon, transfer cauliflower to serving dish and tent with aluminum foil. Stir olives and raisins into sauce and cook, using highest sauté function, until sauce has thickened slightly, about 5 minutes. Season with salt and pepper to taste. Cut cauliflower into wedges and spoon some of sauce over top. Sprinkle with cilantro and pine nuts. Serve, passing remaining sauce separately.

Green Beans with Potatoes and Basil

Prep time: 20 minutes | Cook time: 10 minutes | Serves 4

2 tablespoons extra-virgin olive oil, plus extra for drizzling	
1 onion, chopped fine	¼ teaspoon pepper
2 tablespoons minced fresh oregano or 2 teaspoons dried	1½ pounds (680 g) green beans, trimmed and cut into 2-inch lengths
2 tablespoons tomato paste	1 pound (454 g) Yukon Gold potatoes, peeled and cut into 1-inch pieces
4 garlic cloves, minced	
1 (14½ ounces / 411 g) can whole peeled tomatoes, drained with juice reserved, chopped	3 tablespoons chopped fresh basil or parsley
	2 tablespoons toasted pine nuts
1 cup water	
1 teaspoon table salt	Shaved Parmesan cheese

1. Using highest sauté function, heat oil in Instant Pot until shimmering. Add onion and cook until softened, about 5 minutes. Stir in oregano, tomato paste, and garlic and cook until fragrant, about 30 seconds. Stir in tomatoes and their juice, water, salt, and pepper, then stir in green beans and potatoes. Lock lid in place and close pressure release valve. Select high pressure cook function and cook for 5 minutes. 2. Turn off Instant Pot and quick-release pressure. Carefully remove lid, allowing steam to escape away from you. Season with salt and pepper to taste. Sprinkle individual portions with basil, pine nuts, and Parmesan and drizzle with extra oil. Serve.

Falafel and Lettuce Salad

Prep time: 10 minutes | Cook time: 6 to 8 minutes | Serves 4

1 cup shredded cauliflower	2 cups chopped lettuce
⅓ cup coconut flour	1 cucumber, chopped
1 teaspoon grated lemon zest	1 tablespoon olive oil
1 egg, beaten	1 teaspoon lemon juice
2 tablespoons coconut oil	½ teaspoon cayenne pepper

1. In a bowl, combine the cauliflower, coconut flour, grated lemon zest and egg. Form the mixture into small balls. 2. Set the Instant Pot to the Sauté mode and melt the coconut oil. Place the balls in the pot in a single layer. Cook for 3 to 4 minutes per side, or until they are golden brown. 3. In a separate bowl, stir together the remaining ingredients. 4. Place the cooked balls on top and serve.

Savory and Rich Creamed Kale

Prep time: 10 minutes | Cook time: 5 minutes | Serves 4

2 tablespoons extra-virgin olive oil	1 teaspoon Herbes de Provence
2 cloves garlic, crushed	4 ounces (113 g) cream cheese
1 small onion, chopped	½ cup full-fat heavy cream
12 ounces (340 g) kale, finely chopped	1 teaspoon dried tarragon
½ cup chicken broth	

1. Press the Sauté button on the Instant Pot and heat the olive oil. Add the garlic and onion to the pot and sauté for 2 minutes, or until the onion is soft. Stir in the kale, chicken broth and Herbes de Provence. 2. Lock the lid. Select the Manual mode and set the cooking time for 3 minutes at High Pressure. When the timer goes off, perform a quick pressure release. Carefully open the lid. 3. Stir in the cream cheese, heavy cream and tarragon. Stir well to thicken the dish. Serve immediately.

Garlicky Broccoli with Roasted Almonds

Prep time: 10 minutes | Cook time: 4 minutes | Serves 4 to 6

6 cups broccoli florets	medium lemon
1 cup water	½ teaspoon kosher salt
1½ tablespoons olive oil	Freshly ground black pepper, to taste
8 garlic cloves, thinly sliced	¼ cup chopped roasted almonds
2 shallots, thinly sliced	¼ cup finely slivered fresh basil
½ teaspoon crushed red pepper flakes	
Grated zest and juice of 1	

1. Pour the water into the Instant Pot. Place the broccoli florets in a steamer basket and lower into the pot. 2. Close and secure the lid. Select the Steam setting and set the cooking time for 2 minutes at Low Pressure. Once the timer goes off, use a quick pressure release. Carefully open the lid. 3. Transfer the broccoli to a large bowl filled with cold water and ice. Once cooled, drain the broccoli and pat dry. 4. Select the Sauté mode on the Instant Pot and heat the olive oil. Add the garlic to the pot and sauté for 30 seconds, tossing constantly. Add the shallots and pepper flakes to the pot and sauté for 1 minute. 5. Stir in the cooked broccoli, lemon juice, salt and black pepper. Toss the ingredients together and cook for 1 minute. 6. Transfer the broccoli to a serving platter and sprinkle with the chopped almonds, lemon zest and basil. Serve

immediately.

Parmesan Zoodles

Prep time: 5 minutes | Cook time: 5 minutes | Serves 2

1 large zucchini, trimmed and spiralized	½ teaspoon chili flakes
1 tablespoon butter	3 ounces (85 g) Parmesan cheese, grated
1 garlic clove, diced	

1. Set the Instant Pot on the Sauté mode and melt the butter. Add the garlic and chili flakes to the pot. Sauté for 2 minutes, or until fragrant. 2. Stir in the zucchini spirals and sauté for 2 minutes, or until tender. 3. Add the grated Parmesan cheese to the pot and stir well. Continue to cook it for 1 minute, or until the cheese melts. 4. Transfer to a plate and serve immediately

Zucchini and Daikon Fritters

Prep time: 10 minutes | Cook time: 8 minutes | Serves 4

2 large zucchinis, grated	meal
1 daikon, diced	1 teaspoon salt
1 egg, beaten	1 tablespoon coconut oil
1 teaspoon ground flax	

1. In the mixing bowl, combine all the ingredients, except for the coconut oil. Form the zucchini mixture into fritters. 2. Press the Sauté button on the Instant Pot and melt the coconut oil. 3. Place the zucchini fritters in the hot oil and cook for 4 minutes on each side, or until golden brown. 4. Transfer to a plate and serve.

Simple Cauliflower Gnocchi

Prep time: 5 minutes | Cook time: 2 minutes | Serves 4

2 cups cauliflower, boiled	1 teaspoon salt
½ cup almond flour	1 cup water
1 tablespoon sesame oil	

1. In a bowl, mash the cauliflower until puréed. Mix it up with the almond flour, sesame oil and salt. 2. Make the log from the cauliflower dough and cut it into small pieces. 3. Pour the water in the Instant Pot and add the gnocchi. 4. Lock the lid. Select the Manual mode and set the cooking time for 2 minutes on High Pressure. Once the timer goes off, perform a natural pressure release for 5 minutes, then release any remaining pressure. Carefully open the lid. 5. Remove the cooked gnocchi from the water and serve.

Masala Cauliflower

Prep time: 6 minutes | Cook time: 5 minutes | Serves 4

2 tablespoons olive oil
½ cup chopped scallions
2 cloves garlic, pressed
1 tablespoon garam masala
1 teaspoon curry powder
1 red chili pepper, minced
½ teaspoon ground cumin
Sea salt and ground black pepper, to taste
1 tablespoon chopped fresh coriander
2 tomatoes, puréed
1 pound (454 g) cauliflower, broken into florets
½ cup water
½ cup almond yogurt

1. Press the Sauté button to heat up your Instant Pot. Now, heat the oil and sauté the scallions for 1 minute. 2. Add garlic and continue to cook an additional 30 seconds or until aromatic. 3. Add garam masala, curry powder, chili pepper, cumin, salt, black pepper, coriander, tomatoes, cauliflower, and water. 4. Secure the lid. Choose Manual mode and High Pressure; cook for 3 minutes. Once cooking is complete, use a quick pressure release; carefully remove the lid. 5. Pour in the almond yogurt, stir well and serve warm. Bon appétit!

Garlic Brussels Sprouts with Almonds

Prep time: 5 minutes | Cook time: 15 minutes | Serves 4

1 pound (454 g) Brussels sprouts
1 teaspoon sea salt
1 teaspoon garlic powder
1 tablespoon butter
1 small onion, diced
2 cloves garlic, crushed
3 strips uncured bacon, cut into ½-inch pieces
1 tablespoon extra-fine blanched almond slivers
½ cup chicken broth
2 tablespoons chopped scallions, for garnish

1. Wash the Brussels sprouts well and discard any old and rotten leaves. Trim the ends off and cut the Brussels sprouts in half vertically. Put any loose leaves with the rest of the Brussels sprouts, sea salt and garlic powder in a large mixing bowl and mix. 2. Turn on the Instant Pot by pressing Sauté and set to More. Insert the inner pot and wait until the panel says "Hot." 3. Add the butter, onion and garlic and sauté for 2 minutes or until the onion is soft. Add the bacon and sauté for 3 minutes or until the bacon starts to shrivel. If there's too much bacon grease, you can spoon out some of it now. You want some bacon grease, but not so much that the Brussels sprouts won't brown. 4. Push the bacon to the side and add half of the Brussels sprouts to brown. Place the Brussels sprouts with their flat sides down on the inner pot. Do not to crowd them and don't mix until the sides turn brown. 5. When most of the sides are browned, take them out, place them in a bowl and set aside. Add the remaining Brussels sprouts to the inner pot to brown the sides. If needed, add more bacon grease back so as not to burn the Brussels sprouts. When they are browned, add the first batch of the browned Brussels sprouts back to the inner pot and add the almonds and the chicken broth and mix while scraping the bottom of the inner pot to loosen up all the bits and pieces. 6. Hit Cancel, then press the Manual button and set the timer for 8 minutes on High Pressure. 7. Close the lid tightly and move the steam release handle to Sealing. When the timer goes off, turn the steam release handle to the Venting position carefully for the steam to escape and the float valve to drop down. Press Cancel. Open the lid. 8. Garnish with the chopped scallions and serve immediately.

Caramelized Onions

Prep time: 10 minutes | Cook time: 35 minutes | Serves 8

4 tablespoons margarine
6 large Vidalia or other sweet onions, sliced into
thin half rings
10-ounce can chicken, or vegetable, broth

1. Press Sauté on the Instant Pot. Add in the margarine and let melt. 2. Once the margarine is melted, stir in the onions and sauté for about 5 minutes. Pour in the broth and then press Cancel. 3. Secure the lid and make sure vent is set to sealing. Press Manual and set time for 20 minutes. 4. When cook time is up, release the pressure manually. Remove the lid and press Sauté. Stir the onion mixture for about 10 more minutes, allowing extra liquid to cook off.

Green Cabbage Turmeric Stew

Prep time: 5 minutes | Cook time: 4 minutes | Serves 4

2 tablespoons olive oil
½ cup sliced yellow onion
1 teaspoon crushed garlic
Sea salt and freshly ground black pepper, to taste
1 teaspoon turmeric powder
1 serrano pepper, chopped
1 pound (454 g) green cabbage, shredded
1 celery stalk, chopped
2 tablespoons rice wine
1 cup roasted vegetable broth

1. Place all of the above ingredients in the Instant Pot. 2. Secure the lid. Choose Manual mode and High Pressure; cook for 4 minutes. Once cooking is complete, use a quick pressure release; carefully remove the lid. 3. Divide between individual bowls and serve warm. Bon appétit!

Thyme Cabbage

Prep time: 10 minutes | Cook time: 5 minutes | Serves 4

1 pound (454 g) white cabbage	1 teaspoon dried thyme
2 tablespoons butter	½ teaspoon salt
	1 cup water

1. Cut the white cabbage on medium size petals and sprinkle with the butter, dried thyme and salt. Place the cabbage petals in the Instant Pot pan. 2. Pour the water and insert the trivet in the Instant Pot. Put the pan on the trivet. 3. Set the lid in place. Select the Manual mode and set the cooking time for 5 minutes on High Pressure. When the timer goes off, do a quick pressure release. Carefully open the lid. 4. Serve immediately.

Italian Wild Mushrooms

Prep time: 30 minutes | Cook time: 3 minutes | Serves 10

2 tablespoons canola oil	chopped
2 large onions, chopped	3 fresh bay leaves
4 garlic cloves, minced	10 fresh basil leaves, chopped
3 large red bell peppers, chopped	1 teaspoon salt
3 large green bell peppers, chopped	1½ teaspoons pepper
12 ounces package oyster mushrooms, cleaned and	28 ounces can Italian plum tomatoes, crushed or chopped

1. Press Sauté on the Instant Pot and add in the oil. Once the oil is heated, add the onions, garlic, peppers, and mushroom to the oil. Sauté just until mushrooms begin to turn brown. 2. Add remaining ingredients. Stir well. 3. Secure the lid and make sure vent is set to sealing. Press Manual and set time for 3 minutes. 4. When cook time is up, release the pressure manually. Discard bay leaves.

Cauliflower Rice Curry

Prep time: 5 minutes | Cook time: 2 minutes | Serves 4

1 (9-ounce / 255-g) head cauliflower, chopped	turmeric
½ teaspoon garlic powder	½ teaspoon curry powder
½ teaspoon freshly ground black pepper	½ teaspoon kosher salt
½ teaspoon ground	½ teaspoon fresh paprika
	¼ small onion, thinly sliced

1. Pour 1 cup of filtered water into the inner pot of the Instant Pot, then insert the trivet. In a well-greased, Instant Pot-friendly dish, add the cauliflower. Sprinkle the garlic powder, black pepper, turmeric, curry powder, salt, paprika, and onion over top. 2. Place the dish onto the trivet, and cover loosely with aluminum foil. Close the lid, set the pressure release to Sealing and select Manual. Set the Instant Pot to 2 minutes on High Pressure, and let cook. 3. Once cooked, perform a quick release. 4. Open the Instant Pot, and remove the dish. Serve, and enjoy!

Sauerkraut and Mushroom Casserole

Prep time: 6 minutes | Cook time: 15 minutes | Serves 6

1 tablespoon olive oil	mushrooms, sliced
1 celery rib, diced	1 teaspoon caraway seeds
½ cup chopped leeks	1 teaspoon brown mustard
2 pounds (907 g) canned sauerkraut, drained	1 bay leaf
6 ounces (170 g) brown	1 cup dry white wine

1. Press the Sauté button to heat up your Instant Pot. Now, heat the oil and cook celery and leeks until softened. 2. Add the sauerkraut and mushrooms and cook for 2 minutes more. 3. Add the remaining ingredients and stir to combine well. 4. Secure the lid. Choose Manual mode and High Pressure; cook for 10 minutes. Once cooking is complete, use a natural pressure release; carefully remove the lid. Bon appétit!

Mushroom Stroganoff with Vodka

Prep time: 8 minutes | Cook time: 8 minutes | Serves 4

2 tablespoons olive oil	mushrooms, chopped
½ teaspoon crushed caraway seeds	1 celery stalk, chopped
½ cup chopped onion	1 ripe tomato, puréed
2 garlic cloves, smashed	1 teaspoon mustard seeds
¼ cup vodka	Sea salt and freshly ground pepper, to taste
¾ pound (340 g) button	2 cups vegetable broth

1. Press the Sauté button to heat up your Instant Pot. Now, heat the oil and sauté caraway seeds until fragrant, about 40 seconds. 2. Then, add the onion and garlic, and continue sautéing for 1 to 2 minutes more, stirring frequently. 3. After that, add the remaining ingredients and stir to combine. 4. Secure the lid. Choose Manual mode and High Pressure; cook for 5 minutes. Once cooking is complete, use a quick pressure release; carefully remove the lid. 5. Ladle into individual bowls and serve warm. Bon appétit!

Moroccan Zucchini

Prep time: 10 minutes | Cook time: 6 minutes | Serves 4

2 tablespoons avocado oil
½ medium onion, diced
1 clove garlic, minced
¼ teaspoon cayenne pepper
¼ teaspoon ground coriander
¼ teaspoon ground cumin
¼ teaspoon ground ginger
Pinch of ground cinnamon

1 Roma (plum) tomato, diced
2 medium zucchini, cut into 1-inch pieces
½ tablespoon fresh lemon juice
¼ cup bone broth or vegetable stock

1. Set the Instant Pot to Sauté. When hot, add the oil. Add the onion and sauté, stirring frequently, until translucent, about 2 minutes. Add the garlic, cayenne, coriander, cumin, ginger, and cinnamon and cook until fragrant, about 1 minute. Stir in the tomato and zucchini and cook 2 minutes longer. 2. Press Cancel. Add the lemon juice and broth. Secure the lid and set the steam release valve to Sealing. Press the Manual button, adjust the pressure to Low, and set the cook time to 1 minute. 3. When the Instant Pot beeps, carefully switch the steam release valve to Venting to quick-release the pressure. When fully released, open the lid. Stir and serve warm.

Buttery Whole Cauliflower

Prep time: 5 minutes | Cook time: 8 minutes | Serves 4

1 large cauliflower, rinsed and patted dry
1 cup water
4 tablespoons melted butter
2 cloves garlic, minced

Pinch of sea salt
Pinch of fresh ground black pepper
1 tablespoon chopped fresh flat leaf parsley, for garnish

1. Pour the water into the Instant Pot and put the trivet in the pot. Place the cauliflower on the trivet. 2. Lock the lid. Select the Manual mode and set the cooking time for 3 minutes at High Pressure. 3. Preheat the oven to 550°F (288°C). Line a baking sheet with parchment paper. 4. In a small bowl, whisk together the butter, garlic, sea salt and black pepper. Set aside. 5. When the timer beeps, use a quick pressure release. Carefully open the lid. 6. Transfer the cauliflower to the lined baking sheet. Dab and dry the surface with a clean kitchen towel. Brush the cauliflower with the garlic butter. 7. Place the baking sheet with the cauliflower in the preheated oven and roast for 5 minutes, or until the cauliflower is golden brown. Drizzle with any remaining garlic butter and sprinkle with the chopped parsley. Serve immediately.

Satarash with Eggs

Prep time: 10 minutes | Cook time: 5 minutes | Serves 4

2 tablespoons olive oil
1 white onion, chopped
2 cloves garlic
2 ripe tomatoes, puréed
1 green bell pepper, deseeded and sliced
1 red bell pepper, deseeded and sliced

1 teaspoon paprika
½ teaspoon dried oregano
½ teaspoon turmeric
Kosher salt and ground black pepper, to taste
1 cup water
4 large eggs, lightly whisked

1. Press the Sauté button on the Instant Pot and heat the olive oil. Add the onion and garlic to the pot and sauté for 2 minutes, or until fragrant. Stir in the remaining ingredients, except for the eggs. 2. Lock the lid. Select the Manual mode and set the cooking time for 3 minutes on High Pressure. When the timer goes off, perform a quick pressure release. Carefully open the lid. 3. Fold in the eggs and stir to combine. Lock the lid and let it sit in the residual heat for 5 minutes. Serve warm.

Parmesan Cauliflower Mash

Prep time: 7 minutes | Cook time: 5 minutes | Serves 4

1 head cauliflower, cored and cut into large florets
½ teaspoon kosher salt
½ teaspoon garlic pepper
2 tablespoons plain Greek yogurt

¾ cup freshly grated Parmesan cheese
1 tablespoon unsalted butter or ghee (optional)
Chopped fresh chives

1. Pour 1 cup of water into the electric pressure cooker and insert a steamer basket or wire rack. 2. Place the cauliflower in the basket. 3. Close and lock the lid of the pressure cooker. Set the valve to sealing. 4. Cook on high pressure for 5 minutes. 5. When the cooking is complete, hit Cancel and quick release the pressure. 6. Once the pin drops, unlock and remove the lid. 7. Remove the cauliflower from the pot and pour out the water. Return the cauliflower to the pot and add the salt, garlic pepper, yogurt, and cheese. Use an immersion blender or potato masher to purée or mash the cauliflower in the pot. 8. Spoon into a serving bowl, and garnish with butter (if using) and chives.

Sesame Zoodles with Scallions

Prep time: 10 minutes | Cook time: 3 minutes | Serves 6

2 large zucchinis, trimmed and spiralized
¼ cup chicken broth
1 tablespoon chopped scallions
1 tablespoon coconut aminos

1 teaspoon sesame oil
1 teaspoon sesame seeds
¼ teaspoon chili flakes

1. Set the Instant Pot on the Sauté mode. Add the zucchini spirals to the pot and pour in the chicken broth. Sauté for 3 minutes and transfer to the serving bowls. 2. Sprinkle with the scallions, coconut aminos, sesame oil, sesame seeds and chili flakes. Gently stir the zoodles. 3. Serve immediately.

Steamed Tomato with Halloumi Cheese

Prep time: 5 minutes | Cook time: 3 minutes | Serves 4

8 tomatoes, sliced
1 cup water
½ cup crumbled Halloumi cheese

2 tablespoons extra-virgin olive oil
2 tablespoons snipped fresh basil
2 garlic cloves, smashed

1. Pour the water into the Instant Pot and put the trivet in the pot. Place the tomatoes in the trivet. 2. Lock the lid. Select the Manual mode and set the cooking time for 3 minutes on High Pressure. When the timer goes off, perform a quick pressure release. Carefully open the lid. 3. Toss the tomatoes with the remaining ingredients and serve.

Chapter 7
Snacks and Appetizers

Creamy Scallion Dip

Prep time: 10 minutes | Cook time: 11 minutes | Serves 4

5 ounces (142 g) scallions, diced	1 teaspoon garlic powder
4 tablespoons cream cheese	2 tablespoons coconut cream
1 tablespoon chopped fresh parsley	½ teaspoon salt
	1 teaspoon coconut oil

1. Heat up the instant pot on Sauté mode. 2. Then add coconut oil and melt it. 3. Add diced scallions and sauté it for 6 to 7 minutes or until it is light brown. 4. Add cream cheese, parsley, garlic powder, salt, and coconut cream. 5. Close the instant pot lid and cook the scallions dip for 5 minutes on Manual mode (High Pressure). 6. Make a quick pressure release. Blend the dip will it is smooth if desired.

Parmesan Chicken Balls with Chives

Prep time: 10 minutes | Cook time: 15 minutes | Serves 4

1 teaspoon coconut oil, softened	chives
1 cup ground chicken	1 teaspoon cayenne pepper
¼ cup chicken broth	3 ounces (85 g) Parmesan cheese, grated
1 tablespoon chopped	

1. Set your Instant Pot to Sauté and heat the coconut oil. 2. Add the remaining ingredients except the cheese to the Instant Pot and stir to mix well. 3. Secure the lid. Select the Manual mode and set the cooking time for 15 minutes at High Pressure. 4. Once cooking is complete, do a quick pressure release. Carefully open the lid. 5. Add the grated cheese and stir until combined. Form the balls from the cooked chicken mixture and allow to cool for 10 minutes, then serve.

Rosemary Chicken Wings

Prep time: 10 minutes | Cook time: 16 minutes | Serves 4

4 boneless chicken wings	½ teaspoon garlic powder
1 tablespoon olive oil	¼ teaspoon salt
1 teaspoon dried rosemary	

1. In the mixing bowl, mix up olive oil, dried rosemary, garlic powder, and salt. 2. Then rub the chicken wings with the rosemary mixture and leave for 10 minutes to marinate. 3. After this, put the chicken wings in the instant pot, add the remaining rosemary marinade and cook them on Sauté mode for 8 minutes from each side.

Chinese Spare Ribs

Prep time: 3 minutes | Cook time: 24 minutes | Serves 6

1½ pounds (680 g) spare ribs	1 tablespoon coconut aminos
Salt and ground black pepper, to taste	1 teaspoon ginger-garlic paste
2 tablespoons sesame oil	½ teaspoon crushed red pepper flakes
½ cup chopped green onions	½ teaspoon dried parsley
½ cup chicken stock	2 tablespoons sesame seeds, for serving
2 tomatoes, crushed	
2 tablespoons sherry	

1. Season the spare ribs with salt and black pepper to taste. 2. Set your Instant Pot to Sauté and heat the sesame oil. 3. Add the seasoned spare ribs and sear each side for about 3 minutes. 4. Add the remaining ingredients except the sesame seeds to the Instant Pot and stir well. 5. Secure the lid. Select the Meat/Stew mode and set the cooking time for 18 minutes at High Pressure. 6. When the timer beeps, perform a natural pressure release for 10 minutes, then release any remaining pressure. Carefully remove the lid. 7. Serve topped with the sesame seeds.

Broccoli with Garlic-Herb Cheese Sauce

Prep time: 5 minutes | Cook time: 3 minutes | Serves 4

½ cup water	cheese
1 pound (454 g) broccoli (frozen or fresh)	3 tablespoons garlic and herb cheese spread
½ cup heavy cream	Pinch of salt
1 tablespoon butter	Pinch of black pepper
½ cup shredded Cheddar	

1. Add the water to the pot and place the trivet inside. 2. Put the steamer basket on top of the trivet. Place the broccoli in the basket. 3. Close the lid and seal the vent. Cook on Low Pressure for 1 minute. Quick release the steam. Press Cancel. 4. Carefully remove the steamer basket from the pot and drain the water. If you steamed a full bunch of broccoli, pull the florets off the stem. (Chop the stem into bite-size pieces, it's surprisingly creamy.) 5. Turn the pot to Sauté mode. Add the cream and butter. Stir continuously while the butter melts and the cream warms up. 6. When the cream begins to bubble on the edges, add the Cheddar cheese, cheese spread, salt, and pepper. Whisk continuously until the cheeses are melted and a sauce consistency is reached, 1 to 2 minutes. 7. Top one-fourth of the broccoli with 2 tablespoons cheese sauce.

Sesame Mushrooms

Prep time: 2 minutes | Cook time: 10 minutes | Serves 6

3 tablespoons sesame oil	½ teaspoon smoked paprika
¾ pound (340 g) small button mushrooms	½ teaspoon cayenne pepper
1 teaspoon minced garlic	Salt and ground black pepper, to taste

1. Set your Instant Pot to Sauté and heat the sesame oil. 2. Add the mushrooms and sauté for 4 minutes until just tender, stirring occasionally. 3. Add the remaining ingredients to the Instant Pot and stir to mix well. 4. Lock the lid. Select the Manual mode and set the cooking time for 5 minutes at High Pressure. 5. When the timer beeps, perform a quick pressure release. Carefully remove the lid. 6. Serve warm.

Lemon-Butter Mushrooms

Prep time: 10 minutes | Cook time: 4 minutes | Serves 2

1 cup cremini mushrooms, sliced	
½ cup water	zest
1 tablespoon lemon juice	½ teaspoon salt
1 teaspoon almond butter	½ teaspoon dried thyme
1 teaspoon grated lemon	

1. Combine all the ingredients in the Instant Pot. 2. Secure the lid. Select the Manual mode and set the cooking time for 4 minutes at High Pressure. 3. Once cooking is complete, do a natural pressure release for 5 minutes, then release any remaining pressure. Carefully open the lid. 4. Serve warm.

Fast Spring Kale Appetizer

Prep time: 5 minutes | Cook time: 2 minutes | Serves 6

3 teaspoons butter	½ teaspoon cayenne pepper
1 cup chopped spring onions	Himalayan salt and ground black pepper, to taste
1 pound (454 g) kale, torn into pieces	½ cup shredded Colby cheese, for serving
1 cup water	

1. Set your Instant Pot to Sauté and melt the butter. 2. Add the spring onions and sauté for 1 minute until wilted. 3. Add the remaining ingredients except the cheese to the Instant Pot and mix well. 4. Lock the lid. Select the Manual mode and set the cooking time for 1 minute at High Pressure. 5. When the timer beeps, perform a quick pressure release. Carefully remove the lid. 6. Transfer the kale mixture to a bowl and serve topped with the cheese.

Cabbage and Broccoli Slaw

Prep time: 5 minutes | Cook time: 10 minutes | Serves 6

2 cups broccoli slaw	4 tablespoons butter
½ head cabbage, thinly sliced	1 teaspoon salt
¼ cup chopped kale	¼ teaspoon pepper

1. Press the Sauté button and add all ingredients to Instant Pot. Stir-fry for 7 to 10 minutes until cabbage softens. Serve warm.

Cauliflower Fritters with Cheese

Prep time: 10 minutes | Cook time: 8 minutes | Serves 4

1 cup cauliflower, boiled	cheese, shredded
2 eggs, beaten	½ teaspoon garlic powder
2 tablespoons almond flour	1 tablespoon avocado oil
2 ounces (57 g) Cheddar	

1. In a medium bowl, mash the cauliflower. Add the beaten eggs, flour, cheese, and garlic powder and stir until well incorporated. Make the fritters from the cauliflower mixture. 2. Set your Instant Pot to Sauté and heat the avocado oil. 3. Add the fritters to the hot oil and cook each side for 3 minutes until golden brown. 4. Serve hot.

Garlic Meatballs

Prep time: 20 minutes | Cook time: 15 minutes | Serves 6

7 ounces (198 g) ground beef	3 tablespoons water
7 ounces (198 g) ground pork	1 teaspoon chili flakes
1 teaspoon minced garlic	1 teaspoon dried parsley
	1 tablespoon coconut oil
	¼ cup beef broth

1. In the mixing bowl, mix up ground beef, ground pork, minced garlic, water, chili flakes, and dried parsley. 2. Make the medium size meatballs from the mixture. 3. After this, heat up coconut oil in the instant pot on Sauté mode. 4. Put the meatballs in the hot coconut oil in one layer and cook them for 2 minutes from each side. 5. Then add beef broth and close the lid. 6. Cook the meatballs for 10 minutes on Manual mode (High Pressure). 7. Then make a quick pressure release and transfer the meatballs on the plate.

Mayo Chicken Celery

Prep time: 15 minutes | Cook time: 15 minutes | Serves 4

14 ounces (397 g) chicken breast, skinless, boneless
1 cup water
4 celery stalks
1 teaspoon salt
½ teaspoon onion powder
1 teaspoon mayonnaise

1. Combine all the ingredients except the mayo in the Instant Pot. 2. Secure the lid. Select the Manual mode and set the cooking time for 15 minutes at High Pressure. 3. Once cooking is complete, do a natural pressure release for 6 minutes, then release any remaining pressure. Carefully open the lid. 4. Remove the chicken and shred with two forks, then return to the Instant Pot. 5. Add the mayo and stir well. Serve immediately.

Broccoli Cheese Dip

Prep time: 5 minutes | Cook time: 10 minutes | Serves 6

4 tablespoons butter
½ medium onion, diced
1½ cups chopped broccoli
8 ounces (227 g) cream cheese
½ cup mayonnaise
½ cup chicken broth
1 cup shredded Cheddar cheese

1. Press the Sauté button and then press the Adjust button to set heat to Less. Add butter to Instant Pot. Add onion and sauté until softened, about 5 minutes. Press the Cancel button. 2. Add broccoli, cream cheese, mayo, and broth to pot. Press the Manual button and adjust time for 4 minutes. 3. When timer beeps, quick-release the pressure and stir in Cheddar. Serve warm.

Bok Choy Salad Boats with Shrimp

Prep time: 8 minutes | Cook time: 2 minutes | Serves 8

26 shrimp, cleaned and deveined
2 tablespoons fresh lemon juice
1 cup water
Sea salt and ground black pepper, to taste
4 ounces (113 g) feta cheese, crumbled
2 tomatoes, diced
⅓ cup olives, pitted and sliced
4 tablespoons olive oil
2 tablespoons apple cider vinegar
8 Bok choy leaves
2 tablespoons fresh basil leaves, snipped
2 tablespoons chopped fresh mint leaves

1. Toss the shrimp and lemon juice in the Instant Pot until well coated. Pour in the water. 2. Lock the lid. Select the Manual mode and set the cooking time for 2 minutes at Low Pressure. 3. When the timer beeps, perform a quick pressure release. Carefully remove the lid. 4. Season the shrimp with salt and pepper to taste, then let them cool completely. 5. Toss the shrimp with the feta cheese, tomatoes, olives, olive oil, and vinegar until well incorporated. 6. Divide the salad evenly onto each Bok choy leaf and place them on a serving plate. Scatter the basil and mint leaves on top and serve immediately.

Oregano Sausage Balls

Prep time: 10 minutes | Cook time: 16 minutes | Serves 10

15 ounces (425 g) ground pork sausage
1 teaspoon dried oregano
4 ounces (113 g) Mozzarella, shredded
1 cup coconut flour
1 garlic clove, grated
1 teaspoon coconut oil, melted

1. In the bowl mix up ground pork sausages, dried oregano, shredded Mozzarella, coconut flour, and garlic clove. 2. When the mixture is homogenous, make the balls. 3. After this, pour coconut oil in the instant pot. 4. Arrange the balls in the instant pot and cook them on Sauté mode for 8 minutes from each side.

Southern Boiled Peanuts

Prep time: 5 minutes | Cook time: 1 hour 20 minutes | Makes 8 cups

1 pound raw jumbo peanuts in the shell
3 tablespoons fine sea salt

1. Remove the inner pot from the Instant Pot and add the peanuts to it. Cover the peanuts with water and use your hands to agitate them, loosening any dirt. Drain the peanuts in a colander, rinse out the pot, and return the peanuts to it. Return the inner pot to the Instant Pot housing. 2. Add the salt and 9 cups water to the pot and stir to dissolve the salt. Select a salad plate just small enough to fit inside the pot and set it on top of the peanuts to weight them down, submerging them all in the water. 3. Secure the lid and set the Pressure Release to Sealing. Select the Steam setting and set the cooking time for 1 hour at low pressure. (The pot will take about 20 minutes to come up to pressure before the cooking program begins.) 4. When the cooking program ends, let the pressure release naturally (this will take about 1 hour). Open the pot and, wearing heat-resistant mitts, remove the inner pot from the housing. Let the peanuts cool to room temperature in the brine (this will take about 1½ hours). 5. Serve at room temperature or chilled. Transfer the peanuts with their brine to an airtight container and refrigerate for up to 1 week.

Blackberry Baked Brie

Prep time: 5 minutes | Cook time: 15 minutes | Serves 5

8-ounce round Brie	blackberry preserves
1 cup water	2 teaspoons chopped fresh
¼ cup sugar-free	mint

1. Slice a grid pattern into the top of the rind of the Brie with a knife. 2. In a 7-inch round baking dish, place the Brie, then cover the baking dish securely with foil. 3. Insert the trivet into the inner pot of the Instant Pot; pour in the water. 4. Make a foil sling and arrange it on top of the trivet. Place the baking dish on top of the trivet and foil sling. 5. Secure the lid to the locked position and turn the vent to sealing. 6. Press Manual and set the Instant Pot for 15 minutes on high pressure. 7. When cooking time is up, turn off the Instant Pot and do a quick release of the pressure. 8. When the valve has dropped, remove the lid, then remove the baking dish. 9. Remove the top rind of the Brie and top with the preserves. Sprinkle with the fresh mint.

Creamy Mashed Cauliflower

Prep time: 3 minutes | Cook time: 1 minute | Serves 4

1 head cauliflower, chopped into florets	3 tablespoons butter
1 cup water	2 tablespoons sour cream
1 clove garlic, finely minced	½ teaspoon salt
	¼ teaspoon pepper

1. Place cauliflower on steamer rack. Add water and steamer rack to Instant Pot. Press the Steam button and adjust time to 1 minute. When timer beeps, quick-release the pressure. 2. Place cooked cauliflower into food processor and add remaining ingredients. Blend until smooth and creamy. Serve warm.

Colby Cheese and Pepper Dip

Prep time: 5 minutes | Cook time: 5 minutes | Serves 8

1 tablespoon butter	2 garlic cloves, minced
2 red bell peppers, sliced	1 teaspoon red Aleppo
2 cups shredded Colby cheese	pepper flakes
1 cup cream cheese, room temperature	1 teaspoon sumac
1 cup chicken broth	Salt and ground black pepper, to taste

1. Set your Instant Pot to Sauté and melt the butter. 2. Add the bell peppers and sauté for about 2 minutes until just tender. 3. Add the remaining ingredients to the Instant Pot and gently stir to incorporate. 4. Lock the lid. Select the Manual mode and set the cooking time for 3 minutes at High Pressure. 5. When the timer beeps, perform a quick pressure release. Carefully remove the lid. 6. Allow to cool for 5 minutes and serve warm.

Cauliflower Cheese Balls

Prep time: 5 minutes | Cook time: 21 minutes | Serves 8

1 cup water	2 tablespoons butter
1 head cauliflower, broken into florets	2 tablespoons minced fresh chives
1 cup shredded Asiago cheese	1 garlic clove, minced
½ cup grated Parmesan cheese	½ teaspoon cayenne pepper
2 eggs, beaten	Coarse sea salt and white pepper, to taste

1. Pour the water into the Instant Pot and insert a steamer basket. Place the cauliflower in the basket. 2. Lock the lid. Select the Manual mode and set the cooking time for 3 minutes at High Pressure. 3. When the timer beeps, perform a quick pressure release. Carefully remove the lid. 4. Transfer the cauliflower to a food processor, along with the remaining ingredients. Pulse until everything is well combined. 5. Form the mixture into bite-sized balls and place them on a baking sheet. 6. Bake in the preheated oven at 400ºF (205ºC) for 18 minutes until golden brown. Flip the balls halfway through the cooking time. Cool for 5 minutes before serving.

Spinach and Artichoke Dip

Prep time: 5 minutes | Cook time: 4 minutes | Serves 11

8 ounces low-fat cream cheese	½ cup low-fat sour cream
10-ounce box frozen spinach	½ cup low-fat mayo
½ cup no-sodium chicken broth	3 cloves of garlic, minced
14-ounce can artichoke hearts, drained	1 teaspoon onion powder
	16 ounces reduced-fat shredded Parmesan cheese
	8 ounces reduced-fat shredded mozzarella

1. Put all ingredients in the inner pot of the Instant Pot, except the Parmesan cheese and the mozzarella cheese. 2. Secure the lid and set vent to sealing. Place on Manual high pressure for 4 minutes. 3. Do a quick release of steam. 4. Immediately stir in the cheeses.

Creole Pancetta and Cheese Balls

Prep time: 5 minutes | Cook time: 5 minutes | Serves 6

1 cup water	¼ cup mayonnaise
6 eggs	1 teaspoon Creole
4 slices pancetta, chopped	seasonings
⅓ cup grated Cheddar	Sea salt and ground black
cheese	pepper, to taste
¼ cup cream cheese	

1. Pour the water into the Instant Pot and insert a steamer basket. Place the eggs in the basket. 2. Lock the lid. Select the Manual mode and set the cooking time for 5 minutes at Low Pressure. 3. When the timer beeps, perform a quick pressure release. Carefully remove the lid. 4. Allow the eggs to cool for 10 to 15 minutes. Peel the eggs and chop them, then transfer to a bowl. Add the remaining ingredients and stir to combine well. 5. Shape the mixture into balls with your hands. Serve chilled.

Creamy Spinach Dip

Prep time: 13 minutes | Cook time: 5 minutes | Serves 11

8 ounces low-fat cream	½ teaspoon salt
cheese	¼ teaspoon black pepper
1 cup low-fat sour cream	10 ounces frozen spinach
½ cup finely chopped	12 ounces reduced-fat
onion	shredded Monterey Jack
½ cup no-sodium vegetable	cheese
broth	12 ounces reduced-fat
5 cloves garlic, minced	shredded Parmesan cheese

1. Add cream cheese, sour cream, onion, vegetable broth, garlic, salt, pepper, and spinach to the inner pot of the Instant Pot. 2. Secure lid, make sure vent is set to sealing, and set to the Bean/Chili setting on high pressure for 5 minutes. 3. When done, do a manual release. 4. Add the cheeses and mix well until creamy and well combined.

Candied Pecans

Prep time: 5 minutes | Cook time: 20 minutes | Serves 10

4 cups raw pecans	1 teaspoon cinnamon
1½ teaspoons liquid stevia	¼ teaspoon nutmeg
½ cup plus 1 tablespoon	⅛ teaspoon ground ginger
water, divided	⅛ teaspoon sea salt
1 teaspoon vanilla extract	

1. Place the raw pecans, liquid stevia, 1 tablespoon water, vanilla, cinnamon, nutmeg, ground ginger, and sea salt into the inner pot of the Instant Pot. 2. Press the Sauté button on the Instant Pot and sauté the pecans and other ingredients until the pecans are soft. 3. Pour in the ½ cup water and secure the lid to the locked position. Set the vent to sealing. 4. Press Manual and set the Instant Pot for 15 minutes. 5. Preheat the oven to 350°F. 6. When cooking time is up, turn off the Instant Pot, then do a quick release. 7. Spread the pecans onto a greased, lined baking sheet. 8. Bake the pecans for 5 minutes or less in the oven, checking on them frequently so they do not burn.

Cayenne Beef Bites

Prep time: 5 minutes | Cook time: 23 minutes | Serves 6

2 tablespoons olive oil	1 teaspoon cayenne pepper
1 pound (454 g) beef steak,	½ teaspoon dried marjoram
cut into cubes	Sea salt and ground black
1 cup beef bone broth	pepper, to taste
¼ cup dry white wine	

1. Set your Instant Pot to Sauté and heat the olive oil. 2. Add the beef and sauté for 2 to 3 minutes, stirring occasionally. 3. Add the remaining ingredients to the Instant Pot and combine well. 4. Lock the lid. Select the Manual mode and set the cooking time for 20 minutes at High Pressure. 5. When the timer beeps, perform a natural pressure release for 10 minutes, then release any remaining pressure. Carefully remove the lid. 6. Remove the beef from the Instant Pot to a platter and serve warm.

Lemon-Cheese Cauliflower Bites

Prep time: 5 minutes | Cook time: 8 minutes | Serves 6

1 cup water	2 tablespoons extra-virgin
1 pound (454 g)	olive oil
cauliflower, broken into	2 tablespoons lemon juice
florets	1 cup grated Cheddar
Sea salt and ground black	cheese
pepper, to taste	

1. Pour the water into the Instant Pot and insert a steamer basket. Place the cauliflower florets in the basket. 2. Lock the lid. Select the Manual mode and set the cooking time for 3 minutes at Low Pressure. 3. When the timer beeps, perform a quick pressure release. Carefully remove the lid. 4. Season the cauliflower with salt and pepper. Drizzle with olive oil and lemon juice. Sprinkle the grated cheese all over the cauliflower. 5. Press the Sauté button to heat the Instant Pot. Allow to cook for about 5 minutes, or until the cheese melts. Serve warm.

Brussels Sprouts with Aioli Sauce

Prep time: 5 minutes | Cook time: 7 minutes | Serves 4

1 tablespoon butter	¼ cup mayonnaise
½ cup chopped scallions	1 tablespoon fresh lemon
¾ pound (340 g) Brussels	juice
sprouts	1 garlic clove, minced
Aioli Sauce:	½ teaspoon Dijon mustard

1. Set your Instant Pot to Sauté and melt the butter. 2. Add the scallions and sauté for 2 minutes until softened. Add the Brussels sprouts and cook for another 1 minute. 3. Lock the lid. Select the Manual mode and set the cooking time for 4 minutes at High Pressure. 4. Meanwhile, whisk together all the ingredients for the Aioli sauce in a small bowl until well incorporated. 5. When the timer beeps, perform a quick pressure release. Carefully remove the lid. 6. Serve the Brussels sprouts with the Aioli sauce on the side.

Stuffed Jalapeños with Bacon

Prep time: 10 minutes | Cook time: 6 minutes | Serves 2

1 ounce (28 g) bacon, chopped, fried	cream
2 ounces (57 g) Cheddar cheese, shredded	1 teaspoon chopped green onions
1 tablespoon coconut	2 jalapeños, trimmed and seeded

1. Mix together the chopped bacon, cheese, coconut cream, and green onions in a mixing bowl and stir until well incorporated. 2. Stuff the jalapeños evenly with the bacon mixture. 3. Press the Sauté button to heat your Instant Pot. 4. Place the stuffed jalapeños in the Instant Pot and cook each side for 3 minutes until softened. 5. Transfer to a paper towel-lined plate and serve.

Asparagus with Creamy Dip

Prep time: 5 minutes | Cook time: 1 minute | Serves 6

1 cup water	2 tablespoons chopped
1½ pounds (680 g)	scallions
asparagus spears, trimmed	2 tablespoons fresh chervil
Dipping Sauce:	1 teaspoon minced garlic
½ cup mayonnaise	Salt, to taste
½ cup sour cream	

1. Pour the water into the Instant Pot and insert a steamer basket. Place the asparagus in the basket. 2. Lock the lid. Select the Manual mode and set the cooking time for 1 minute at High Pressure. 3. When the timer beeps, perform a quick pressure release. Carefully remove the lid. Transfer the asparagus to a plate. 4. Whisk together the remaining ingredients to make your dipping sauce. Serve the asparagus with the dipping sauce on the side.

Red Wine Mushrooms

Prep time: 5 minutes | Cook time: 15 minutes | Serves 2

8 ounces (227 g) sliced mushrooms	¼ teaspoon Worcestershire sauce
¼ cup dry red wine	Pinch of salt
2 tablespoons beef broth	Pinch of black pepper
½ teaspoon garlic powder	¼ teaspoon xanthan gum

1. Add the mushrooms, wine, broth, garlic powder, Worcestershire sauce, salt, and pepper to the pot. 2. Close the lid and seal the vent. Cook on High Pressure for 13 minutes. Quick release the steam. Press Cancel. 3. Turn the pot to Sauté mode. Add the xanthan gum and whisk until the juices have thickened, 1 to 2 minutes.

Curried Broccoli Skewers

Prep time: 15 minutes | Cook time: 1 minute | Serves 2

1 cup broccoli florets	cream
½ teaspoon curry paste	1 cup water, for cooking
2 tablespoons coconut	

1. In the shallow bowl mix up curry paste and coconut cream. 2. Then sprinkle the broccoli florets with curry paste mixture and string on the skewers. 3. Pour water and insert the steamer rack in the instant pot. 4. Place the broccoli skewers on the rack. Close and seal the lid. 5. Cook the meal on Manual mode (High Pressure) for 1 minute. 6. Make a quick pressure release.

Garlic Herb Butter

Prep time: 10 minutes | Cook time: 8 minutes | Serves 4

⅓ cup butter	½ teaspoon minced garlic
1 teaspoon dried parsley	¼ teaspoon dried thyme
1 tablespoon dried dill	

1. Preheat the instant pot on Sauté mode. 2. Then add butter and melt it. 3. Add dried parsley, dill, minced garlic, and thyme. Stir the butter mixture well. 4. Transfer it in the butter mold and refrigerate until it is solid.

Herbed Mushrooms

Prep time: 5 minutes | Cook time: 10 minutes | Serves 4

2 tablespoons butter	1 bay leaf
2 cloves garlic, minced	Sea salt, to taste
20 ounces (567 g) button mushrooms	½ teaspoon freshly ground black pepper
1 tablespoon coconut aminos	½ cup chicken broth
1 teaspoon dried rosemary	½ cup water
1 teaspoon dried basil	1 tablespoon roughly chopped fresh parsley
1 teaspoon dried sage	leaves, for garnish

1. Set your Instant Pot to Sauté and melt the butter. 2. Add the garlic and mushrooms and sauté for 3 to 4 minutes until the garlic is fragrant. 3. Add the remaining ingredients except the parsley to the Instant Pot and stir well. 4. Lock the lid. Select the Manual mode and set the cooking time for 5 minutes at High Pressure. 5. When the timer beeps, perform a quick pressure release. Carefully open the lid. 6. Remove the mushrooms from the pot to a platter. Serve garnished with the fresh parsley leaves.

Hummus with Chickpeas and Tahini Sauce

Prep time: 10 minutes | Cook time: 55 minutes | Makes 4 cups

4 cups water	3 tablespoons fresh lemon juice
1 cup dried chickpeas	
2½ teaspoons fine sea salt	1 garlic clove
½ cup tahini	¼ teaspoon ground cumin

1. Combine the water, chickpeas, and 1 teaspoon of the salt in the Instant Pot and stir to dissolve the salt. 2. Secure the lid and set the Pressure Release to Sealing. Select the Bean/Chili, Pressure Cook, or Manual setting and set the cooking time for 40 minutes at high pressure. (The pot will take about 15 minutes to come up to pressure before the cooking program begins.) 3. When the cooking program ends, let the pressure release naturally for 15 minutes, then move the Pressure Release to Venting to release any remaining steam. 4. Place a colander over a bowl. Open the pot and, wearing heat-resistant mitts, lift out the inner pot and drain the beans in the colander. Return the chickpeas to the inner pot and place it back in the Instant Pot housing on the Keep Warm setting. Reserve the cooking liquid. 5. In a blender or food processor, combine 1 cup of the cooking liquid, the tahini, lemon juice, garlic, cumin, and 1 teaspoon salt. Blend or process on high speed, stopping to scrape down the sides of the container as needed, for about 30 seconds, until smooth and a little fluffy. Scoop

out and set aside ½ cup of this sauce for the topping. 6. Set aside ½ cup of the chickpeas for the topping. Add the remaining chickpeas to the tahini sauce in the blender or food processor along with ½ cup of the cooking liquid and the remaining ½ teaspoon salt. Blend or process on high speed, stopping to scrape down the sides of the container as needed, for about 1 minute, until very smooth. 7. Transfer the hummus to a shallow serving bowl. Spoon the reserved tahini mixture over the top, then sprinkle on the reserved chickpeas. The hummus will keep in an airtight container in the refrigerator for up to 3 days. Serve at room temperature or chilled.

Creamed Onion Spinach

Prep time: 3 minutes | Cook time: 5 minutes | Serves 6

4 tablespoons butter	frozen spinach
¼ cup diced onion	½ cup chicken broth
8 ounces (227 g) cream cheese	1 cup shredded whole-milk Mozzarella cheese
1 (12 ounces / 340 g) bag	

1. Press the Sauté button and add butter. Once butter is melted, add onion to Instant Pot and sauté for 2 minutes or until onion begins to turn translucent. 2. Break cream cheese into pieces and add to Instant Pot. Press the Cancel button. Add frozen spinach and broth. Click lid closed. Press the Manual button and adjust time for 5 minutes. When timer beeps, quick-release the pressure and stir in shredded Mozzarella. If mixture is too watery, press the Sauté button and reduce for additional 5 minutes, stirring constantly.

Cheddar Cauliflower Rice

Prep time: 3 minutes | Cook time: 1 minute | Serves 4

1 head fresh cauliflower, chopped into florets	1 cup shredded sharp Cheddar cheese
1 cup water	½ teaspoon salt
3 tablespoons butter	¼ teaspoon pepper
1 tablespoon heavy cream	¼ teaspoon garlic powder

1. Place cauliflower in steamer basket. Pour water into Instant Pot and lower steamer rack into pot. Click lid closed. Press the Steam button and adjust time for 1 minute. When timer beeps, quick-release the pressure. 2. Remove steamer basket and place cauliflower in food processor. Pulse until cauliflower is broken into small pearls. Place cauliflower into large bowl, and add remaining ingredients. Gently fold until fully combined.

Zucchini and Cheese Tots

Prep time: 15 minutes | Cook time: 10 minutes | Serves 6

4 ounces (113 g) Parmesan, grated	1 zucchini, grated
4 ounces (113 g) Cheddar cheese, grated	1 egg, beaten
	1 teaspoon dried oregano
	1 tablespoon coconut oil

1. In the mixing bowl, mix up Parmesan, Cheddar cheese, zucchini, egg, and dried oregano. 2. Make the small tots with the help of the fingertips. 3. Then melt the coconut oil in the instant pot on Sauté mode. 4. Put the prepared zucchini tots in the hot coconut oil and cook them for 3 minutes from each side or until they are light brown. Cool the zucchini tots for 5 minutes.

Green Goddess White Bean Dip

Prep time: 1 minutes | Cook time: 45 minutes | Makes 3 cups

1 cup dried navy, great Northern, or cannellini beans	oil, plus 1 tablespoon
	¼ cup firmly packed fresh flat-leaf parsley leaves
4 cups water	1 bunch chives, chopped
2 teaspoons fine sea salt	Leaves from 2 tarragon sprigs
3 tablespoons fresh lemon juice	Freshly ground black pepper
¼ cup extra-virgin olive	

1. Combine the beans, water, and 1 teaspoon of the salt in the Instant Pot and stir to dissolve the salt. 2. Secure the lid and set the Pressure Release to Sealing. Select the Bean/Chili, Pressure Cook, or Manual setting and set the cooking time for 30 minutes at high pressure if using navy or Great Northern beans or 40 minutes at high pressure if using cannellini beans. (The pot will take about 15 minutes to come up to pressure before the cooking program begins.) 3. When the cooking program ends, let the pressure release naturally for 15 minutes, then move the Pressure Release to Venting to release any remaining steam. Open the pot and scoop out and reserve ½ cup of the cooking liquid. Wearing heat-resistant mitts, lift out the inner pot and drain the beans in a colander. 4. In a food processor or blender, combine the beans, ½ cup cooking liquid, lemon juice, ¼ cup olive oil, ½ teaspoon parsley, chives, tarragon, remaining 1 teaspoon salt, and ½ teaspoon pepper. Process or blend on medium speed, stopping to scrape down the sides of the container as needed, for about 1 minute, until the mixture is smooth. 5. Transfer the dip to a serving bowl. Drizzle with the remaining 1 tablespoon olive oil and sprinkle with a few grinds of pepper. The dip will keep in an airtight container in the refrigerator for up to 1 week. Serve at room temperature or chilled.

Ground Turkey Lettuce Cups

Prep time: 5 minutes | Cook time: 30 minutes | Serves 8

3 tablespoons water	1 yellow onion, diced
2 tablespoons soy sauce, tamari, or coconut aminos	2 pounds 93 percent lean ground turkey
3 tablespoons fresh lime juice	½ teaspoon fine sea salt
2 teaspoons Sriracha, plus more for serving	Two 8-ounce cans sliced water chestnuts, drained and chopped
2 tablespoons cold-pressed avocado oil	1 tablespoon cornstarch
2 teaspoons toasted sesame oil	2 hearts romaine lettuce or 2 heads butter lettuce, leaves separated
4 garlic cloves, minced	½ cup roasted cashews (whole or halves and pieces), chopped
1-inch piece fresh ginger, peeled and minced	1 cup loosely packed fresh cilantro leaves
2 carrots, diced	
2 celery stalks, diced	

1. In a small bowl, combine the water, soy sauce, 2 tablespoons of the lime juice, and the Sriracha and mix well. Set aside. 2. Select the Sauté setting on the Instant Pot and heat the avocado oil, sesame oil, garlic, and ginger for 2 minutes, until the garlic is bubbling but not browned. Add the carrots, celery, and onion and sauté for about 3 minutes, until the onion begins to soften. 3. Add the turkey and salt and sauté, using a wooden spoon or spatula to break up the meat as it cooks, for about 5 minutes, until cooked through and no streaks of pink remain. Add the water chestnuts and soy sauce mixture and stir to combine, working quickly so not too much steam escapes. 4. Secure the lid and set the Pressure Release to Sealing. Press the Cancel button to reset the cooking program, then select the Pressure Cook or Manual setting and set the cooking time for 5 minutes at high pressure. (The pot will take about 10 minutes to come up to pressure before the cooking program begins.) 5. When the cooking program ends, perform a quick pressure release by moving the Pressure Release to Venting, or let the pressure release naturally. Open the pot. 6. In a small bowl, stir together the remaining 1 tablespoon lime juice and the cornstarch, add the mixture to the pot, and stir to combine. Press the Cancel button to reset the cooking program, then select the Sauté setting. Let the mixture come to a boil and thicken, stirring often, for about 2 minutes, then press the Cancel button to turn off the pot. 7. Spoon the turkey mixture onto the lettuce leaves and sprinkle the cashews and cilantro on top. Serve right away, with additional Sriracha at the table.

7-Layer Dip

Prep time: 10 minutes | Cook time: 35 minutes | Serves 6

Cashew Sour Cream
1 cup raw whole cashews, soaked in water to cover for 1 to 2 hours and then drained
½ cup avocado oil
½ cup water
¼ cup fresh lemon juice
2 tablespoons nutritional yeast
1 teaspoon fine sea salt
Beans
½ cup dried black beans
2 cups water
½ teaspoon fine sea salt

½ teaspoon chili powder
¼ teaspoon garlic powder
½ cup grape or cherry tomatoes, halved
1 avocado, diced
¼ cup chopped yellow onion
1 jalapeño chile, sliced
2 tablespoons chopped cilantro
6 ounces baked corn tortilla chips
1 English cucumber, sliced
2 carrots, sliced
6 celery stalks, cut into sticks

1. To make the cashew sour cream: In a blender, combine the cashews, oil, water, lemon juice, nutritional yeast, and salt. Blend on high speed, stopping to scrape down the sides of the container as needed, for about 2 minutes, until very smooth. (The sour cream can be made in advance and stored in an airtight container in the refrigerator for up to 5 days.) 2. To make the beans: Pour 1 cup water into the Instant Pot. In a 1½-quart stainless-steel bowl, combine the beans, the 2 cups water, and salt and stir to dissolve the salt. Place the bowl on a long-handled silicone steam rack, then, holding the handles of the steam rack, lower it into the Instant Pot. (If you don't have the long-handled rack, use the wire metal steam rack and a homemade sling) 3. Secure the lid and set the Pressure Release to Sealing. Select the Bean/Chili, Pressure Cook, or Manual setting and set the cooking time for 25 minutes at high pressure. (The pot will take about 10 minutes to come up to pressure before the cooking program begins.) 4. When the cooking program ends, let the pressure release naturally for at least 20 minutes, then move the Pressure Release to Venting to release any remaining steam. 5. Place a colander over a bowl. Open the pot and, wearing heat-resistant mitts, lift out the inner pot and drain the beans in the colander. Transfer the liquid captured in the bowl to a measuring cup, and pour the beans into the bowl. Add ¼ cup of the cooking liquid to the beans and, using a potato masher or fork, mash the beans to your desired consistency, adding more cooking liquid as needed. Stir in the chili powder and garlic powder. 6. Using a rubber spatula, spread the black beans in an even layer in a clear-glass serving dish. Spread the cashew sour cream in an even layer on top of the beans. Add layers of the tomatoes, avocado, onion, jalapeño, and cilantro. (At this point, you can cover and refrigerate the assembled dip for up to 1 day.) Serve accompanied with the tortilla chips, cucumber, carrots, and celery on the side.

Chapter 8
Desserts

Cocoa Cookies

Prep time: 15 minutes | Cook time: 25 minutes | Serves 4

½ cup coconut flour	1 teaspoon apple cider
3 tablespoons cream cheese	vinegar
1 teaspoon cocoa powder	1 tablespoon butter
1 tablespoon erythritol	1 cup water, for cooking
¼ teaspoon baking powder	

1. Make the dough: Mix up coconut flour, cream cheese, cocoa powder, erythritol, baking powder, apple cider vinegar, and butter. Knead the dough, 2. Then transfer the dough in the baking pan and flatten it in the shape of a cookie. 3. Pour water and insert the steamer rack in the instant pot. 4. Put the pan with a cookie in the instant pot. Close and seal the lid. 5. Cook the cookie on Manual (High Pressure) for 25 minutes. Make a quick pressure release. Cool the cookie well.

Caramelized Pumpkin Cheesecake

Prep time: 15 minutes | Cook time: 45 minutes | Serves 8

Crust:

1½ cups almond flour	erythritol
4 tablespoons butter, melted	½ teaspoon ground cinnamon
1 tablespoon Swerve	Cooking spray
1 tablespoon granulated	

Filling:

16 ounces (454 g) cream cheese, softened	3 tablespoons Swerve
	1 teaspoon vanilla extract
½ cup granulated erythritol	¼ teaspoon pumpkin pie spice
2 eggs	
¼ cup pumpkin purée	1½ cups water

1. To make the crust: In a medium bowl, combine the almond flour, butter, Swerve, erythritol, and cinnamon. Use a fork to press it all together. 2. Spray the pan with cooking spray and line the bottom with parchment paper. 3. Press the crust evenly into the pan. Work the crust up the sides of the pan, about halfway from the top, and make sure there are no bare spots on the bottom. 4. Place the crust in the freezer for 20 minutes while you make the filling. 5. To make the filling: In a large bowl using a hand mixer on medium speed, combine the cream cheese and erythritol. Beat until the cream cheese is light and fluffy, 2 to 3 minutes. 6. Add the eggs, pumpkin purée, Swerve, vanilla, and pumpkin pie spice. Beat until well combined. 7. Remove the crust from the freezer and pour in the filling. Cover the pan with aluminum foil and place

it on the trivet. 8. Add the water to the pot and carefully lower the trivet into the pot. 9. Set the lid in place. Select the Manual mode and set the cooking time for 45 minutes on High Pressure. When the timer goes off, do a quick pressure release. Carefully open the lid. 10. Remove the trivet and cheesecake from the pot. Remove the foil from the pan. The center of the cheesecake should still be slightly jiggly. 11. Let the cheesecake cool for 30 minutes on the counter before placing it in the refrigerator to set. Leave the cheesecake in the refrigerator for at least 6 hours before removing the sides and serving.

Almond Pie with Coconut

Prep time: 5 minutes | Cook time: 41 minutes | Serves 8

1 cup almond flour	softened
½ cup coconut milk	1 tablespoon Truvia
1 teaspoon vanilla extract	¼ cup shredded coconut
2 tablespoons butter,	1 cup water

1. In the mixing bowl, mix up almond flour, coconut milk, vanilla extract, butter, Truvia, and shredded coconut. 2. When the mixture is smooth, transfer it in the baking pan and flatten. 3. Pour water and insert the trivet in the instant pot. 4. Put the baking pan with cake on the trivet. 5. Lock the lid. Select the Manual mode and set the cooking time for 41 minutes on High Pressure. Once the timer goes off, perform a natural pressure release for 10 minutes, then release any remaining pressure. Carefully open the lid. 6. Serve immediately.

Chocolate Fondue

Prep time: 5 minutes | Cook time: 2 minutes | Serves 4

2 ounces (57 g) unsweetened baking chocolate, finely chopped, divided	Fine sea salt
	1 cup cold water
	Special Equipment:
	Set of fondue forks or
1 cup heavy cream, divided	wooden skewers
⅓ cup Swerve, divided	

1. Divide the chocolate, cream, and sweetener evenly among four ramekins. Add a pinch of salt to each one and stir well. Cover the ramekins with aluminum foil. 2. Place a trivet in the bottom of your Instant Pot and pour in the water. Place the ramekins on the trivet. 3. Lock the lid. Select the Manual mode and set the cooking time for 2 minutes at High Pressure. 4. When the timer beeps, perform a natural pressure release for 10 minutes. Carefully remove the lid. 5. Use tongs to remove the ramekins from the pot. Use a fork to stir the fondue until smooth. 6. Use immediately.

Glazed Pumpkin Bundt Cake

Prep time: 7 minutes | Cook time: 35 minutes | Serves 12

Cake:

3 cups blanched almond flour	¼ teaspoon ground cloves
1 teaspoon baking soda	6 large eggs
½ teaspoon fine sea salt	2 cups pumpkin purée
2 teaspoons ground cinnamon	1 cup Swerve
1 teaspoon ground nutmeg	¼ cup (½ stick) unsalted butter (or coconut oil for dairy-free), softened
1 teaspoon ginger powder	

Glaze:

1 cup (2 sticks) unsalted butter (or coconut oil for	dairy-free), melted
	½ cup Swerve

1. In a large bowl, stir together the almond flour, baking soda, salt, and spices. In another large bowl, add the eggs, pumpkin, sweetener, and butter and stir until smooth. Pour the wet ingredients into the dry ingredients and stir well. 2. Grease a 6-cup Bundt pan. Pour the batter into the prepared pan and cover with a paper towel and then with aluminum foil. 3. Place a trivet in the bottom of the Instant Pot and pour in 2 cups of cold water. Place the Bundt pan on the trivet. 4. Lock the lid. Select the Manual mode and set the cooking time for 35 minutes at High Pressure. 5. When the timer beeps, use a natural pressure release for 10 minutes. Carefully remove the lid. 6. Let the cake cool in the pot for 10 minutes before removing. 7. While the cake is cooling, make the glaze: In a small bowl, mix the butter and sweetener together. Spoon the glaze over the warm cake. 8. Allow to cool for 5 minutes before slicing and serving.

Vanilla Crème Brûlée

Prep time: 7 minutes | Cook time: 9 minutes | Serves 4

1 cup heavy cream (or full-fat coconut milk for dairy-free)	vanilla bean (about 8 inches long), or 1 teaspoon vanilla extract
2 large egg yolks	1 cup cold water
2 tablespoons Swerve, or more to taste	4 teaspoons Swerve, for topping
Seeds scraped from ½	

1. Heat the cream in a pan over medium-high heat until hot, about 2 minutes. 2. Place the egg yolks, Swerve, and vanilla seeds in a blender and blend until smooth. 3. While the blender is running, slowly pour in the hot cream. Taste and adjust the sweetness to your liking. 4. Scoop the mixture into four ramekins with a spatula. Cover the ramekins with aluminum foil. 5. Add the water to the Instant Pot and insert a trivet. Place the ramekins on the trivet. 6. Lock the lid. Select the Manual mode and set the cooking time for 7 minutes at High Pressure. 7. When the timer beeps, perform a quick pressure release. Carefully remove the lid. 8. Keep the ramekins covered with the foil and place in the refrigerator for about 2 hours until completely chilled. 9. Sprinkle 1 teaspoon of Swerve on top of each crème brûlée. Use the oven broiler to melt the sweetener. 10. Allow the topping to cool in the fridge for 5 minutes before serving.

Egg Custard Tarts

Prep time: 10 minutes | Cook time: 20 minutes | Serves 2

¼ cup almond flour	1 tablespoon erythritol
1 tablespoon coconut oil	1 teaspoon vanilla extract
2 egg yolks	1 cup water, for cooking
¼ cup coconut milk	

1. Make the dough: Mix up almond flour and coconut oil. 2. Then place the dough into 2 mini tart molds and flatten well in the shape of cups. 3. Pour water in the instant pot. Insert the steamer rack. 4. Place the tart mold in the instant pot. Close and seal the lid. 5. Cook them for 3 minutes on Manual mode (High Pressure). Make a quick pressure release. 6. Then whisk together vanilla extract, erythritol, coconut milk, and egg yolks. 7. Pour the liquid in the tart molds and close the lid. 8. Cook the dessert for 7 minutes on Manual mode (High Pressure). 9. Then allow the natural pressure release for 10 minutes more.

Vanilla Poppy Seed Cake

Prep time: 10 minutes | Cook time: 25 minutes | Serves 6

1 cup almond flour	¼ cup heavy cream
2 eggs	⅛ cup sour cream
½ cup erythritol	½ teaspoon baking powder
2 teaspoons vanilla extract	1 cup water
1 teaspoon lemon extract	¼ cup powdered erythritol, for garnish
1 tablespoon poppy seeds	
4 tablespoons melted butter	

1. In large bowl, mix almond flour, eggs, erythritol, vanilla, lemon, and poppy seeds. 2. Add butter, heavy cream, sour cream, and baking powder. 3. Pour into 7-inch round cake pan. Cover with foil. 4. Pour water into Instant Pot and place steam rack in bottom. Place baking pan on steam rack and click lid closed. Press the Cake button and press the Adjust button to set heat to Less. Set time for 25 minutes. 5. When timer beeps, allow a 15-minute natural release, then quick-release the remaining pressure. Let cool completely. Sprinkle with powdered erythritol for serving.

Spiced Pear Applesauce

Prep time: 15 minutes | Cook time: 5 minutes | Makes: 3½ cups

1 pound pears, peeled, cored, and sliced	or cinnamon
	Pinch kosher salt
2 teaspoons apple pie spice	Juice of ½ small lemon

1. In the electric pressure cooker, combine the apples, pears, apple pie spice, salt, lemon juice, and ¼ cup of water. 2. Close and lock the lid of the pressure cooker. Set the valve to sealing. 3. Cook on high pressure for 5 minutes. 4. When the cooking is complete, hit Cancel and let the pressure release naturally. 5. Once the pin drops, unlock and remove the lid. 6. Mash the apples and pears with a potato masher to the consistency you like. 7. Serve warm, or cool to room temperature and refrigerate.

Crustless Key Lime Cheesecake

Prep time: 15 minutes | Cook time: 35 minutes | Serves 8

Nonstick cooking spray	Joe's Famous Key West Lime Juice)
16 ounces light cream cheese (Neufchâtel), softened	½ teaspoon vanilla extract
⅔ cup granulated erythritol sweetener	¼ cup plain Greek yogurt
	1 teaspoon grated lime zest
	2 large eggs
¼ cup unsweetened Key lime juice (I like Nellie &	Whipped cream, for garnish (optional)

1. Spray a 7-inch springform pan with nonstick cooking spray. Line the bottom and partway up the sides of the pan with foil. 2. Put the cream cheese in a large bowl. Use an electric mixer to whip the cream cheese until smooth, about 2 minutes. Add the erythritol, lime juice, vanilla, yogurt, and zest, and blend until smooth. Stop the mixer and scrape down the sides of the bowl with a rubber spatula. With the mixer on low speed, add the eggs, one at a time, blending until just mixed. (Don't overbeat the eggs.) 3. Pour the mixture into the prepared pan. Drape a paper towel over the top of the pan, not touching the cream cheese mixture, and tightly wrap the top of the pan in foil. (Your goal here is to keep out as much moisture as possible.) 4. Pour 1 cup of water into the electric pressure cooker. 5. Place the foil-covered pan onto the wire rack and carefully lower it into the pot. 6. Close and lock the lid of the pressure cooker. Set the valve to sealing. 7. Cook on high pressure for 35 minutes. 8. When the cooking is complete, hit Cancel. Allow the pressure to release naturally for 20 minutes, then quick release any remaining pressure. 9. Once the pin drops, unlock and remove the lid.

10. Using the handles of the wire rack, carefully transfer the pan to a cooling rack. Cool to room temperature, then refrigerate for at least 3 hours. 11. When ready to serve, run a thin rubber spatula around the rim of the cheesecake to loosen it, then remove the ring. 12. Slice into wedges and serve with whipped cream (if using).

Apple Crunch

Prep time: 13 minutes | Cook time: 2 minutes | Serves 4

3 apples, peeled, cored, and sliced (about 1½ pounds)	or ground cinnamon
	¼ cup unsweetened apple juice, apple cider, or water
1 teaspoon pure maple syrup	¼ cup low-sugar granola
1 teaspoon apple pie spice	

1. In the electric pressure cooker, combine the apples, maple syrup, apple pie spice, and apple juice. 2. Close and lock the lid of the pressure cooker. Set the valve to sealing. 3. Cook on high pressure for 2 minutes. 4. When the cooking is complete, hit Cancel and quick release the pressure. 5. Once the pin drops, unlock and remove the lid. 6. Spoon the apples into 4 serving bowls and sprinkle each with 1 tablespoon of granola.

Chocolate Macadamia Bark

Prep time: 5 minutes | Cook time: 20 minutes | Serves 20

16 ounces (454 g) raw dark chocolate	nuts
	1 tablespoon almond butter
3 tablespoons raw coconut butter	½ teaspoon salt
	⅓ cup Swerve, or more to taste
2 tablespoons coconut oil	
2 cups chopped macadamia	

1. In a large bowl, mix together the chocolate, coconut butter, coconut oil, macadamia nuts, almond butter, salt, and Swerve. Combine them very thoroughly, until a perfectly even mixture is obtained. 2. Pour 1 cup of filtered water into the Instant Pot, and insert the trivet. Transfer the mixture from the bowl into a well-greased, Instant Pot-friendly dish. 3. Place the dish onto the trivet, and cover loosely with aluminum foil. Close the lid, set the pressure release to Sealing, and select Manual. Set the Instant Pot to 20 minutes on High Pressure, and let cook. 4. Once cooked, let the pressure naturally disperse from the Instant Pot for about 10 minutes, then carefully switch the pressure release to Venting. 5. Open the Instant Pot and remove the dish. Cool in the refrigerator until set. Break into pieces, serve, and enjoy! Store remaining bark in the refrigerator or freezer.

Espresso Cheesecake with Raspberries

Prep time: 5 minutes | Cook time: 35 minutes | Serves 8

1 cup blanched almond flour	16 ounces (454 g) cream cheese
½ cup plus 2 tablespoons Swerve	1 cup water
3 tablespoons espresso powder, divided	6 ounces (170 g) dark chocolate (at least 80% cacao)
2 tablespoons butter	8 ounces (227 g) full-fat heavy whipping cream
1 egg	2 cups raspberries
½ cup full-fat heavy cream	

1. In a small mixing bowl, combine the almond flour, 2 tablespoons of Swerve, 1 tablespoon of espresso powder and the butter. 2. Line the bottom of a springform pan with parchment paper. Press the almond flour dough flat on the bottom and about 1 inch on the sides. Set aside. 3. In a food processor, mix the egg, heavy cream, cream cheese, remaining Swerve and remaining espresso powder until smooth. 4. Pour the cream cheese mixture into the springform pan. Loosely cover with aluminum foil. 5. Put the water in the Instant Pot and place the trivet inside. 6. Close the lid. Select Manual button and set the timer for 35 minutes on High pressure. 7. When timer beeps, use a natural pressure release for 15 minutes, then release any remaining pressure. Open the lid. 8. Remove the springform pan and place it on a cooling rack for 2 to 3 hours or until it reaches room temperature. Refrigerate overnight. 9. Melt the chocolate and heavy whipping cream in the double boiler. Cool for 15 minutes and drizzle on top of the cheesecake, allowing the chocolate to drip down the sides. 10. Add the raspberries on top of the cheesecake before serving.

Lemon Vanilla Cheesecake

Prep time: 15 minutes | Cook time: 20 minutes | Serves 6

2 teaspoons freshly squeezed lemon juice	Swerve
2 teaspoons vanilla extract or almond extract	8 ounces (227 g) cream cheese, at room temperature
½ cup sour cream, divided, at room temperature	2 eggs, at room temperature
½ cup plus 2 teaspoons	

1. Pour 2 cups of water into the inner cooking pot of the Instant Pot, then place a trivet (preferably with handles) in the pot. Line the sides of a 6-inch springform pan with parchment paper. 2. In a food processor, put the lemon juice, vanilla, ¼ cup of sour cream, ½ cup of Swerve, and the cream cheese. 3. Gently but thoroughly blend all the ingredients, scraping down the sides of the bowl as needed. 4. Add the eggs and blend only as long as you need to in order to get them well incorporated, 20 to 30 seconds. Your mixture will be pourable by now. 5. Pour the mixture into the prepared pan. Cover the pan with aluminum foil and place on the trivet. (If your trivet doesn't have handles, you may wish to use a foil sling to make removing the pan easier.) 6. Lock the lid into place. Select Manual and adjust the pressure to High. Cook for 20 minutes. When the cooking is complete, let the pressure release naturally. Unlock the lid. 7. Meanwhile, in a small bowl, mix together the remaining ¼ cup of sour cream and 2 teaspoons of Swerve for the topping. 8. Take out the cheesecake and remove the foil. Spread the topping over the top. Doing this while the cheesecake is still hot helps melt the topping into the cheesecake. 9. Put the cheesecake in the refrigerator and leave it alone. Seriously. Leave it alone and let it chill for at least 6 to 8 hours. It won't taste right hot. 10. When you're ready to serve, open the sides of the pan and peel off the parchment paper. Slice and serve.

Southern Almond Pie

Prep time: 10 minutes | Cook time: 35 minutes | Serves 12

2 cups almond flour	1 egg
1½ cups powdered erythritol	1 teaspoon vanilla extract
1 teaspoon baking powder	Cooking spray
Pinch of salt	1½ teaspoons ground cinnamon
½ cup sour cream	1½ teaspoons Swerve
4 tablespoons butter, melted	1 cup water

1. In a large bowl, whisk together the almond flour, powdered erythritol, baking powder, and salt. 2. Add the sour cream, butter, egg, and vanilla and whisk until well combined. The batter will be very thick, almost like cookie dough. 3. Grease the baking dish with cooking spray. Line with parchment paper, if desired. 4. Transfer the batter to the dish and level with an offset spatula. 5. In a small bowl, combine the cinnamon and Swerve. Sprinkle over the top of the batter. 6. Cover the dish tightly with aluminum foil. Add the water to the pot. Set the dish on the trivet and carefully lower it into the pot. 7. Set the lid in place. Select the Manual mode and set the cooking time for 35 minutes on High Pressure. When the timer goes off, do a quick pressure release. Carefully open the lid. 8. Remove the trivet and pie from the pot. Remove the foil from the pan. The pie should be set but soft, and the top should be slightly cracked. 9. Cool completely before cutting.

Hearty Crème Brûlée

Prep time: 5 minutes | Cook time: 30 minutes | Serves 4

5 egg yolks	1½ cups heavy cream
5 tablespoons powdered erythritol	2 teaspoons vanilla extract
	2 cups water

1. In a small bowl, use a fork to break up the egg yolks. Stir in the erythritol. 2. Pour the cream into a small saucepan over medium-low heat and let it warm up for 3 to 4 minutes. Remove the saucepan from the heat. 3. Temper the egg yolks by slowly adding a small spoonful of the warm cream, keep whisking. Do this three times to make sure the egg yolks are fully tempered. 4. Slowly add the tempered eggs to the cream, whisking the whole time. Add the vanilla and whisk again. 5. Pour the cream mixture into the ramekins. Each ramekin should have ½ cup liquid. Cover each with aluminum foil. 6. Place the trivet inside the Instant Pot. Add the water. Carefully place the ramekins on top of the trivet. 7. Close the lid. Select Manual mode and set cooking time for 11 minutes on High Pressure. 8. When timer beeps, use a natural release for 15 minutes, then release any remaining pressure. Open the lid. 9. Carefully remove a ramekin from the pot. Remove the foil and check for doneness. The custard should be mostly set with a slightly jiggly center. 10. Place all the ramekins in the fridge for 2 hours to chill and set. Serve chilled.

Pumpkin Pie Spice Pots De Crème

Prep time: 5 minutes | Cook time: 7 minutes | Serves 4

2 cups heavy cream (or full-fat coconut milk for dairy-free)	2 teaspoons pumpkin pie spice
4 large egg yolks	1 teaspoon vanilla extract
¼ cup Swerve, or more to taste	Pinch of fine sea salt
	1 cup cold water

1. Heat the cream in a pan over medium-high heat until hot, about 2 minutes. 2. Place the remaining ingredients except the water in a medium bowl and stir until smooth. 3. Slowly pour in the hot cream while stirring. Taste and adjust the sweetness to your liking. Scoop the mixture into four ramekins with a spatula. Cover the ramekins with aluminum foil. 4. Place a trivet in the Instant Pot and pour in the water. Place the ramekins on the trivet. 5. Lock the lid. Select the Manual mode and set the cooking time for 5 minutes at High Pressure. 6. When the timer beeps, use a quick pressure release. Carefully remove the lid.

7. Remove the foil and set the foil aside. Let the pots de crème cool for 15 minutes. Cover the ramekins with the foil again and place in the refrigerator to chill completely, about 2 hours. 8. Serve.

Blackberry Crisp

Prep time: 5 minutes | Cook time: 5 minutes | Serves 1

10 blackberries	¼ cup chopped pecans
½ teaspoon vanilla extract	3 teaspoons almond flour
2 tablespoons powdered erythritol	½ teaspoon cinnamon
⅛ teaspoon xanthan gum	2 teaspoons powdered erythritol
1 tablespoon butter	1 cup water

1. Place blackberries, vanilla, erythritol, and xanthan gum in 4-inch ramekin. Stir gently to coat blackberries. 2. In small bowl, mix remaining ingredients. Sprinkle over blackberries and cover with foil. Press the Manual button and set time for 4 minutes. When timer beeps, quick-release the pressure. Serve warm. Feel free to add scoop of whipped cream on top.

Cocoa Custard

Prep time: 5 minutes | Cook time: 7 minutes | Serves 4

2 cups heavy cream (or full-fat coconut milk for dairy-free)	teaspoon unsweetened cocoa powder, or more to taste
4 large egg yolks	½ teaspoon almond extract
¼ cup Swerve, or more to taste	Pinch of fine sea salt
1 tablespoon plus 1	1 cup cold water

1. Heat the cream in a pan over medium-high heat until hot, about 2 minutes. 2. Place the remaining ingredients except the water in a blender and blend until smooth. 3. While the blender is running, slowly pour in the hot cream. Taste and adjust the sweetness to your liking. Add more cocoa powder, if desired. 4. Scoop the custard mixture into four ramekins with a spatula. Cover the ramekins with aluminum foil. 5. Place a trivet in the Instant Pot and pour in the water. Place the ramekins on the trivet. 6. Lock the lid. Select the Manual mode and set the cooking time for 5 minutes at High Pressure. 7. When the timer beeps, use a quick pressure release. Carefully remove the lid. 8. Remove the foil and set the foil aside. Let the custard cool for 15 minutes. Cover the ramekins with the foil again and place in the refrigerator to chill completely, about 2 hours. 9. Serve.

Cinnamon Roll Cheesecake

Prep time: 15 minutes | Cook time: 35 minutes | Serves 12

Crust:

3½ tablespoons unsalted butter or coconut oil	⅓ cup Swerve
1½ ounces (43 g) unsweetened baking chocolate, chopped	2 teaspoons ground cinnamon
	1 teaspoon vanilla extract
1 large egg, beaten	¼ teaspoon fine sea salt

Filling:

4 (8 ounces / 227 g) packages cream cheese, softened	6 tablespoons (¾ stick) unsalted butter (or butter flavored coconut oil for dairy-free)
¾ cup Swerve	½ cup Swerve
½ cup unsweetened almond milk (or hemp milk for nut-free)	Seeds scraped from ½ vanilla bean (about 8 inches long), or 1 teaspoon vanilla extract
1 teaspoon vanilla extract	
¼ teaspoon almond extract (omit for nut-free)	
	1 tablespoon ground cinnamon
¼ teaspoon fine sea salt	¼ teaspoon fine sea salt
3 large eggs	1 cup cold water
Cinnamon Swirl:	

1. Line a baking pan with two layers of aluminum foil. 2. Make the crust: Melt the butter in a pan over medium-low heat. Slowly add the chocolate and stir until melted. Stir in the egg, sweetener, cinnamon, vanilla extract, and salt. 3. Transfer the crust mixture to the prepared baking pan, spreading it with your hands to cover the bottom completely. 4. Make the filling: In the bowl of a stand mixer, add the cream cheese, sweetener, milk, extracts, and salt and mix until well blended. Add the eggs, one at a time, mixing on low speed after each addition just until blended. Then blend until the filling is smooth. Pour half of the filling over the crust. 5. Make the cinnamon swirl: Heat the butter over high heat in a pan until the butter froths and brown flecks appear, stirring occasionally. Stir in the sweetener, vanilla seeds, cinnamon, and salt. Remove from the heat and allow to cool slightly. 6. Spoon half of the cinnamon swirl on top of the cheesecake filling in the baking pan. Use a knife to cut the cinnamon swirl through the filling several times for a marbled effect. Top with the rest of the cheesecake filling and cinnamon swirl. Cut the cinnamon swirl through the cheesecake filling again several times. 7. Place a trivet in the bottom of the Instant Pot and pour in the water. Use a foil sling to lower the baking pan onto the trivet. Cover the cheesecake with 3 large sheets of paper towel to ensure that condensation doesn't leak onto it. Tuck in the sides of the sling. 8. Lock the lid. Select the Manual mode and set the cooking time for 26 minutes at High Pressure. 9. When the timer beeps, use a natural pressure release for 10 minutes. Carefully remove the lid. 10. Use the foil sling to lift the pan out of the Instant Pot. 11. Let the cheesecake cool, then place in the refrigerator for 4 hours to chill and set completely before slicing and serving.

Espresso Cream

Prep time: 10 minutes | Cook time: 9 minutes | Serves 4

1 cup heavy cream	¼ cup low-carb chocolate chips
½ teaspoon espresso powder	½ cup powdered erythritol
½ teaspoon vanilla extract	3 egg yolks
2 teaspoons unsweetened cocoa powder	1 cup water

1. Press the Sauté button and add heavy cream, espresso powder, vanilla, and cocoa powder. Bring mixture to boil and add chocolate chips. Press the Cancel button. Stir quickly until chocolate chips are completely melted. 2. In medium bowl, whisk erythritol and egg yolks. Fold mixture into Instant Pot chocolate mix. Ladle into four (4-inch) ramekins. 3. Rinse inner pot and replace. Pour in 1 cup of water and place steam rack on bottom of pot. Cover ramekins with foil and carefully place on top of steam rack. Click lid closed. 4. Press the Manual button and adjust time for 9 minutes. Allow a full natural release. When the pressure indicator drops, carefully remove ramekins and allow to completely cool, then refrigerate. Serve chilled with whipped topping.

Goat Cheese–Stuffed Pears

Prep time: 6 minutes | Cook time: 2 minutes | Serves 4

2 ounces goat cheese, at room temperature	2 ripe, firm pears, halved lengthwise and cored
2 teaspoons pure maple syrup	2 tablespoons chopped pistachios, toasted

1. Pour 1 cup of water into the electric pressure cooker and insert a wire rack or trivet. 2. In a small bowl, combine the goat cheese and maple syrup. 3. Spoon the goat cheese mixture into the cored pear halves. Place the pears on the rack inside the pot, cut-side up. 4. Close and lock the lid of the pressure cooker. Set the valve to sealing. 5. Cook on high pressure for 2 minutes. 6. When the cooking is complete, hit Cancel and quick release the pressure. 7. Once the pin drops, unlock and remove the lid. 8. Using tongs, carefully transfer the pears to serving plates. 9. Sprinkle with pistachios and serve immediately.

Pumpkin Pie Pudding

Prep time: 10 minutes | Cook time: 20 minutes | Serves 6

Nonstick cooking spray	1 (15 ounces / 425 g) can
2 eggs	pumpkin purée
½ cup heavy (whipping)	1 teaspoon pumpkin pie
cream or almond milk (for	spice
dairy-free)	1 teaspoon vanilla extract
¾ cup Swerve	
For Serving:	
½ cup heavy (whipping) cream	

1. Grease a 6-by-3-inch pan extremely well with the cooking spray, making sure it gets into all the nooks and crannies. 2. In a medium bowl, whisk the eggs. Add the cream, Swerve, pumpkin purée, pumpkin pie spice, and vanilla, and stir to mix thoroughly. 3. Pour the mixture into the prepared pan and cover it with a silicone lid or aluminum foil. 4. Pour 2 cups of water into the inner cooking pot of the Instant Pot, then place a trivet in the pot. Place the covered pan on the trivet. 5. Lock the lid into place. Select Manual and adjust the pressure to High. Cook for 20 minutes. When the cooking is complete, let the pressure release naturally for 10 minutes, then quick-release any remaining pressure. Unlock the lid. 6. Remove the pan and place it in the refrigerator. Chill for 6 to 8 hours. 8. When ready to serve, finish by making the whipped cream. Using a hand mixer, beat the heavy cream until it forms soft peaks. Do not overbeat and turn it to butter. Serve each pudding with a dollop of whipped cream.

Nutmeg Cupcakes

Prep time: 5 minutes | Cook time: 30 minutes | Serves 7

Cake:

2 cups blanched almond	milk
flour	½ cup Swerve, or more to
2 tablespoons grass-fed	taste
butter, softened	½ teaspoon ground nutmeg
2 eggs	½ teaspoon baking powder
½ cup unsweetened almond	

Frosting:

4 ounces (113 g) full-fat	1 teaspoon vanilla extract
cream cheese, softened	½ cup Swerve, or more to
4 tablespoons grass-fed	taste
butter, softened	6 tablespoons sugar-free
2 cups heavy whipping	chocolate chips (optional)
cream	

1. Pour 1 cup of filtered water into the inner pot of the Instant Pot, then insert the trivet. In a large bowl, combine the flour, butter, eggs, almond milk, Swerve, nutmeg, and baking powder. Mix thoroughly. Working in batches if needed, transfer this mixture into a well-greased, Instant Pot-friendly muffin (or egg bites) mold. 2. Place the molds onto the trivet, and cover loosely with aluminum foil. Close the lid, set the pressure release to Sealing, and select Manual. Set the Instant Pot to 30 minutes on High Pressure, and let cook. 3. While you wait, in a large bowl, combine the cream cheese, butter, whipping cream, vanilla, Swerve, and chocolate chips. Use an electric hand mixer until you achieve a light and fluffy texture. Place frosting in refrigerator. 4. Once the cupcakes are cooked, let the pressure release naturally, for about 10 minutes. Then, switch the pressure release to Venting. Open the Instant Pot, and remove the food. Let cool, top each cupcake evenly with a scoop of frosting.

Chipotle Black Bean Brownies

Prep time: 15 minutes | Cook time: 30 minutes | Serves 8

Nonstick cooking spray	⅓ cup honey
½ cup dark chocolate	1 teaspoon vanilla extract
chips, divided	⅓ cup white wheat flour
¾ cup cooked calypso	½ teaspoon chipotle chili
beans or black beans	powder
½ cup extra-virgin olive oil	½ teaspoon ground
2 large eggs	cinnamon
¼ cup unsweetened dark	½ teaspoon baking powder
chocolate cocoa powder	½ teaspoon kosher salt

1. Spray a 7-inch Bundt pan with nonstick cooking spray. 2. Place half of the chocolate chips in a small bowl and microwave them for 30 seconds. Stir and repeat, if necessary, until the chips have completely melted. 3. In a food processor, blend the beans and oil together. Add the melted chocolate chips, eggs, cocoa powder, honey, and vanilla. Blend until the mixture is smooth. 4. In a large bowl, whisk together the flour, chili powder, cinnamon, baking powder, and salt. Pour the bean mixture from the food processor into the bowl and stir with a wooden spoon until well combined. Stir in the remaining chocolate chips. 5. Pour the batter into the prepared Bundt pan. Cover loosely with foil. 6. Pour 1 cup of water into the electric pressure cooker. 7. Place the Bundt pan onto the wire rack and lower it into the pressure cooker. 8. Close and lock the lid of the pressure cooker. Set the valve to sealing. 9. Cook on high pressure for 30 minutes. 10. When the cooking is complete, hit Cancel and quick release the pressure. 11. Once the pin drops, unlock and remove the lid. 12. Carefully transfer the pan to a cooling rack for about 10 minutes, then invert the cake onto the rack and let it cool completely. 13. Cut into slices and serve.

Coconut Lemon Squares

Prep time: 5 minutes | Cook time: 40 minutes | Serves 5 to 6

3 eggs	½ cup Swerve, or more to
2 tablespoons grass-fed	taste
butter, softened	¼ cup lemon juice
½ cup full-fat coconut milk	1 cup blanched almond
½ teaspoon baking powder	flour
½ teaspoon vanilla extract	

1. In a large bowl, mix together the eggs, butter, coconut milk, baking powder, vanilla, Swerve, lemon juice, and flour. Stir thoroughly, until a perfectly even mixture is obtained. 2. Next, pour 1 cup filtered water into the Instant Pot, and insert the trivet. Transfer the mixture from the bowl into a well-greased, Instant Pot-friendly pan (or dish). 3. Using a sling if desired, place the dish onto the trivet, and cover loosely with aluminum foil. Close the lid, set the pressure release to Sealing, and select Manual. Set the Instant Pot to 40 minutes on High Pressure, and let cook. 4. Once cooked, let the pressure naturally disperse from the Instant Pot for about 10 minutes, then carefully switch the pressure release to Venting. 5. Open the Instant Pot, and remove the dish. Let cool, cut into 6 squares, serve, and enjoy!

Deconstructed Tiramisu

Prep time: 5 minutes | Cook time: 9 minutes | Serves 4

1 cup heavy cream (or	1 teaspoon rum extract
full-fat coconut milk for	1 teaspoon unsweetened
dairy-free)	cocoa powder, or more to
2 large egg yolks	taste
2 tablespoons brewed decaf	Pinch of fine sea salt
espresso or strong brewed	1 cup cold water
coffee	4 teaspoons Swerve, for
2 tablespoons Swerve, or	topping
more to taste	

1. Heat the cream in a pan over medium-high heat until hot, about 2 minutes. 2. Place the egg yolks, coffee, sweetener, rum extract, cocoa powder, and salt in a blender and blend until smooth. 3. While the blender is running, slowly pour in the hot cream. Taste and adjust the sweetness to your liking. Add more cocoa powder, if desired. 4. Scoop the mixture into four ramekins with a spatula. Cover the ramekins with aluminum foil. 5. Place a trivet in the bottom of the Instant Pot and pour in the water. Place the ramekins on the trivet. 6. Lock the lid. Select the Manual mode and set the cooking time for 7 minutes at High Pressure. 7. When the timer beeps, use a quick pressure release. Carefully remove the lid. 8.

Keep the ramekins covered with the foil and place in the refrigerator for about 2 hours until completely chilled. 9. Sprinkle 1 teaspoon of Swerve on top of each tiramisu. Use the oven broiler to melt the sweetener. 10. Put in the fridge to chill the topping, about 20 minutes. 11. Serve.

Greek Yogurt Strawberry Pops

Prep time: 5 minutes | Cook time: 0 minutes | Serves 6

2 ripe bananas, peeled, cut	Greek yogurt
into ½-inch pieces, and	1 cup chopped fresh
frozen	strawberries
½ cup plain 2 percent	

1. In a food processor, combine the bananas and yogurt and process at high speed for 2 minutes, until mostly smooth (it's okay if a few small chunks remain). Scrape down the sides of the bowl, add the strawberries, and process for 1 minute, until smooth. 2. Divide the mixture evenly among six ice-pop molds. Tap each mold on a countertop a few times to get rid of any air pockets, then place an ice-pop stick into each mold and transfer the molds to the freezer. Freeze for at least 4 hours, or until frozen solid. 3. To unmold each ice pop, run it under cold running water for 5 seconds, taking care not to get water inside the mold, then remove the ice pop from the mold. Eat the ice pops right away or store in a ziplock plastic freezer bag in the freezer for up to 2 months.

Thai Pandan Coconut Custard

Prep time: 10 minutes | Cook time: 30 minutes | Serves 4

Nonstick cooking spray	⅓ cup Swerve
1 cup unsweetened coconut	3 to 4 drops pandan extract,
milk	or use vanilla extract if you
3 eggs	must

1. Grease a 6-inch heatproof bowl with the cooking spray. 2. In a large bowl, whisk together the coconut milk, eggs, Swerve, and pandan extract. Pour the mixture into the prepared bowl and cover it with aluminum foil. 3. Pour 2 cups of water into the inner cooking pot of the Instant Pot, then place a trivet in the pot. Place the bowl on the trivet. 4. Lock the lid into place. Select Manual and adjust the pressure to High. Cook for 30 minutes. When the cooking is complete, let the pressure release naturally. Unlock the lid. 5. Remove the bowl from the pot and remove the foil. A knife inserted into the custard should come out clean. Cool in the refrigerator for 6 to 8 hours, or until the custard is set.

Vanilla Butter Curd

Prep time: 5 minutes | Cook time: 6 hours | Serves 3

4 egg yolks, whisked	½ cup organic almond milk
2 tablespoon butter	1 teaspoon vanilla extract
1 tablespoon erythritol	

1. Set the instant pot to Sauté mode and when the "Hot" is displayed, add butter. 2. Melt the butter but not boil it and add whisked egg yolks, almond milk, and vanilla extract. 3. Add erythritol. Whisk the mixture. 4. Cook the meal on Low for 6 hours.

Lemon and Ricotta Torte

Prep time: 15 minutes | Cook time: 35 minutes | Serves 12

Cooking spray	cheese
Torte:	¼ cup lemon juice
1⅓ cups Swerve	1 cup cold water
½ cup (1 stick) unsalted butter, softened	Lemon Glaze:
2 teaspoons lemon or vanilla extract	½ cup (1 stick) unsalted butter
5 large eggs, separated	¼ cup Swerve
2½ cups blanched almond flour	2 tablespoons lemon juice
1¼ (10 ounces / 284 g) cups whole-milk ricotta	2 ounces (57 g) cream cheese (¼ cup)
	Grated lemon zest and lemon slices, for garnish

1. Line a baking pan with parchment paper and spray with cooking spray. Set aside. 2. Make the torte: In the bowl of a stand mixer, place the Swerve, butter, and extract and blend for 8 to 10 minutes until well combined. Scrape down the sides of the bowl as needed. 3. Add the egg yolks and continue to blend until fully combined. Add the almond flour and mix until smooth, then stir in the ricotta and lemon juice. 4. Whisk the egg whites in a separate medium bowl until stiff peaks form. Add the whites to the batter and stir well. Pour the batter into the prepared pan and smooth the top. 5. Place a trivet in the bottom of your Instant Pot and pour in the water. Use a foil sling to lower the baking pan onto the trivet. Tuck in the sides of the sling. 6. Seal the lid, press Pressure Cook or Manual, and set the timer for 30 minutes. Once finished, let the pressure release naturally. 7. Lock the lid. Select the Manual mode and set the cooking time for 30 minutes at High Pressure. 8. When the timer beeps, perform a natural pressure release for 10 minutes. Carefully remove the lid. 9. Use the foil sling to lift the pan out of the Instant Pot. Place the torte in the fridge for 40 minutes to chill before glazing. 10. Meanwhile, make the glaze: Place the butter in a large pan over high heat and cook for about 5 minutes until brown, stirring occasionally. Remove from the heat. While stirring the browned butter, add the Swerve. 11. Carefully add the lemon juice and cream cheese to the butter mixture. Allow the glaze to cool for a few minutes, or until it starts to thicken. 12. Transfer the chilled torte to a serving plate. Pour the glaze over the torte and return it to the fridge to chill for an additional 30 minutes. 13. Scatter the lemon zest on top of the torte and arrange the lemon slices on the plate around the torte. 14. Serve.

Traditional Cheesecake

Prep time: 30 minutes | Cook time: 45 minutes | Serves 8

For Crust:	
1½ cups almond flour	1 tablespoon granulated erythritol
4 tablespoons butter, melted	½ teaspoon ground cinnamon
1 tablespoon Swerve	

For Filling:	
16 ounces (454 g) cream cheese, softened	1 teaspoon vanilla extract
½ cup granulated erythritol	½ teaspoon lemon extract
2 eggs	1½ cups water

1. To make the crust: In a medium bowl, combine the almond flour, butter, Swerve, erythritol, and cinnamon. Use a fork to press it all together. When completed, the mixture should resemble wet sand. 2. Spray the springform pan with cooking spray and line the bottom with parchment paper. 3. Press the crust evenly into the pan. Work the crust up the sides of the pan, about halfway from the top, and make sure there are no bare spots on the bottom. 4. Place the crust in the freezer for 20 minutes while you make the filling. 5. To make the filling: In the bowl of a stand mixer using the whip attachment, combine the cream cheese and erythritol on medium speed until the cream cheese is light and fluffy, 2 to 3 minutes. 6. Add the eggs, vanilla extract, and lemon extract. Mix until well combined. 7. Remove the crust from the freezer and pour in the filling. Cover the pan tightly with aluminum foil and place it on the trivet. 8. Add the water to the pot and carefully lower the trivet into the pot. 9. Close the lid. Select Manual mode and set cooking time for 45 minutes on High Pressure. 10. When timer beeps, use a quick pressure release and open the lid. 11. Remove the trivet and cheesecake from the pot. Remove the foil from the pan. The center of the cheesecake should still be slightly jiggly. If the cheesecake is still very jiggly in the center, cook for an additional 5 minutes on High pressure until the appropriate doneness is reached. 12. Let the cheesecake cool for 30 minutes on the counter before placing it in the refrigerator to set. Leave the cheesecake in the refrigerator for at least 6 hours before removing the sides of the pan, slicing, and serving.

Ultimate Chocolate Cheesecake

Prep time: 10 minutes | Cook time: 50 minutes | Serves 12

2 cups pecans	powder
2 tablespoons butter	2 teaspoons vanilla extract
16 ounces (454 g) cream cheese, softened	2 cups low-carb chocolate chips
1 cup powdered erythritol	1 tablespoon coconut oil
¼ cup sour cream	2 eggs
2 tablespoons cocoa	2 cups water

1. Preheat oven to 400°F (205°C). Place pecans and butter into food processor. Pulse until dough-like consistency. Press into bottom of 7-inch springform pan. Bake for 10 minutes then set aside to cool. 2. While crust bakes, mix cream cheese, erythritol, sour cream, cocoa powder, and vanilla together in large bowl using a rubber spatula. Set aside. 3. In medium bowl, combine chocolate chips and coconut oil. Microwave in 20-second increments until chocolate begins to melt and then stir until smooth. Gently fold chocolate mixture into cheesecake mixture. 4. Add eggs and gently fold in, careful not to overmix. Pour mixture over cooled pecan crust. Cover with foil. 5. Pour water into Instant Pot and place steam rack on bottom. Place cheesecake on steam rack and click lid closed. Press the Manual button and adjust time for 40 minutes. When timer beeps, allow a natural release. Carefully remove and let cool completely. Serve chilled.

Fudgy Walnut Brownies

Prep time: 10 minutes | Cook time: 1 hour | Serves 12

¾ cup walnut halves and pieces	1 cup Lakanto Monkfruit Sweetener Golden
½ cup unsalted butter, melted and cooled	¼ teaspoon fine sea salt
4 large eggs	¾ cup almond flour
1½ teaspoons instant coffee crystals	¾ cup natural cocoa powder
1½ teaspoons vanilla extract	¾ cup stevia-sweetened chocolate chips

1. In a dry small skillet over medium heat, toast the walnuts, stirring often, for about 5 minutes, until golden. Transfer the walnuts to a bowl to cool. 2. Pour 1 cup water into the Instant Pot. Line the base of a 7 by 3-inch round cake pan with a circle of parchment paper. Butter the sides of the pan and the parchment or coat with nonstick cooking spray. 3. Pour the butter into a medium bowl. One at a time, whisk in the eggs, then whisk in the coffee crystals, vanilla, sweetener, and salt. Finally, whisk in the flour and cocoa powder just until combined. Using a rubber spatula, fold in the chocolate chips and walnuts. 4. Transfer the batter to the prepared pan and, using the spatula, spread it in an even layer. Cover the pan tightly with aluminum foil. Place the pan on a long-handled silicone steam rack, then, holding the handles of the steam rack, lower it into the Instant Pot. 5. Secure the lid and set the Pressure Release to Sealing. Select the Cake, Pressure Cook, or Manual setting and set the cooking time for 45 minutes at high pressure. (The pot will take about 10 minutes to come up to pressure before the cooking program begins.) 6. When the cooking program ends, let the pressure release naturally for 10 minutes, then move the Pressure Release to Venting to release any remaining steam. Open the pot and, wearing heat-resistant mitts, grasp the handles of the steam rack and lift it out of the pot. Uncover the pan, taking care not to get burned by the steam or to drip condensation onto the brownies. Let the brownies cool in the pan on a cooling rack for about 2 hours, to room temperature. 7. Run a butter knife around the edge of the pan to make sure the brownies are not sticking to the pan sides. Invert the brownies onto the rack, lift off the pan, and peel off the parchment paper. Invert the brownies onto a serving plate and cut into twelve wedges. The brownies will keep, stored in an airtight container in the refrigerator for up to 5 days, or in the freezer for up to 4 months.

Cardamom Rolls with Cream Cheese

Prep time: 20 minutes | Cook time: 18 minutes | Serves 5

½ cup coconut flour	¼ cup almond milk
1 tablespoon ground cardamom	1 tablespoon butter, softened
2 tablespoon Swerve	1 tablespoon cream cheese
1 egg, whisked	⅓ cup water

1. Combine together coconut flour, almond milk, and softened butter. 2. Knead the smooth dough. 3. Roll up the dough with the help of the rolling pin. 4. Then combine together Swerve and ground cardamom. 5. Sprinkle the surface of the dough with the ground cardamom mixture. 6. Roll the dough into one big roll and cut them into servings. 7. Place the rolls into the instant pot round mold. 8. Pour water in the instant pot (⅓ cup) and insert the mold inside. 9. Set Manual mode (High Pressure) for 18 minutes. 10. Then use the natural pressure release method for 15 minutes. 11. Chill the rolls to the room temperature and spread with cream cheese.

Candied Mixed Nuts

Prep time: 5 minutes | Cook time: 15 minutes | Serves 8

1 cup pecan halves	⅓ cup grass-fed butter
1 cup chopped walnuts	1 teaspoon ground
⅓ cup Swerve, or more to taste	cinnamon

1. Preheat your oven to 350ºF (180ºC), and line a baking sheet with aluminum foil. 2. While your oven is warming, pour ½ cup of filtered water into the inner pot of the Instant Pot, followed by the pecans, walnuts, Swerve, butter, and cinnamon. Stir nut mixture, close the lid, and then set the pressure valve to Sealing. Use the Manual mode to cook at High Pressure, for 5 minutes. 3. Once cooked, perform a quick release by carefully switching the pressure valve to Venting, and strain the nuts. Pour the nuts onto the baking sheet, spreading them out in an even layer. Place in the oven for 5 to 10 minutes (or until crisp, being careful not to overcook). Cool before serving. Store leftovers in the refrigerator or freezer.

Coconut Cupcakes

Prep time: 5 minutes | Cook time: 10 minutes | Serves 6

4 eggs, beaten	2 tablespoons erythritol
4 tablespoons coconut milk	1 teaspoon baking powder
4 tablespoons coconut flour	1 cup water
½ teaspoon vanilla extract	

1. In the mixing bowl, mix up eggs, coconut milk, coconut flour, vanilla extract, erythritol, and baking powder. 2. Then pour the batter in the cupcake molds. 3. Pour the water and insert the trivet in the instant pot. 4. Place the cupcakes on the trivet. 5. Lock the lid. Select the Manual mode and set the cooking time for 10 minutes on High Pressure. Once the timer goes off, perform a natural pressure release for 5 minutes, then release any remaining pressure. Carefully open the lid. 6. Serve immediately.

Pine Nut Mousse

Prep time: 5 minutes | Cook time: 35 minutes | Serves 8

1 tablespoon butter	1 cup Swerve, reserve 1 tablespoon
1¼ cups pine nuts	
1¼ cups full-fat heavy cream	1 c water
2 large eggs	1 cup full-fat heavy whipping cream
1 teaspoon vanilla extract	

1. Butter the bottom and the side of a pie pan and set aside. 2. In a food processor, blend the pine nuts and heavy cream. Add the eggs, vanilla extract and Swerve and pulse a few times to incorporate. 3. Pour the batter into the pan and loosely cover with aluminum foil. Pour the water in the Instant Pot and place the trivet inside. Place the pan on top of the trivet. 4. Close the lid. Select Manual mode and set the timer for 35 minutes on High pressure. 5. In a small mixing bowl, whisk the heavy whipping cream and 1 tablespoon of Swerve until a soft peak forms. 6. When timer beeps, use a natural pressure release for 15 minutes, then release any remaining pressure and open the lid. 7. Serve immediately with whipped cream on top.

Strawberry Cheesecake

Prep time: 20 minutes | Cook time: 10 minutes | Serves 2

1 tablespoon gelatin	1 strawberry, chopped
4 tablespoon water (for gelatin)	¼ cup coconut milk
	1 tablespoon Swerve
4 tablespoon cream cheese	

1. Mix up gelatin and water and leave the mixture for 10 minutes. 2. Meanwhile, pour coconut milk in the instant pot. 3. Bring it to boil on Sauté mode, about 10 minutes. 4. Meanwhile, mash the strawberry and mix it up with cream cheese. 5. Add the mixture in the hot coconut milk and stir until smooth. 6. Cool the liquid for 10 minutes and add gelatin. Whisk it until gelatin is melted. 7. Then pour the cheesecake in the mold and freeze in the freezer for 3 hours.

Chai Pear-Fig Compote

Prep time: 20 minutes | Cook time: 3 minutes | Serves 4

1 vanilla chai tea bag	1½ pounds pears, peeled and chopped (about 3 cups)
1 (3-inch) cinnamon stick	
1 strip lemon peel (about 2-by-½ inches)	½ cup chopped dried figs
	2 tablespoons raisins

1. Pour 1 cup of water into the electric pressure cooker and hit Sauté/More. When the water comes to a boil, add the tea bag and cinnamon stick. Hit Cancel. Let the tea steep for 5 minutes, then remove and discard the tea bag. 2. Add the lemon peel, pears, figs, and raisins to the pot. 3. Close and lock the lid of the pressure cooker. Set the valve to sealing. 4. Cook on high pressure for 3 minutes. 5. When the cooking is complete, hit Cancel and quick release the pressure. 6. Once the pin drops, unlock and remove the lid. 7. Remove the lemon peel and cinnamon stick. Serve warm or cool to room temperature and refrigerate.

Appendix 1:
Instant Pot Cooking Timetable

Dried Beans, Legumes and Lentils

Dried Beans and Legume	Dry (Minutes)	Soaked (Minutes)
Soy beans	25 – 30	20 – 25
Scarlet runner	20 – 25	10 – 15
Pinto beans	25 – 30	20 – 25
Peas	15 – 20	10 – 15
Navy beans	25 – 30	20 – 25
Lima beans	20 – 25	10 – 15
Lentils, split, yellow (moong dal)	15 – 18	N/A
Lentils, split, red	15 – 18	N/A
Lentils, mini, green (brown)	15 – 20	N/A
Lentils, French green	15 – 20	N/A
Kidney white beans	35 – 40	20 – 25
Kidney red beans	25 – 30	20 – 25
Great Northern beans	25 – 30	20 – 25
Pigeon peas	20 – 25	15 – 20
Chickpeas (garbanzo bean chickpeas)	35 – 40	20 – 25
Cannellini beans	35 – 40	20 – 25
Black-eyed peas	20 – 25	10 – 15
Black beans	20 – 25	10 – 15

Fish and Seafood

Fish and Seafood	Fresh (minutes)	Frozen (minutes)
Shrimp or Prawn	1 to 2	2 to 3
Seafood soup or stock	6 to 7	7 to 9
Mussels	2 to 3	4 to 6
Lobster	3 to 4	4 to 6
Fish, whole (snapper, trout, etc.)	5 to 6	7 to 10
Fish steak	3 to 4	4 to 6
Fish fillet	2 to 3	3 to 4
Crab	3 to 4	5 to 6

Fruits

Fruits	Fresh (in Minutes)	Dried (in Minutes)
Raisins	N/A	4 to 5
Prunes	2 to 3	4 to 5
Pears, whole	3 to 4	4 to 6
Pears, slices or halves	2 to 3	4 to 5
Peaches	2 to 3	4 to 5
Apricots, whole or halves	2 to 3	3 to 4
Apples, whole	3 to 4	4 to 6
Apples, in slices or pieces	2 to 3	3 to 4

Meat

Meat and Cuts	Cooking Time (minutes)	Meat and Cuts	Cooking Time (minutes)
Veal, roast	35 to 45	Duck, with bones, cut up	10 to 12
Veal, chops	5 to 8	Cornish Hen, whole	10 to 15
Turkey, drumsticks (leg)	15 to 20	Chicken, whole	20 to 25
Turkey, breast, whole, with bones	25 to 30	Chicken, legs, drumsticks, or thighs	10 to 15
Turkey, breast, boneless	15 to 20	Chicken, with bones, cut up	10 to 15
Quail, whole	8 to 10	Chicken, breasts	8 to 10
Pork, ribs	20 to 25	Beef, stew	15 to 20
Pork, loin roast	55 to 60	Beef, shanks	25 to 30
Pork, butt roast	45 to 50	Beef, ribs	25 to 30
Pheasant	20 to 25	Beef, steak, pot roast, round, rump, brisket or blade, small chunks, chuck,	25 to 30
Lamb, stew meat	10 to 15		
Lamb, leg	35 to 45	Beef, pot roast, steak, rump, round, chuck, blade or brisket, large	35 to 40
Lamb, cubes	10 t0 15		
Ham slice	9 to 12	Beef, ox-tail	40 to 50
Ham picnic shoulder	25 to 30	Beef, meatball	10 to 15
Duck, whole	25 to 30	Beef, dressed	20 to 25

Vegetables (fresh/frozen)

Vegetable	Fresh (minutes)	Frozen (minutes)	Vegetable	Fresh (minutes)	Frozen (minutes)
Zucchini, slices or chunks	2 to 3	3 to 4	Mixed vegetables	2 to 3	3 to 4
Yam, whole, small	10 to 12	12 to 14	Leeks	2 to 4	3 to 5
Yam, whole, large	12 to 15	15 to 19	Greens (collards, beet greens, spinach, kale, turnip greens, swiss chard) chopped	3 to 6	4 to 7
Yam, in cubes	7 to 9	9 to 11			
Turnip, chunks	2 to 4	4 to 6	Green beans, whole	2 to 3	3 to 4
Tomatoes, whole	3 to 5	5 to 7	Escarole, chopped	1 to 2	2 to 3
Tomatoes, in quarters	2 to 3	4 to 5	Endive	1 to 2	2 to 3
Sweet potato, whole, small	10 to 12	12 to 14	Eggplant, chunks or slices	2 to 3	3 to 4
Sweet potato, whole, large	12 to 15	15 to 19	Corn, on the cob	3 to 4	4 to 5
Sweet potato, in cubes	7 to 9	9 to 11	Corn, kernels	1 to 2	2 to 3
Sweet pepper, slices or chunks	1 to 3	2 to 4	Collard	4 to 5	5 to 6
Squash, butternut, slices or chunks	8 to 10	10 to 12	Celery, chunks	2 to 3	3 to 4
Squash, acorn, slices or chunks	6 to 7	8 to 9	Cauliflower flowerets	2 to 3	3 to 4
Spinach	1 to 2	3 to 4	Carrots, whole or chunked	2 to 3	3 to 4
Rutabaga, slices	3 to 5	4 to 6	Carrots, sliced or shredded	1 to 2	2 to 3
Rutabaga, chunks	4 to 6	6 to 8	Cabbage, red, purple or green, wedges	3 to 4	4 to 5
Pumpkin, small slices or chunks	4 to 5	6 to 7	Cabbage, red, purple or green, shredded	2 to 3	3 to 4
Pumpkin, large slices or chunks	8 to 10	10 to 14	Brussel sprouts, whole	3 to 4	4 to 5
Potatoes, whole, large	12 to 15	15 to 19	Broccoli, stalks	3 to 4	4 to 5
Potatoes, whole, baby	10 to 12	12 to 14	Broccoli, flowerets	2 to 3	3 to 4
Potatoes, in cubes	7 to 9	9 to 11	Beets, small roots, whole	11 to 13	13 to 15
Peas, in the pod	1 to 2	2 to 3	Beets, large roots, whole	20 to 25	25 to 30
Peas, green	1 to 2	2 to 3	Beans, green/yellow or wax, whole, trim ends and strings	1 to 2	2 to 3
Parsnips, sliced	1 to 2	2 to 3			
Parsnips, chunks	2 to 4	4 to 6	Asparagus, whole or cut	1 to 2	2 to 3
Onions, sliced	2 to 3	3 to 4	Artichoke, whole, trimmed without leaves	9 to 11	11 to 13
Okra	2 to 3	3 to 4	Artichoke, hearts	4 to 5	5 to 6

Rice and Grains

Rice & Grain	Water Quantity (Grain: Water ratios)	Cooking Time (in Minutes)	Rice & Grain	Water Quantity (Grain: Water ratios)	Cooking Time (in Minutes)
Wheat berries	1:3	25 to 30	Oats, steel-cut	1:1	10
Spelt berries	1:3	15 to 20	Oats, quick cooking	1:1	6
Sorghum	1:3	20 to 25	Millet	1:1	10 to 12
Rice, wild	1:3	25 to 30	Kamut, whole	1:3	10 to 12
Rice, white	1:1.5	8	Couscous	1:2	5 to 8
Rice, Jasmine	1:1	4 to 10	Corn, dried, half	1:3	25 to 30
Rice, Brown	1:1.3	22 to 28	Congee, thin	1:6 ~ 1:7	15 to 20
Rice, Basmati	1:1.5	4 to 8	Congee, thick	1:4 ~ 1:5	15 to 20
Quinoa, quick cooking	1:2	8	Barley, pot	1:3 ~ 1:4	25 to 30
Porridge, thin	1:6 ~ 1:7	15 to 20	Barley, pearl	1:4	25 to 30

Appendix 2:
Recipe Index

Made in the USA
Las Vegas, NV
15 January 2024